BOOKS BY A. T. ROBERTSON

PUBLISHED BY

CHARLES SCRIBNER'S SONS

EPOCHS IN THE LIFE OF SIMON PETER

JOHN THE LOYAL

LUKE THE HISTORIAN IN THE LIGHT OF RESEARCH

THE PHARISEES AND JESUS (Stone Lectures for 1916)

EPOCHS IN THE LIFE OF PAUL

EPOCHS IN THE LIFE OF JESUS

OTHER BOOKS BY A. T. ROBERTSON

A HARMONY OF THE GOSPELS FOR STUDENTS OF THE LIFE OF CHRIST (Many editions)

THE MOTHER OF JESUS

THE CHRIST OF THE LOGIA

STUDIES IN MARK'S GOSPEL

A TRANSLATION OF LUKE'S GOSPEL

A NEW SHORT GRAMMAR OF THE GREEK TESTAMENT (9th edition)

A GRAMMAR OF THE GREEK NEW TESTAMENT IN THE LIGHT OF HISTORICAL RESEARCH (5th edition)

WORD PICTURES IN THE NEW TESTAMENT (6 volumes)

AN INTRODUCTION TO THE TEXTUAL CRITICISM OF THE NEW TESTAMENT

STUDIES IN THE TEXT OF THE NEW TESTAMENT

THE MINISTER AND HIS GREEK NEW TESTAMENT

PAUL AND THE INTELLECTUALS (Stone Lectures for 1926)

SOME MINOR CHARACTERS IN THE NEW TESTAMENT

STUDIES IN THE EPISTLE OF JAMES

MAKING GOOD IN THE MINISTRY

A SYLLABUS FOR NEW TESTAMENT STUDY

THE GLORY OF THE MINISTRY

PAUL'S JOY IN CHRIST

THE STUDENT'S CHRONOLOGICAL NEW TESTAMENT

THE DIVINITY OF CHRIST IN THE GOSPEL OF JOHN

EPOCHS IN THE LIFE OF
SIMON PETER

EPOCHS IN THE LIFE
OF SIMON PETER

BY

A. T. ROBERTSON, D.D., LL.D, Litt.D.

PROFESSOR OF NEW TESTAMENT INTERPRETATION IN THE SOUTHERN BAPTIST
THEOLOGICAL SEMINARY, LOUISVILLE, KENTUCKY

Jesus to Peter: "Follow me."
—*John 21 : 19*

CHARLES SCRIBNER'S SONS
NEW YORK : : LONDON
1935

TO

MY SON

CARY ROBERTSON

PREFACE

Ever since the appearance of my *Epochs in the Life of Jesus* (1907), *Epochs in the Life of Paul* (1909), and *John the Loyal* (1911), I have cherished the hope that some day I should be able to do *Epochs in the Life of Simon Peter*. Until now my grammatical and expository works have claimed my time. But with the completion of the last volume of *Word Pictures in the New Testament* (Vol. VI.—*The General Epistles and the Apocalypse*) no excuse remains for not doing this book if I ever mean to do it. I cannot claim unusual qualifications for doing it beyond an intense admiration for Simon Peter and sympathy with him in his slips and weaknesses of nature. We are told more about him than about any of the twelve apostles in the Gospels and in the Acts. He is the only one of the number of whom the New Testament has much to tell after the Ascension of Christ, though Luke drops him from his story after Acts 15 and follows Paul's career to Rome. There are those who lose interest in Peter because of the extreme claims made by the Roman Catholics that Peter is the founder of the church in Rome and the first pope. A legendary literature of Gospels, Acts, and Apocalypse has gathered around his name and early Christian writers give a confused account of his doings and death. These have been duly considered, but shall not be used save where clearly probable

in drawing the picture of Simon Peter. It is possible
to follow the rapid changes in the growth of Simon,
the simple fisherman of Galilee, into Peter the "Prince
of Apostles" (Foakes-Jackson). He came to justify
the promise of service held out by Jesus, but only
after severe sifting by Satan. When he did turn, he
strengthened his brethren. The process by which this
goal was reached will repay the study of any one who
seeks to grow in grace and in the knowledge of the
Lord Jesus Christ. Simon appealed to the heart of
Jesus in a special way and he touches our hearts today with the note of reality in spite of all the legends
gathered around his name. Christ's hopes about
Simon's usefulness finally came true. There is thus
hope for us all.

The useful Index to New Testament Passages has
been prepared by my former student, Reverend Joseph
Nordenhaug, Ph.D., of Oslo, Norway.

A. T. ROBERTSON.

LOUISVILLE, KY.

TABLE OF CONTENTS

xi

TABLE OF CONTENTS

EPOCHS IN THE LIFE OF
SIMON PETER

CHAPTER I

THE CHARM IN SIMON PETER

1. *A Winsome Personality.*—There is a fascination for most of us in Simon Peter that justifies a new interpretation of his life and work. The sheer humanity of the man appeals to the average individual who feels that he can understand Peter better than he can Paul or John. Peter's very winsomeness drew Jesus to him at the start and won him friends at every turn. He will win every heart today that tries to understand him.

2. *Overshadowed by Paul.*—Peter plays a large part in the Gospels, though he was not acknowledged to be first by the other apostles. The frequent disputes over the primacy during Christ's ministry prove this. In the Acts Peter starts out in the lead after the coming of the Holy Spirit in power. For the opening chapters he is constantly to the fore, but in the middle of the book Luke drops him for Paul, who is henceforth Luke's hero. The fortunes of Paul are recorded by Luke after chapter 12. To this day the figure of Paul stands in front of Peter save in Roman Catholic circles. My own feeling is that Paul deserves the place of pre-eminence because of his gifts and achievements for Christ.

3. *And Not Equal to John.*—Peter did precede John in energy and activity after the great Pente-

cost, though John was associated with him in the Acts. And yet the Beloved Disciple had come closer to the heart of Christ even in the Inner Circle of three (Peter, James and John). John outlived both Peter and Paul and at last produced the Fourth Gospel, the greatest book of all time. Peter did not rise to heights like this Gospel, nor did he write Epistles equal to those by Paul, nor did he do as far-reaching mission work in the Roman Empire as did Paul. In sheer genius John the Eagle soared above Peter. And yet Peter is not to be neglected.

4. *His Very Impulsiveness Appeals to Us.*—He had a way of speaking up on the spur of the moment, that is so natural to all of us; once "not knowing what he was saying," as Luke explains. This natural ebullition of spirits illustrates his interest and eagerness. Sometimes it would lead him too far, as when he dared to rebuke the Master for talking about his approaching death, a daring that brought on him the sharp retort that he was acting the part of Satan even in his ignorance.

5. *His Great Sin Awakens Sympathy.*—There is no real excuse for Peter's shameful denials of his Master. And yet we all see how he was caught in the toils between love and fear. It was not deliberately planned sin. He stumbled into it in spite of plain warning. He was the victim of his own self-confidence. He felt superior to temptation, but the look of Jesus broke Peter's heart and won him back after days of agony. Peter could be counted on to come back. Jesus knew that he would.

6. *Final Sturdy Manhood.*—It was slow in coming, but, when the fruit was ripe, it was rich and gracious. He was a man worth the making and Jesus knew it. He loved Peter from the start and to the end. Peter came to justify Christ's love and patience with him.

CHAPTER II

THE ROCK THAT IS TO BE
(John 1:35–42)

Bernard thinks that the call of Simon in the Synoptic Gospels (Mark 1:16–20; Matt. 4:18–22; Luke 5:1–11) "may be another version" of John 1:35–42, though probably "a more formal call to apostleship." Pretty clearly not that, for that came still later, just before the Sermon on the Mount (Mark 3:13–19; Luke 6:12–16). Matthew gives the list of the Twelve when they are sent out by twos over Galilee (10:4). Case (Hastings, *Dictionary of the Apostolic Church*) considers it doubtful which of the three calls of Simon is historically true. Why not all three? The call here (John 1:42) is to discipleship, that in Mark 1:16–20 is to continuous following of Christ, that in Mark 3:13–19 is to formal apostleship. They are merely three stages in Simon's relationship to Jesus. Let us then look at Simon when he is first introduced to Jesus and to us.

1. *Andrew a Disciple of John the Baptist.*—There are here two disciples of the Baptist who hear his witness to Jesus as the Lamb of God (1:35) shortly before the passover (2:13). He had borne like witness to Jesus the day before (1:29) at Bethany beyond Jordan, which Andrew may not have heard (Dods) or may have heard without being as much impressed by it as on this day. Andrew was one of

4

two (the other not named, but clearly the future Beloved Disciple, the author of this Gospel) disciples of the Baptist who heard and believed his witness to Jesus as the Messiah. Andrew and his brother Simon were from Bethsaida in Galilee (1:44). The implication is that Simon was also a disciple of the Baptist since he was here at Bethany beyond Jordan though not with Andrew on this day when the Baptist bore direct witness to Jesus as the Messiah.

2. *The Baptist's Interpretation of Jesus.*—The preaching of the Baptist about the Messiah had been precise and definite even before the baptism of Jesus (Mark 1:7 f.; Matt. 3:11 f.; Luke 3:15–18). Some even then wondered "concerning John whether haply he were the Christ" (Luke 3:15), to whom he replied that he was not worthy to unloose the latchet of the Messiah's sandals. Even after Christ's baptism a formal committee of Sadducees (priests and Levites) had been sent to John from the Sanhedrin by the Pharisees (John 1:24), perhaps with vivid memories of the Baptist's denunciation of both Pharisees and Sadducees as "offspring of vipers" (Matt. 3:7–10; Luke 3:7–14). John boldly told the committee that he himself was not the Messiah, not Elijah in person, not the prophet foretold by Moses, but only "the voice of one crying in the wilderness" (John 1:20–23). To their surprise, however, John added that the Messiah was already standing among them and that they did not know him (John 1:26). On the next day, possibly after the committee had departed, the Baptist saw Jesus himself (John 1:29)

who had come to Bethany after the forty days of
temptation in the wilderness (Mark 1:12; Matt.
4:1–11; Luke 4:1–13) and was actually nearer than
when John spoke so confidently the day before (John
1:26). John now knew Jesus by face for he had pre-
viously baptized him (Mark 1:9–11; Matt. 3:13–17;
Luke 3:21–23) and he instantly bore a glad and
triumphant witness to the mission and Messiahship
of Jesus (John 1:29–34. He pictured him as "the
Lamb of God, which taketh away the sin of the
world," applying to Jesus the words of Isaiah 53:7
concerning the "suffering servant" of the Lord.

It is objected that the Baptist could not have had
this theological conception, because the rabbis of the
time did not have it. But it is surely poor criticism
as well as injustice to hold him in the bonds of the
ignorance of the rabbis whom Jesus will later accuse
of rejecting the commandment of God to preserve
their own tradition (Mark 7:9; Matt. 15:3). In the
wilderness John had ample opportunity, by the help
of the Holy Spirit who was guiding him, to study
Isaiah and to gain a proper interpretation and per-
spective of the Messiah whose forerunner he knew
himself to be. I would rather believe that than to
say that the author of the Fourth Gospel has put
into the Baptist's mouth the high view of the Messiah of a later time. This view of Jesus was held,
of course, when this Gospel was written, but the
Synoptic Gospels present an equally high view of
Jesus as the Son of God when John baptized him
(Mark 1:10 f.; Matt. 3:16 f.; Luke 3:21–23).

John here alludes to the descent of the Holy Spirit on Jesus at the baptism as proof of the identity of Jesus as the Messiah. Hence John refers to the witness of the Father to the Sonship of Jesus: "I have seen, and have borne witness that this is the Son of God" (John 1:34). So then, according to both the Synoptics and John's Gospel, the Baptist gives clear-cut and unequivocal testimony to the Messiahship and deity (Sonship) of Jesus. He had pictured the Messiah in broad outline before he saw him. He recognized him when he appeared at the Jordan asking baptism at his hands, and after the baptism had seen the coming of the Holy Spirit as a dove out of the opened heaven and had heard the Father's audible approval of Jesus as "My beloved Son, in whom I am well pleased" (Mark 1:11; Matt. 3:17; Luke 3:22), and now the Baptist has identified Jesus to his own disciples as the Lamb of God and the Messiah, the Son of God. On the next day he has repeated his witness in a single exclamation of rapture to two of his disciples: "Behold, the Lamb of God" (John 1:36). Whether it was a fresh identification for Andrew and John the son of Zebedee or the power of repetition upon them we do not know. In any case the Baptist is very much in earnest in his witness as he looks in ecstasy upon Jesus whom he never sees more on earth. Jesus is to the Baptist the goal of all his ministry. There he is, walking before him again. The very soul of John goes out after him as he gazes upon him who is the long hoped for Messiah of Israel. Others may have

heard the Baptist witness on this second day, but, if
so, Andrew and John the son of Zebedee were nearer
to him and it was almost as if he spoke directly to
them. If the Baptist was sincere in this open and
specific witness to Jesus, what was the duty of the
two disciples of John?

3. *Andrew's Visit to Jesus.*—The effect of John's
direct witness to Jesus on Andrew and his companion (John the brother of James) was electric and
called for instantaneous action on their part. If
John meant what he said (and they heard him say it
as he looked and pointed at Jesus), the best that
they could do was to go and see Jesus. John had
insisted that Jesus was superior to him and that he
had preached and baptized in order to manifest him
to Israel as the Messiah (John 1:27, 30 f.). God
who sent John to baptize had expressly told him how
to recognize the Messiah who was to baptize in the
Holy Spirit and not just in water (John 1:26, 33).
Andrew was a loyal disciple of John and for long
some clung to him instead of following Jesus (John
3:26; 4:1 f.; Acts 19:1–7). But John wanted his
own disciples to follow Jesus (John 3:27–29). The
wonder is that only Andrew and his companion acted
on John's witness at this time. Which of the two
took the initiative we do not know. But they both
"followed Jesus." They wanted to investigate for
themselves the tremendous statement made by John
about Jesus. We are told that Jesus "turned" as
one naturally would when he felt that he was followed. He beheld them following him, perhaps for

some distance. The question of Jesus is not abrupt, but a polite and courteous inquiry: "What seek ye?" These are the first words of Jesus preserved in John's Gospel. He did not say "whom" but "what." The two disciples evidently felt embarrassed at this sudden turn of affairs, for they said, "Rabbi, where abidest thou?" It was, in fact, a request for an interview with Jesus, who, like them, was a visitor in Bethany beyond Jordan and probably had his tent near by. "They were in need of Christ first and not of any special gift of Christ. They desired a quiet place for converse" (Westcott). The reply of Jesus (Come, and ye shall see) was a common formula inviting one to one's home. It is frequent in Talmudic authors. In John 1:46 and 11:34 we have two imperatives (come and see) rather than one imperative and a future as here. John repeats both verbs in the sententious phrase: "They came therefore and saw where he abode." Yes, but they did more; they spent the rest of the day from ten o'clock in the morning (Roman time, for there was no Jewish time when John wrote this Gospel).

Through the long years John never forgot that blessed day by the side of Jesus. It was the first of many more, but the witchery and the wonder of this first charm never left the aged disciple. He does not tell us what the conversation turned upon, but all the day John and Andrew were testing Jesus to see if he measured up to the high words used of him that morning by the Baptist. It was a proper attitude on their part. They could not afford to make a mistake

in so vital a matter. They were already disciples
(learners) of the Baptist, but even he might be deceived, though to say so was to brand the Baptist's
work and mission a sad failure for he had placed the
crown upon the head of Jesus. Andrew and his companion were simple fishermen from Galilee and not
scribes from either of the Jerusalem theological sem-
inaries. They were not skilled in Jewish rabbinical
subtleties and dialectics. They did not wish to be
credulous or gullible, and no rabbis were present to
help them. And if there had been some, the Scribes
and Pharisees had rejected the preaching and the
baptism of the Baptist who had even dared to brand
them a brood of vipers. These two disciples had to
make up their own minds about Jesus and the Baptist's interpretation of him, as indeed is true of all
men. Personal experiences lie at the root of one's
relation to Jesus. It was fitting that the first men to
turn to Jesus as the Messiah the Son of God after
the temptation in the wilderness should come from
the circle of the Baptist's disciples and as a result
of his direct tribute to Jesus. So Andrew and John
decided before the day was gone that the Baptist
was right, that Jesus was in reality all that he had
been pictured before them, the Lamb of God. It was
a tremendous fact and one that stirred their very
souls. They knew something of the Messianic hope
in the prophets of the Old Testament and in the
Pharisaic teaching. They do not pause here to in-
quire what sort of a Messiah (political or spiritual)
Jesus was. Apparently they accepted him first as

the political Messiah of the Pharisaic type, though
the Baptist had described him as "the Lamb of God
that takes away the sin of the world" (John 1:29),
the suffering Messiah and Redeemer, wholly out of
line with the Pharisaic Messiah who was not to die
(John 12:34). But with simple and daring faith
these two men alone with Jesus made the bold step
and took their stand with the Baptist in hailing
Jesus as the Messiah of Jewish hope and longing.
Long years afterwards the aged disciple John will
refer to the days of which this was the first when he
saw, heard, and touched this wondrous being, the
Jesus of history and the Messiah of God (I John
1:1-4). Andrew and John have found the Messiah,
the mystery of the ages, the great secret now unfolded. Shall they keep it to themselves?

4. *Andrew's Eager Proclamation of the New Discovery to Simon.*—There were many things that Andrew could have done with his great discovery. He
could have taken it out in dreaming, in disputing, in
reading in the Old Testament, in consulting the rabbis, in revisiting the Baptist, in deciding to tell some-
body sometime after matters of business and personal
interest had been settled. But the very first thing that
he does is to find his own brother Simon. We do not
know which was older, Andrew or Simon. Andrew is
here called the brother of Simon as in Mark 1:16
because the Gospels are written after Simon came to
be so prominent. So it is in John 6:8 when Andrew
tells of the boy with the loaves and fishes. Philip
appears again (cf. vs. 7) with Andrew in John 12:22

(the visit of the Greeks). Andrew was clearly a man of wise counsel. He showed his wisdom in thinking of his own brother Simon before any one else. Clearly Andrew had a high opinion of Simon and there was a bond of fellowship and camaraderie between them, as should always be true of brothers. Unfortunately today with some men so personal an experience as surrender to the Lord Jesus is not a secret that one confides to his own brother first of all. Simon was probably already a disciple of the Baptist also and evidently nearby. But Andrew had to tell Simon what "was and is the Great Discovery" (Bernard): "We have found the Messiah." He included John his companion in the discovery, and used a word equivalent to our *Eureka*. He had found the pearl of great price and must tell about it. The narrative is brief at this point and we are told nothing of the reply of Simon or of his attitude toward Andrew's great discovery. Apparently Simon was a bit sceptical, as was natural, particularly if Simon had not heard the Baptist's clear-cut identification of Jesus as the Messiah on two successive days. Simon, of course, knew that the Baptist had proclaimed the coming of the Kingdom and of the Messiah as at hand. But here Andrew had named the man himself which was a matter that called for certainty. It is probable that Andrew's companion John went and told his brother James.

5. *Bringing Simon to Jesus.*—It is possible that Simon expressed some reluctance to take the step of full allegiance to Jesus as Messiah on the enthusi-

astic statement of Andrew alone. There may have
been some argument or even some protest on Simon's part. Bernard comments on the "swift and
unhesitating" recognition of Jesus by Andrew, by
Philip, and by Nathanael after he actually saw Jesus
(vss. 41, 45), but he wonders if this has not been
"antedated" or then "dulled" in view of the later
confessions of Peter (John 6:65 f.; Matt. 16:16).
But these later confessions come when multitudes
are deserting Christ and they rather mean that the
Apostles are true to Jesus. Andrew brought by skill
and tact his gifted, but hesitating, brother to Jesus.
That is the crowning act in Andrew's life and it
came to be his chief glory to be known as the brother
of Simon. There is never a sign of pique on Andrew's
part. He had influence for good with his own brother
and used it with fine effect. What flimsy excuses we
invent to the Lord Jesus for failing our own flesh
and blood instead of claiming the proud privilege of
bringing them to Jesus. This Andrew did even if he
did not wholly win him to Christ before he came. He
brought Simon face to face with Jesus. It was that
experience that had settled all of Andrew's doubt
and now the same thing happened to Simon. If John
used Roman time, he may have brought Simon that
same evening. If it is Jewish time, it would probably be the next day. But the idea of all that day
in verse 39 would have little meaning if it was only
from four o'clock in the afternoon (ten o'clock Jewish time) till sunset.

6. *The New Name for Simon.*—It is plain that

Simon had not met Jesus before and we are told
nothing of his first impressions, unlike the previous
record about Andrew. But we are told succinctly
the reaction of Jesus toward Simon the brother of
Andrew who is already an avowed disciple of Jesus
and one of the two first to align themselves definitely
with him. Jesus gave Simon an eager and a penetrating look. It is the very idiom used in verse 36
about the rapturous gaze of the Baptist at Jesus as
he was walking, and it occurs also in Mark 10:21
of the look that Jesus gave the rich young ruler
when he loved him at sight. Besides, it is the word
used by Luke (22:61) of the sorrowing look that
Jesus gave Simon after his three denials. We are not
told here, as in Mark 10:21, that Jesus fell in love
with Simon at first sight, but the words of Jesus
reveal insight into the possibilities of usefulness for
the Kingdom of God wrapped up in Simon. Jesus
evidently accepts Simon as a disciple on the same
terms as Andrew (confession of the Messiahship of
Jesus). It is a misreading of the situation to post-
pone Simon's full allegiance to the confession in
Matthew 16:16. The prophecy that Jesus here makes
is not that Simon will in the future confess him as
Messiah, but that he will rise to a high plane of
service, and be a very rock for stability. Jesus calls
him "Simon the son of John." That was the name
in current use for him (cf. John 21:15–17) to distinguish him from the many other Simons, as seen
in Josephus. It is simply the Greek form of Simeon
or Symeon, the Aramaic form used by James for

Simon in Acts 15:14 and by many manuscripts in II Peter 1:1. The original etymology of the word is unknown, but it is the name given the second son of Jacob and Leah (Gen. 29:33) and seems to be connected there with the Hebrew verb *shama'*, to hear. "The reason of this utterance to Simon is understood when it is considered that the name he as yet bore, Simon Barjona, was identified with a character full of impulsiveness, which might well lead him to suppose he would only bring mischief to the Messiah's kingdom" (Dods).

It is easy to admit that Jesus read correctly on the spur of the moment the true character of Simon, as he soon will that of Nathanael (John 1:47). Soon John will say in his Gospel (2:25) that Jesus had no need that any one should bear witness concerning man for he himself knew what was in man. He had this knowledge, not just as the religious genius of the race, but as the Son of God and the Son of Man. That fact in itself is such a supreme miracle that one need not pause here to parley concerning how Jesus possessed such supernatural knowledge of man and of this man now before him. It is clear that Jesus yearned for Simon and rejoiced in his surrender to him. He knows at a glance the limitations and weaknesses in Simon's nature, but he sees also what others had not seen, unless Andrew had glimmerings of it, the enormous possibilities of good in Simon if properly trained for service. Is this not true of every servant of Christ who is called to high service? He is chosen, not because of his perfections, but because of the latent power in him, in spite of many manifest shortcomings. The problem with each of us is how to outgrow and overcome the weakness and how to gain increasing strength for Christ. So Jesus makes a prophecy concerning Simon. He sees the angel in this rough stone and foretells the day when he will be called "Cephas," which, John explains, is the Greek transliteration of the Aramaic *kipho* for *petros* in Greek or rock in English.

Bernard wonders if the Aramaic Cephas is not the same as Caiaphas. The Aramaic Cephas occurs in the New Testament only here and in I Corinthians 1:12; 3:22; 9:5; 15:5; Galatians 1:18; 2:9; 11, 14. But in Galatians 2:7 f. Paul uses Peter, not Cephas. This prophecy of Jesus as to the new name for Simon came true. Jesus continues to address him as Simon in the Gospels (Mark 14:37; Matt. 17:25; Luke 22:31; John 21:15–17), even when he assures him that he is now living up to the prophecy of being a rock (Matt. 16:17). It would seem that Jesus and the disciples continued to use the name Simon for him, but that gradually the surname Peter, repeated by Jesus when the Twelve were set apart (Mark 3:16; Luke 6:14), began to displace the name Simon (Acts 1:13), or both were used together (II Peter 1:1). Matthew uses Peter 19 times, Mark 18 times, Luke 16 times. Bernard notes how giving a new name sometimes in the Old Testament "marked the beginning of a new relation to God; e. g. Jacob was called Israel (Gen. 32:28), and Abram became Abraham

(Gen. 17:5), after a spiritual crisis." Moffatt (*Introduction to the Literature of the N. T.*, p. 524) comments on the habit in the Fourth Gospel of noting a mystical sense in names as an Alexandrian trait to some extent like Philo. The Greek *petros* was commonly used of a detached fragment of a massive ledge of rock (*petra*) like Stone Mountain, a distinction that may be preserved in Matt. 16:18, though it does not exist in the Aramaic word *kipho*. It is not to be overlooked that Peter will later apply this metaphor of Jesus to all believers whom he will describe as "living stones" in I Peter 2:5 with the same phrase applied first to Jesus (vs. 4) as rejected by men as a corner stone (Mark 12:10; Matt. 21:42; Luke 20:17). There is nothing here to indicate the slightest jealousy on the part of Andrew, but only joy that he has brought his brother Simon to Jesus who has placed before him a future of high service.

There is thus beyond a doubt the making of a rock in Simon, but he has a long way to go before he will be in reality "the rock man" pictured here by Jesus. Rocks are made slowly by heat and pressure, upheaval and denudation. But Jesus will keep his eye on Simon and will pray for him in particular when Satan sifts the disciples like wheat (Luke 22:31 f.). In the end, as we see Peter in Acts 1 to 5, he is a rock of defense for Christ and a pillar in the temple of Christ (Gal. 2:9). One can only be grateful for the patience of Jesus with us all as well as the wonder of his mercy and grace in putting us into the ministry, as Paul, the greatest of all ministers of Christ, felt to the very end (I Tim. 1:12–17). It is all of God and for God's glory (II Cor. 4:7). So the outcome with the versatile and volatile Simon, when he does become a *Petros*, is not so much to his credit as it is proof of the power of Jesus to make a mighty engine of power out of frail material. It will pay us all to watch the steps of Simon and the dealings of Jesus with him after this noble prophecy of his future.

CHAPTER III

THE FISHER OF MEN IN PROSPECT
(Mark 1:16–20; Matthew 4:18–22; Luke 5:1–11)

1. *Simon Back at His Regular Work.*—The Fourth Gospel (2:2) first employs the word "disciples" or "learners" of the six who came to the side of Jesus at Bethany beyond Jordan. They are Andrew and Simon, John and James, Philip and Nathanael (later called Bartholomew). It is the word used of Andrew and John as followers of the Baptist (John 1:35). The first occasion for the use of the word for followers of Jesus is at the wedding at Cana (2:2), the second at Capernaum (2:12), the third at Jerusalem at the first passover in Christ's ministry (2:22), the fourth and fifth still in Judea (3:22; 4:2), the sixth in Samaria (4:8, 27, 31, 33). It was concerning believers in the Messiahship of Jesus as the Baptist had proclaimed. Jesus had, indeed, already won many more "disciples" in a looser sense, even more than followed the Baptist (John 4:1), but not quite of a piece with this first half dozen from the circle of the Baptist's followers. There is no indication that these six had given up their business in Bethsaida and Capernaum. The Synoptics do not give this early ministry of Jesus after the temptations till he appears in Galilee. Jesus here is apparently at first preaching and healing alone (Mark

19

1:14 f.; Matt. 4:13–17; Luke, 4:14–31). There is
no relapse or loss of faith or of interest on the part
of the six disciples. They had avowed their faith in
and adherence to Jesus as the Messiah, but they had
not given up their regular vocation. Four of them,
the two pairs of brothers (Andrew and Simon, James
and John), were fishermen and partners, apparently
with Simon as the head of the company, "partners
with Simon" (Luke 5:10), with Zebedee, father of
James and John, also in the company (Mark 1:20;
Matt. 4:21 f.). The business was normally a flourish-
ing one for "hired servants" were engaged (Mark
1:20). It is wholly unnecessary to ignore John's
narrative previous to the record in the Synoptics of
the second call of the four fishermen. There is nothing in the Synoptic account that excludes the fact
that these men were already disciples of Jesus. These
were at this stage what we call laymen. They had followed Jesus steadily for a while, but had not been
called upon to give up their regular work.

2. *But Making a Failure as a Fisherman.*—Luke
gives more details than Mark and Matthew that explain the call that Jesus now makes. But even so
there is no real reason to confuse Luke's narrative
with the much later one in John 21:1–19. Each has a
verisimilitude of its own. Ragg rather timidly suggests that "in view of the naturalness of each narrative, it may be that the *facts* are duplicate, not
merely the records." Mark (1:16) and Matthew (4:
18) simply picture Jesus as walking by the sea of
Galilee when he sees first Andrew and Simon "cast-

ing a net in the sea," "casting to and fro now to one
side now to the other" as Mark has it (1:16),
"throwing a fishing net" as Matthew has it (4:18).
Jesus gives them a definite call to follow him continuously with a remarkable promise: "And I will
make you to become fishers of men." They were
"fishers" by profession, but Jesus takes the metaphor and uses it for evangelism. This term for sea-
folk "is one of many Homeric words which seems to
have gone out of use and then to have reappeared in
late Greek" (Plummer). The use of this metaphor
here is in no way inconsistent with that of "rock"
applied to Simon in John 1:42. A little farther on
Jesus saw James and John mending their nets and
he called them likewise. But Luke analyzes this stage
of the episode and paints a graphic portrait of
Simon that throws a light upon his whole career.
The multitude "pressed" upon Jesus to hear the
word of God spoken by Jesus. "Only in Luke is
Christ's preaching called the word of God (8:11,
21; 11:28)" (Easton). Jesus "was standing" by the
lake at this juncture (cf. "walking" in Mark and
Matthew) and saw two boats standing still and the
fishermen washing the nets as if the work was over
for the time being. They were getting ready to hang
up the nets to dry. Foakes-Jackson (*Peter, Prince
of Apostles*, p. 47) thinks that Luke has "indulged
his literary and artistic sense" and "by allowing his
fancy fuller play" he "has painted a picture of rare
beauty." But why cannot Luke's narrative be simply a fuller account of one phase of the "sublime"

and "simpler narrative" of Mark and Matthew? It was apparent that they had caught nothing. They had fishermen's luck and no doubt it was not the first time, but they could hope for better luck next time.

3. *Simon's Boat as a Pulpit for Jesus.*—Jesus made himself at home in Simon's boat, clearly implying previous acquaintance and fellowship (cf. John 1:40–42). At a later time (the first great group of parables) Jesus entered into a boat and taught the multitudes (Mark 4:1). "This may have become habitual with him" (Ragg) and had obvious advantages as an escape from the pressure of the crowd upon him (Luke 5:1; Mark 4:1; Matt. 13:2). "Christ uses Peter's boat as a pulpit, whence to throw the net of the Gospel over his hearers" (Plummer). There was no reluctance on Simon's part to this use of his boat. He asked Simon "to put out a little from the land" in order to get a better view of the crowd as a whole. So Peter jumped back into the boat and steered it off a bit. Jesus sat down in the boat as also in Mark 4:1 and Matthew 13:2 according to the Jewish custom in the synagogues (Luke 4:20). Then he began teaching out of the boat. No doubt Simon felt a certain pride in this use of his boat by the Master who was now the centre of all eyes. Jesus had grown rapidly in prestige and power with the people since the day of decision by Simon at Bethany beyond Jordan about a year ago. The crowds here have literally pushed Jesus into the sea in their eagerness to hear him. It makes a vivid picture.

4. *Simon Challenged by Jesus to Fish Again Right Where He Had Failed.*—When Jesus had ceased speaking to the multitude, he turned directly to the master of the craft: "Put out into the deep." Perhaps both Andrew and the hired servants helped Simon since James and John and Zebedee were in the other boat. The word in Luke 5:4 for "draught" or "catch" is as old as Homer, but in the New Testament only here and verse 9. Simon was at once challenged by Jesus to fish again in the very waters where he had fished all night and caught nothing. He does not hesitate to tell Jesus his experience of failure. Simon was an expert fisherman and he evidently felt that he knew more about fishing than Jesus did. He readily admitted that Jesus was his superior in all spiritual things, the Messiah in truth. So he calls him "Master," employing an old word for overseer or superintendent that occurs in the New Testament only in Luke and always in addresses to Christ (5:5; 8:24, 45; 9:33, 49, 17:13), a word that recognizes Christ's authority and right to give orders. It is hardly likely that at this stage Simon had a very definite Christology. Luke never employs "Rabbi" (so common in the other Gospels), for he has Gentiles in mind. It is doubtful if Simon saw anything of particular moment in the command to go "into the deep," though it often happens that fish can be caught in the deeper waters while absent from the shallow places. At any rate Simon makes a vigorous protest against fishing again in the very portion of the lake where he had so miserably failed all night

long. He had no heart for such an enterprise, fond of fishing as he was and expert though he claimed to be. "The work of fishers is best carried on at night" (Easton), and night had failed Simon utterly. "Success was doubly improbable: it was *day* and in *deep* water; fish were got at night and near shore" (Bruce). "The symbolical significance of this 'acted parable' is among the richest in the New Testament. This is an ever-fresh message to exhausted and disappointed missioners. The expert thinks he knows that there is no chance of success; yet the moment of utter hopelessness brings a call to new ventures of faith" (Ragg). If we could only learn the lesson of going in deeper right where we are, and when we have apparently done all that seems possible or have even failed to do anything at all. Between Los Angeles and Long Beach is one of the deepest and richest groups of oil wells in the world. They are dug right where the field seemed exhausted till a hopeful and persevering man dug deeper and struck the oil lower down and far richer than that nearer the surface. Simon had not yet learned this lesson. Then he had the pessimistic mood so common in ministers and all Christian workers who feel sure that they can do wonders somewhere else instead of going in deeper where they are.

5. *Reluctant Compliance by Simon.*—Simon made his protest, but he recognized Jesus as Master with the right to give orders. "But at thy word I will let down the nets." He will give orders to let down the nets again, which had just been washed and were

ready to dry, even though he had no confidence in
the wisdom of this particular command and no hope
of success. Edersheim views this word of Simon as
showing "the new trust, and the new work spring-
ing out of that trust," but I fail to see "the new
trust" in such reluctant obedience (see vs. 8). On
the basis of the word of Jesus Simon as a disciple
could do nothing else than obey after his vigorous
protest against its lack of wisdom. It is a fair question to ask whether Christian workers do not often
approach their tasks today with no more hope of
success than spurred Simon on this occasion. We are
too easily held back and down by the dead weight of
past failures. Nothing unusual has happened in so
long a time that we come to expect nothing this time
and usually we are not disappointed, for nothing
happens. Later we shall see an element of daring ad-
venture in Simon in walking on the water (Matt. 14:
28), but that spirit is absent here. Simon is absolutely certain that no fish are in the waters where
they are and he expects to be vindicated in his protest by the outcome. But all the same he is willing
to carry on. That is more than some will do who question the wisdom of this plan or that. They protest
and object and then hang back in order to prove
that they are right. But Simon obeys like a loyal
soldier even though he expects defeat.

6. *The Amazing Success That Humbled Simon.*—
"They inclosed a great multitude of fishes." The
nets "shut together" so many fish that they "were
breaking." That was not all. They beckoned (pos-

sibly because too far away for a call to be heard)
unto their partners in the other boat to come and
take hold together with them. They were in danger
of losing the nets and the fishes also. It was an exciting moment. They filled both boats with the fishes
so full that they began to sink into the depth. This
verb occurs once more in the New Testament (I Tim.
6:9) of money "drowning" men. Every preacher
has had surprising experiences like this in character.
An instance came under my own observation a good
many years ago. I had been making talks on some
portions of the New Testament at the First Baptist
Church in Oklahoma City. I had noticed that the
Sunday School had a large number of unconverted
young people in it. So I asked the privilege of speaking ten minutes to the Sunday School on the closing
Sunday. The pastor, Doctor S. J. Porter, got the
teachers to coöperate and to shorten the class peri-
ods and they were all prayerful and hopeful. The
invitation that came after the short talk lasted for
an hour to the dismay of the organist and the choir
who had an elaborate program, but ninety-three
young people joined the church that morning. It
was the greatest single service of my experience. I
was myself deeply humbled by this token of God's
blessing. Simon (here called Simon Peter, the only
place in Luke with both names, and the first mention
of the surname by Luke) was wholly sincere when he
fell on his knees in the boat and cried out: "Depart
from me; for I am a sinful man, O Lord!" "He saw
the glory of Messiah's Godhead streaming through

the miracle" (W. M. Taylor, *Peter the Apostle*, p. 39). His doubt of success was sinful. It was doubt of the knowledge and the power of Jesus as well as confidence in his own expert knowledge of the situation. Simon had overlooked the deity of Jesus with his omniscience and omnipotence. Now he calls him "Lord," with the full meaning of *Kurios*. It is a full confession of his own sinfulness and of the holiness and deity of Jesus. Simon perhaps unconsciously recognizes the deity of Jesus "which inevitably thrills him through with a sense of unworthiness" (Ragg). Simon does not regard himself as a criminal, but as a sinner. There is no basis for the notion that the Twelve Apostles were exceptionally wicked before their conversion. Simon is overawed by the supernatural power and holiness of Jesus. The contrast between Simon's sinfulness and the holiness of Jesus "is felt to be so intense as to be intolerable" (Plummer). Simon does not, like Jonah, jump into the sea, but he asks Jesus to depart from him, using the very word of Jesus to the demon in Luke 4:35. There are those today who try to explain away this miracle as being only a miracle of knowledge and not of power as in the feeding of the five thousand and of the four thousand. But if it is only a matter of superior knowledge as to the presence of so many fish where Simon had caught none, it is still a miracle of nature and we gain little by trying to explain it away. "Moreover, this was a miracle in Peter's own craft, and therefore was likely to make a special impression on him, just as the healing of a disease,

known to the profession as incurable, would specially
impress a physician" (Plummer). There is not the
slightest doubt about the profound impression made
on Simon by this miracle. He here makes a noble confession of faith in Jesus as Lord quite in contrast
to the doubt and reluctance just before. He will
make other confessions of his faith hereafter, but he
is here in a wholesome frame of mind for service to
Christ. Simon was not alone in his amazement, for
the same wonder and fear held fast or encompassed
all the others in both boats at the catch of fish.
Their surprise was complete, for undoubtedly they
had sympathized with Simon's protest against let-
ting down the nets for this attempt to catch fish.

7. *To Catch Men Alive.*—Jesus still addresses
Peter, clear proof of his interest in Simon and dis-
proof of the modern notion that Luke depreciates
Simon Peter while Matthew exalts him. Jesus bids
Simon not to fear, using the very phrase of the angel
to Zacharias (Luke 1:13). "Peter's sense of unworthiness was in itself a reason for courage"
(Plummer). He was unduly depressed by a kind of
natural inferiority complex in the presence of one so
high and holy as Jesus. "From henceforth," says
Jesus to Peter, thus marking this occasion as a distinct crisis or epoch in his life. Simon will recognize
the crisis when the second miraculous draught of
fishes takes place (John 21:7 f.). Jesus makes a
prophecy about Simon: "Thou shalt catch men,"
using a periphrastic future which "implies permanent occupation" (Bruce). The verb used here means

to catch alive, not to kill. That is a difficult kind of
sport, but a fascinating one. With the nets fish were
easily caught alive. And Simon is to catch alive men,
not fish. Men are more difficult to catch alive in
spiritual nets than fish in the ordinary nets. Homer
uses the verb for sparing men captured in battle.
The prophecy is apparently inopportune, for Simon
deserves no credit for the huge number of fish just
caught after his prediction of failure in view of his
previous experience. As a matter of fact Simon will
deserve no credit when he does become a fisher of men
on a large scale as in Acts 2 and 3. It is interesting
to note how Paul, the greatest of all preachers, will
speak of himself as the least of the apostles (I Cor.
15:9), less than the least of all saints (Eph. 3:8),
the chief of sinners (I Tim. 1:15), progressive de-
preciation of self and increasing exaltation of Christ.
There seemed little enough basis in the conduct and
character of Simon for the forecast of Jesus concerning the future work of Simon. Left to himself
Peter certainly would have failed to fulfil this
prophecy as many men and ministers have failed to
realize the hopes and promises of youth to the sorrow of loved ones and friends. Paul saw just this
thing happen to Hymenæus and Alexander and he
is anxious that it shall not come to pass in the case
of Timothy (I Tim. 1:18–20). There are special
perils before Simon of which he is doubtless unaware
as he hears the rich and glowing picture of evangel-
istic powers here drawn by Jesus. The hope for
Simon as for each of us today is precisely the fact

that Jesus who called us and put us into the ministry watches over us and helps us in the sharp turns in our lives and rescues us from the pitfalls into which we may fall. All this is most strikingly illustrated in the case of Simon Peter. He has an impulsive nature that exposed him to special snares of the devil who sets many for preachers (I Tim. 3:6; II Tim. 2:26), who will catch Judas Iscariot till he becomes a devil himself (John 6:70), and who will sift sorely each of the Twelve (Luke 22:31), and the pressure on Simon will call forth special prayer from Jesus (Luke 22:32). It will be worth while for each of us to watch the ups and downs in Simon's life after this brilliant prophecy of his future. Jesus had already given him a new name (Cephas, Peter, Rock) to live up to. Now another metaphor is applied to him. In simple truth, there seems to us at this juncture little foundation for either figure of speech as a just portrayal of Simon. Paul will never cease to marvel that Jesus found anything in him, once a blasphemer, a persecutor, an insolent man (I Tim. 1:12). Paul's solution of this mystery is that Jesus uses him as a specimen sinner to show what the grace of God can do with a man (I Tim. 1:16). It is God's way to use earthen vessels, broken pieces of pottery, for the highest service that the glory may be of God and not of man (II Cor. 4:7). There is no evidence that Simon was unduly elated or exalted by this prophecy. Jesus may have included the others (Andrew, James, John) in the prophecy, though he singles out Simon. Simon's sense of humiliation (Luke 5:9) was so profound that there was small danger, emotional as he was, of a violent rebound to self conceit.

8. *Leaving All to Follow Jesus.*—Luke does not mention the specific call to follow him, "Come ye after me" given in Mark (1:17) and Matthew (4: 19), but it is evidently implied by the conduct of the group: "And when they had brought their boats to land, they left all, and followed him." Easton calls the plural here "abrupt" after the words of Jesus to Simon. Easton remarks about the fish: "Older commentators sometimes puzzled over the fate of the fish caught in the miraculous draught." Surely that is a side issue after the turn given to the miracle by Jesus. At any rate Zebedee was quite able to dispose of the fish in the market. The miracle under the hands of Jesus becomes a parable for all these four disciples, who now are called upon by Jesus to leave their nets and to follow Jesus continuously. In our modern phraseology these laymen are asked to become travelling evangelists with Jesus. They left their nets then and there without the common excuses so often made by those reluctant to cut loose from business and to devote themselves wholly to Christ's service. Later a man expressed his willingness to follow Jesus, but he wished first to bury his father (still alive) and another wanted first to bid farewell to those at home (Luke 9:59–62). There are sad cases of men who have fought against a call to the ministry half their lives before they are willing to leave all and follow Jesus. On the other hand there are laymen who look on their service to Christ

as their chief business and making money as a side-
line to help on the work of the Kingdom and provide a living for the family. As a matter of fact, all
ministers are made out of laymen, a fact that some
laymen overlook in their criticism of preachers. The
call of Christ to active and permanent service came
with tremendous force after the great miracle. "Even
the large draught of fishes does not detain them.
They are sure that he who has given them such marvellous returns from their usual business will be
ready to provide for them when, at his summons,
they abandon their business" (Plummer). It is a
serious matter for men with an established business
to drop it all and to trust to the uncertainties of
religious service for a livelihood. No sensible or con-
secrated minister expects to make money even if
pastor of a strong and well-established church. But
these four men made a plunge of faith to follow
steadily Jesus who had no organization of any kind
and apparently had no financial resources. Even in
Paul's time after he had established many mission
churches there was still need to work with his hands
at his trade to support himself though he ably
argued in I Corinthians 9 that the minister was entitled to adequate support. This is not the place to
discuss the problem of ministerial support, but we
should note carefully the step taken by Simon when
he joyfully gave up a lucrative business in order to
follow Jesus in his work as Messiah for the kingdom
of God. The sons of Zebedee left their father and the
hired servants and Simon left his wife and home

except for occasional visits to Capernaum (Mark 1:
29; Luke 4:38; Mark 2:1; Matt. 9:1; Luke 5:19).
It was an irrevocable decision. Simon and the rest
burned their bridges behind them and stepped out
into the open. As we have already seen, they had
travelled with Jesus before to Cana, to Capernaum,
to Jerusalem, to Sychar in Samaria. That was the
enthusiasm of a first devotion, but this is the deliberate decision to cast in their lot with Jesus and
his fortune for better or worse. Already the ecclesiastical leaders in Jerusalem (John 2 and 3) had
shown antipathy to Jesus as an upstart from Galilee
with no prestige from either of their theological
schools in Jerusalem. These four men were just fishermen untrained in the rabbinical schools following a
carpenter from Nazareth. It was unthinkable that
the religious leaders, whether Pharisee or Sadducee,
would acknowledge the right of these men to lead a
theological revolution. And yet the people flocked to
Jesus in great throngs. But what cared the ecclesiastics for the ignorant masses? Simon and the rest
counted the cost and put their hands to the plow
with Jesus. Will they live to regret the decision made
that day?

CHAPTER IV

CHRIST'S CHAMPION IN THE MAKING
(Mark 1:21–8:37; Matthew 4:23–16:26; Luke 4:31–44; 5:12–9:25)

Simon now becomes the partisan of Jesus as every disciple has to be who expects to win men to his service. One will be a poor fisher for men and will never catch men alive if he is merely playing at the business. The fish will not even nibble at such bait offered in a half-hearted way. The note of sincerity is absolutely essential in the preacher. Many a man with doubts himself has loved to hear a preacher preach who really believed his own message. No gospel of "perhaps" will ever win the world to Christ. Simon does not apprehend clearly the person of Jesus as the Son of God and the Son of Man. He has accepted him as the Messiah of promise as pointed out by the Baptist. And he will grow in his knowledge of the work of Jesus. Like the others Simon has come to Jesus out of a Pharisaic environment and atmosphere and is looking for a political kingdom. "It was only very slowly that they appreciated its true significance. To do so they had to undergo the training of constant companionship with the Master, and to learn by varied experience the real object of His mission to mankind" (Foakes-Jackson, *Peter, Prince of Apostles*, p. 56). It will require the cata-

clysm of the crucifixion and resurrection of Jesus
with the coming of the Holy Spirit to open Simon's
eyes to the heart of Christ's mission and message.
But meanwhile he is a rock in the making. He is
learning how to catch men alive and he is loyal to
Jesus. He will slip sadly when Jesus is on trial, but
he will come back. There is always this element of
resilient buoyancy in Simon. This sheer humanness
of the man appeals to us all with our many and
varied weaknesses and shortcomings. In order to see
Simon growing in loyal adherence to Jesus we must
note also some of the instances when his name is not
mentioned as well as those that single him out
sharply. It is quite probable that he was the moving
spirit at times when the disciples acted together. At
any rate he acquiesced in what was said and done.

1. *In His Own Home.*—Simon was married and
had a home in Capernaum with his mother-in-law
(Mark 1:29–34; Matt. 8:14–17; Luke 4:38–41).
Luke mentions this visit of Jesus to Capernaum before the call of Simon in 5:1–11, as does Matthew
(8:14–17) but Mark gives it afterwards, probably
following Peter's own story, calling it "the home of
Simon and Andrew" who also lived with Simon. While
Matthew simply says "Peter's house." There is a
life-like touch in Mark 1:33 picturing the crowds
that came to Peter's house at sunset after the "new
teaching" and great miracle in the synagogue and
the healing of Peter's mother-in-law of a fever
(Mark 1:21–31), all on the Sabbath. Already Jesus
was teaching in the synagogues and creating a sen-

sation by the novelty and power in his teaching with
a note of reality and charm strangely unlike the
perfunctory parrot-like speaking of the Pharisaic
rabbis. This and Christ's power over unclean spirits
spread his fame "everywhere into all the region of
Galilee round about." The synagogue was the one
best means of reaching the people and Jesus used it
constantly though not an accepted rabbi of the
schools. What these crowds really thought of Jesus
matters little to us now, for they saw only the beginning, not the final stage of the picture. There
have been many modern efforts to restore this early
conception of Jesus by the Galilean crowds by trying to get behind the Gospels by *Formgeschichte*
and other methods more or less praiseworthy in
themselves. But even if we could do that and restore
the early view of the so-called historical Jesus, very
little would be gained for our knowledge. One thing
is certain and it is that these early disciples did not
understand Jesus as they came to do after his resurrection and ascension. Foakes-Jackson has a sane
word concerning some of the modern attempts to
eliminate the supernatural elements in the life of
Jesus: "The result of the impression thus produced
has been seen in the many attempts to rationalise,
liberalise, and even to vulgarise the so-called historical Jesus" (*op. cit.* p. 61). The Jewish Sabbath ended at sunset and so "all the city was gathered at the door," at the door of Peter's house, for
Mark is here using Peter's eyes as he had heard him
tell of this unforgettable scene, "when the sun was

setting" (Luke 4:40; Mark 1:32). The sick with manifold (many-colored) diseases passed in glad procession before the door as Jesus "laid his hands on every one of them" (Luke 4:40) and healed them "with a word" (Matt. 8:16). Curiously the demons knew that Jesus was the Messiah (Mark 1:24, 34; Luke 4:41) and hence he forbade their testifying to him. Witness from such a source would discredit rather than help him and already Jesus saw that the public would take him as a political Messiah as they openly did later (John 6:15). The early claim of Jesus to be Messiah in no way contradicts the silence here imposed. It is not difficult to imagine the effect of this wonderful sunset experience on Simon as he stood in his own doorway and saw the might of the Master with men.

Next morning the crowds came early to Peter's house to see and hear Jesus, but he was gone. A great while before day Jesus rose up and went out into a desert place and prayed (Mark 1:35). It is Mark again who adds that "Simon and they that were with him followed," a natural leadership on Simon's part for the group (Simon, Andrew, James, John, Mark 1:29) were at Simon's house and Mark reflects Simon's own attitude, all rejoicing in the prowess of the Master with the people. But Jesus had apparently slipped away without the knowledge of Simon, apparently while Simon was still asleep, who had a habit of sleeping at an important crisis (Transfiguration and Gethsemane). So the four disciples, unable to teach or to heal the crowds already

come, went in search of Jesus till they found him.
Luke (4:42 f.) has some of the crowd going along
also, as was natural, probably at a distance and
finally overtaking them. "All are seeking thee," the
disciples said to Jesus, but he would not come back
to Peter's house and duplicate the experience of the
evening before. They had had their opportunity and
Jesus felt the urge to go on "into the next towns."
So he made this tour of Galilee with the band of
four disciples, a tour that carried his fame into all
Syria, Decapolis, Perea, Jerusalem and Judea besides all Galilee (Mark 1:39; Matt. 4:23–25; Luke
4:44). There was a stirring in the synagogues such
as was never known before. Simon was in the thick
of it all with Jesus.

Once again Jesus is back in Capernaum and in
Peter's house (Mark 2:1; Matt. 9:1; Luke 5:19).
The report spread all over the city that Jesus was
"at home" (in the house) again in Peter's house and
they recalled the former experience there at sunset.
Luke adds (5:17) that "the Pharisees and doctors
of the law" were also there, "which were come out
of every village of Galilee and Judea and Jerusalem"
just as the Pharisees and Sadducees had once flocked
to the Jordan to see and hear the Baptist (Matt.
3:7), tremendous witness to the attractiveness of
Christ's preaching. But these men had not come as
penitents, rather as spies to report to Jerusalem
headquarters (broods of vipers according to the
Baptist). They were in Peter's house "sitting by"
as Jesus "was teaching" to see if they could pick

a flaw somewhere. Already then the ecclesiastics have
lined up against Jesus in Galilee as they did in
Jerusalem before he left Judea for Galilee. Mark
(2:2), using Peter's eyes again, observes that on this
occasion the crowd was so great that "there was no
longer room, no, not even about the door." Jesus was
on the inside, probably near the door, when a notable
incident occurred, graphically told by Mark and
followed by Matthew and Luke. It is the story of
how four men, who bore a paralytic on his pallet,
climbed up the outside stairway to the roof, dug a
hole through the tile roof, and let the man on his
pallet down right before Jesus. Here was a challenge for Jesus with the Pharisees seated nearby to
watch him and with Simon Peter standing eagerly
by also. Jesus accepts the challenge, but forgives the
man's sins first and this assumption of the preroga-
tive of God angers the Pharisees so that they charge
Jesus with blasphemy. Jesus with calm deliberation
then heals the man, "that ye may know that the Son
of Man has power on earth to forgive sins." There
is a remarkable proof that Matthew (9:6) and Luke
(5:24) follow the text of Mark (2:10), since they
both insert the parenthetical comment (he says to
the sick of the palsy) in the midst of the words of
Jesus. The effect of this miracle was electrical. Peter
and all the rest were filled with amazement and fear
and glorified God. "We never saw it on this fashion." Indeed "the power of the Lord was with him
to heal."

Simon reclined with Jesus and the disciples along

with the publicans and sinners at the reception given
by Levi (Matthew) in honor of Jesus after his ac-
ceptance of the call. Simon with the rest stood the
chiding of the Pharisees and their pupils (Luke
5:30) who murmured loudly at a professed rabbi
associating on a social level with such outcasts, one
of whom Jesus had called to his group of a half-
dozen. Such social slurs are hard to bear. The Pharisees looked on the publicans as the modern Hindus
regard the outcastes (the untouchables). But another
shock followed this one when some of the disciples
of the Baptist, as six of these disciples used to be,
actually joined with the Pharisees and their disciples in protest to Jesus for not observing the Jewish
fast days and apparently attending Levi's reception
on one of those very days. Here again it is Jesus
who justifies his conduct by three striking, even startling, parables about the bridegroom, the piece of
undressed cloth as a patch, new wine in old wine-
skins (Mark 2:18–22). Both of these experiences
were illuminating to Simon and to all, though they
remained steadfast to Jesus. Another enlightening
experience was the independence of Jesus concerning the Pharisaic regulations about Sabbath observance. Three of these experiences followed in quick
succession, one at Jerusalem at an unknown feast
(John 5:1–47) when Jesus justified his healing a
man on the Sabbath by claiming equality with God
his Father to the murderous rage of the Pharisees.
Another time was back in Galilee as the disciples
appeased their hunger (Matt. 12:1) by plucking

and eating the ripe grain as they passed through the
fields, whose conduct Jesus defended by revolutionary arguments (Mark 2:23–28; Matt. 12:1–8;
Luke 6:1–5). And then in a synagogue in Galilee on
a Sabbath Jesus deliberately healed a man's withered hand, as the Pharisees watched him, and defied
them for caring more for a sheep than for a man,
a defence that led the Pharisees and the Herodians
to plot to kill him (Mark 3:6). We are told nothing
about the effect of all this fiery hostility on the disciples. So far they seem to be wholly loyal to their first
love. Simon was seeing the fighting side of Christ's
nature as he made his way against the bitter ecclesiastics. It is literally true that Jesus in his Messianic work was opposed by the devil and the current
Pharisaic preachers (rabbis).

2. *Simon Chosen as Apostle.*—The selection of the
Twelve Apostles came at a crisis in the ministry of
Jesus when the organized opposition by the Jerusalem Pharisees showed the sheer necessity for some
definite organization. Mark (3:13–19) and Luke
(6:12–16) locate this important event on a mountain whither Jesus went to pray "and he continued
all night in prayer to God" (Luke). So Jesus ex-
horted prayer for laborers to go into the harvest
(Matt. 9:38). Mark and Luke both say that he
called "unto him whom he himself would" (Mark)
"and he chose from them twelve whom also he named
Apostles" (Luke). It was a solemn appointment by
Jesus who assumed full responsibility for the choice
of these men out of the whole number of disciples

who now followed him. Luke makes it plain that the choice came in the early dawn after the night of prayer just before the Sermon on the Mount (Matt. 5:1 f.), a level place on the mountain (Luke 6:17) where Jesus stood with the newly chosen Twelve beside him and delivered this marvellous address on his conception of righteousness in contrast to that of the current Jewish teachers (Matt. 5:20). To the Twelve it was an Inaugural Lecture (Broadus) by Jesus, but to the multitude of disciples and to the crowds from Idumea to Tyre and Sidon (Mark 3:7 f.; Luke 6:17; Matt. 5:1) a discourse utterly unlike any that had ever been heard from the rabbis (Matt. 7:28 f.). The list of the Twelve is not given by Matthew till they were sent out by twos on a tour of Galilee, but Matthew does not say that they were not chosen till then. He simply states (10:1–5) that Jesus called the Twelve to him, whose names he now gives, and sends them forth on this particular tour. In each instance Simon is named first (Judas Iscariot always last), as also in the list in Acts 1:13, but we are not to understand that Jesus appointed him leader of the Twelve at this time or ever at a later time. It is by no means certain that Simon was acknowledged as leader before the great Pentecost, for there was continuous rivalry among the Twelve (see Chapter VI, "Rivalry for the Primacy"). The lists in the Gospels and the Acts all reflect the feeling of a later time after Simon had come to the front. But the list includes the four fishermen (Andrew and Simon, James and John),

Philip and Nathanael (Bartholomew), all previous
disciples of the Baptist and the first disciples won
by Jesus at Bethany beyond Jordan, as well as Levi
(Matthew) the publican. The other five (Thomas,
James the son of Alphaeus, Simon Zelotes=Thad-
deus, Judas—son or brother of James—and Judas
Iscariot) have not heretofore been named in the
Gospels. They were all Galileans save Judas Iscariot.
No one of them was a scribe or a rabbi and apparently no one was a Pharisee or a Sadducee. No one
of them had technical theological training from the
Pharisees. They were as little under the influence of
the Pharisees as it was possible to find men in Palestine. Each had his own gifts and graces and the
making of an apostle worthy of the choice made by
Jesus. It is certain that Jesus made the wisest selection with the material before him. We should
never forget that God has, from the nature of the
case, in every emergency to use the men on hand at
the time. Jesus had had his eye on Simon from the
very start, as we have seen. He had the making of
a rock in him. He was to be a fisher of men as
Jesus promised for him and for the three other
fishermen: "I will make you fishers of men" (Matt.
4:19). Jesus had tested these men for some months
and now he called them out of the rest "that they
might be with him" (Mark 3:14), a personal body-
guard and more, that they might come to understand Jesus and his mission and message "that he
might send them forth to preach." So he keeps them
by his side for a year or more and then sent them

forth over Galilee "by two and two" (Mark 6:7) with authority to heal and to preach. They were not novices (I Tim. 3:6) when sent forth, but men trained by Jesus himself, the greatest of all teachers, in a sort of peripatetic (after the method of Aristotle) theological seminary.

Luke (6:14) adds about the choice of Simon by Jesus, "whom he also named Peter," while Mark (3:16) says "and Simon he surnamed Peter" in a parenthetical clause ("almost intolerable" in such a context, Swete) which is not clear as to the date of this surname. One naturally thinks of John 1:42. Swete is probably right in thinking that Mark merely means that the name "Peter" was now actually applied to Simon as fact and not mere prophecy. "The name was actually given at the first call of Simon (John 1:42), but apparently not appropriated till he became an Apostle." We are told nothing of Simon Peter's own reaction to the choice of Jesus in selecting him or in the choice of the other eleven. In Paul's case both Luke and Paul tell us a good deal about this great decision that we call the conversion of Saul. But we do know that Simon responded wholly to this third call by Christ, this time to the apostolic circle.

The duties of these men they were to learn from Jesus as he unfolded them and led them on step by step. The mere fact of this selection is proof that the purely eschatological interpretation of Christ's teaching is erroneous. He is laying plans for a campaign, not looking for a sudden catastrophe. Certainly these Twelve men were not the local church seen in the Acts nor the kingdom or general church of Matthew 16:18, though they were chosen for the work of the kingdom and to establish local churches also. If the gospel of Jesus was to go on, there must be competent interpreters of it. These men by association and training should be able to do that. We shall see how hard it was for them, even for Simon, in particular Simon, to do this before Christ's death and resurrection, and the coming of the Holy Spirit at Pentecost. If these men, thus trained by Jesus, had so tremendous a task in comprehending Christ, it is easy to see how necessary it was to have such a group of men, prepared soil at any rate, when the day of understanding did come. We must not picture Palestine as a land of ignoramuses. "It is no exaggeration to say that the intellectuality of the Jew is due to centuries of discipline in the study of his religion. It is quite a mistake to suppose that Jesus addressed his words to ignorant crowds, or chose entirely uneducated men as His disciples. His words could only be understood by those who were familiar from their earliest days with the scriptures of Israel" (Foakes-Jackson op. cit. p. 54). To be sure the Sanhedrin will sneer at Jesus because he had not studied in their schools (John 7:15) and at Peter and John as unlearned and ignorant men for the same reason (Acts 4:13). But here is Simon face to face with his life opportunity. He has been chosen by Jesus a member of the college of the Apostles (missionaries sent forth by Jesus) with the companionship of the greatest of men, to say no more, and the fellowship of a choice body of fellow spirits in the furtherance of the greatest revolution of earth, with a boundless future before it, with no earthly capital or power to push it forward. What will be Simon's part in this golden dream with this group of young men as they confront ecclesiastical hatred and hostility and a world wholly out of sympathy with spiritual and mystical hopes?

3. *Like the Others Simon Is Puzzled by the Parables.*—Jesus had used brief occasional parables before, as about fasting (Mark 2:18–22) and in the Sermon on the Mount (Matt. 5 to 7), but the Pharisees had accused Jesus of being in league with Beelzebub (Mark 3:19–30) and even the brothers of Jesus had come to take him for a rest under the fear that he was beside himself from overstrain (Mark 3:21, 31–35). Now once again Jesus was teaching great crowds by the sea side and entered into a boat and sat in it ("sat in the sea," Mark) and began speaking in parables (Mark 4:1 f.; Matt. 13:1 f.). "And when he was alone, they that were about him with the twelve asked him of the parables" (Mark 4:10). According to Matthew (13:10) they asked why he spoke to the people in parables and evidently felt difficulty in understanding what this parable of the sower really meant (Luke 8:9). Peter may have been the spokesman in this inquiry, though it is not so stated. Certainly he shared in the doubt and the desire for more light concerning this new method of teaching on such a scale by Jesus. Parables occur

in the Old Testament and in the rabbinical teaching, but no parables compare with these of Jesus. The answer of Jesus contains a reflection on the apostles and other disciples, for "unto you is given the mystery of the kingdom of God: but unto them that are without, all things are done in parables" (Mark 4:11). We have here the only use in the Gospels of the word "mystery" so common in Paul (twenty-one times, four times in the Apocalypse). And yet Peter and the rest utterly failed to grasp this secret meant for them. Jesus explains "by an adaptation" (Swete) of Isaiah 6:9 f. how his use of parables was a sentence of judicial blindness on those unable to see (Mark 4:12; Matt. 13:13–15; Luke 8:10). Then Jesus explained the parable of the sower and gave still others. After leaving the crowds Jesus went into the house, and again the disciples asked for an explanation of the parable of the tares (Matt. 13:36). After other parables were spoken Jesus asked the disciples: "Have ye understood all these things?" (Matt. 13:51). "They say unto him, Yea." This answer of self-confidence sounds like Simon Peter, but Matthew credits it to all. They were quick learners in their own estimation and soon forgot how to interpret parables as we shall see (Mark 8:14–21). Peter was not duller than the other apostles and they were above the average in intelligence, but the message of Jesus was so essentially spiritual and original and his method was so different from the traditional parrot-like quotation style of the rabbis that even this chosen group of "learners" (disciples) had trouble in catching the meaning of this greatest of all teachers. We shall see Jesus using repetition and variety and practising patience with these men and even then often unable to lift them out of the Pharisaic cobwebs of external ceremonialism and political literalism. Peter by his very volative impulsiveness is the looking-glass by which we can read the attitude of the rest.

4. *Like the Others Terrified by the Storm.*—It was the evening of this same day when so many parables (ten at least) were spoken by Jesus that he proposed to the disciples to go over to the other side (the eastern) of the Sea of Galilee. It had been a hard day and soon Jesus was asleep on the cushion in the stern of the boat (Mark 4:38). A quick tempest rushed down the gorge of the Jordan from Mount Hermon and lashed the lake into fury to the terror of the apostles who in a panic awoke Jesus with a pathetic plea: "Master, Master, we are perishing" (Luke 8:24), and with a reproach in it according to Mark (4:38): "Master, carest thou not that we are perishing?" They had with them in the boat the Lord of life and yet they had lost heart and hope. Jesus spoke a calm to the wind and the waves and then asked "why" they were fearful (Mark 4:40; Matt. 8:26) and "where" was their faith (Luke 8:25), such "little faith" (Matt. 8:26). "Have ye not yet faith?" Mark picturesquely preserves it. Peter with the rest flounders in his faith in this crisis, fears exceedingly, and asks: "Who then is this, that even the wind and the sea obey him?"

(Mark 4:41). "Faith in its fulness (Matt. 8:26) was still wanting to them. . . . This is the first of a series of censures on the apostles for their lack of faith or understanding" (Swete). They had witnessed the Messianic power of Jesus in the miraculous draught of fishes, in healing the demoniacs and multitudes of sick all over Galilee, but here there is a new revelation of the majesty and might of Jesus in the realm of nature. This nature miracle troubled the apostles as it disturbs some critics today who are willing to admit the reality of the healing miracles by Jesus, especially where the influence of mind upon mind is possible, but who balk at the nature miracles or power over inaminate matter and do not hesitate to apply the term legend to these narratives. This present-day doubt is rendered less creditable in view of the new theories of matter presented by Jeans and Eddington, but at any rate we are able to sympathize with the amazement of the apostles, including Peter, as to "what manner of man" this was in the boat with them who had received instant obedience of wind and wave to his word. "They might have been sure that the Messiah would not perish, and that their prayer for help would be answered" (Plummer). Silently and with reverent awe they row on to the land of the Gerasenes to see fresh power by Jesus over a raging demoniac in the hills.

5. *Peter One of the Inner Circle in the Home of Jairus.*—The urgent and tender request of Jairus, one of the rulers of the synagogue, for Jesus to

come and save his little daughter who is at the point
of death (Mark 5:23) touches the heart of Jesus. On
the way the crowds pressed upon Jesus so that, when
a poor woman touched the hem of his garment for
healing and Jesus asked who had touched him (Luke
8:45), Peter spoke up as if to rebuke Jesus for an
idle question: "Master, the multitudes press and
crowd thee" (Luke 8:45). The other disciples shared
in Peter's protest (Mark 5:31), though he was the
spokesman for them all. All in the crowd apparently denied touching Jesus (Luke 8:45). "This explains, and to some extent excuses, Peter's characteristic interference" (Plummer). Jesus repeated
his statement in a way that Peter did not then understand: "Some one did touch me, for I perceived
that power had gone forth from me" (Luke 8:46).
Before Jesus reaches the home of Jairus word comes
that it is useless to trouble Jesus further for the
child is dead (Mark 5:35). But Jesus overheard and
disregarded the message, and urged that Jairus
should "fear not, only believe," and went on to his
home. Jesus respected the seclusion of the home life
and chose only three of the disciples (Peter and
James and John), perhaps for the sake of the
Twelve, whose faith thus witnessed would be strengthened by this miracle. Precisely these three will be
taken by Jesus to the Mount of Transfiguration and
will be with him as he prays in the Garden of Gethsemane. They constitute a sort of inner circle in the
group of apostles (more select of the select, according to Clement of Alexandria). Plummer thinks

that these "were in character most fitted to profit by the miracle." Jesus seems to feel that it is a crisis for the apostles who are now to see his power to restore the dead to life. There was tumult in the house by the flute-players and other hired mourners (Matt. 9:23), according to Jewish custom and probably congregated in the courtyard, and not in the bedroom (McNeile). Jesus sternly cast out these professional mourners whose interest it was to remain. "He ejects the jeering hirelings who were not in sympathy with his purpose" (Swete). The Synoptics all speak of their laughing Jesus to scorn and of the tenderness of Jesus in taking the little girl by the hand (Mark 5:40 f.; Matt. 9:24 f.; Luke 8:53 f.). The amazement of all was great and Jesus "charged them that no man should know this" (Mark 5:43; Luke 8:56), but all the same "the fame thereof went forth into all that land" (Matt. 9:26). Nothing is said about the immediate effect on Peter and James and John, nor how soon they told the other nine. But they had had an epochal experience of Christ's power and they had stepped up to a still higher level in the growing apprehension of Jesus as the Christ, one beyond the wonder when he stilled the wind and the waves. Here Jesus revealed himself as Master over life and death. By and by Peter will call Jesus: "The Prince of life" (Acts 3:15). Here he had seen the Prince of life in action.

6. *Peter Sent with the Others on a Tour of Galilee.*—Both Mark (6:1–6) and Matthew (13: 54–58) give a last visit to Nazareth, later than the

one in Luke 4:16–31. It is fitting that Jesus should give the people of his home town another opportunity to hear him. His own mother and brothers had already shown concern about his health. The people then recognized that he has brothers and sisters still with his mother Mary and are greatly puzzled to explain his manifest prowess. Their disbelief was so great that he left Nazareth for good and all.

There have been two tours of Galilee before, but now Jesus sends the Twelve by twos (Mark 6:7). If we may judge by later instances (Luke 22:8; John 20:2–10) Peter and John went together. It was an important experiment by Jesus to see how these chosen apostles could carry on the work without his personal presence. They had had over a year of definite training since they had been chosen and set apart by the Master. The immediate occasion was the compassion of Jesus for the multitudes "as sheep not having a shepherd" (Matt. 9:36). So Jesus urged prayer that the Lord would send forth more workers into the harvest (no unemployment here) and then sent them forth with special instructions for this particular time, some of which were changed afterwards. It was not a preparation for the world tour later after the Ascension (Matt. 28:16–20), but just for this Galilean campaign. They were not even to go this time to the Samaritans, but only to the lost sheep of the house of Israel (Matt. 10:6). But even so in this limited experimental tour of healing and preaching (Matt. 10:7 f.) they would meet real perils that called for great

wisdom and courage. With no equipment of money
or baggage they would need the innocence of doves
and the wisdom of serpents. They would go as sheep
in the midst of the same wolves that had been yelp-
ing at the heels of Jesus. But they will have the help
of the Holy Spirit. Doctor John A. Broadus used to
say that the only way to learn how to preach is to
preach. At the Baptist Seminary in Louisville, Kentucky, the students find street preaching an invalu-
able experience with many blessed results. So they
went forth "preaching the gospel, and healing everywhere" (Luke 9:6). Jesus himself then went on to
teach and preach in the cities of Galilee (Matt.
11:1). His path probably overlapped that of the
apostles as we know was the case when the seventy
were sent out in Judea "whither he himself was
about to come" (Luke 10:1). We may be sure that
Peter did his share of the preaching and healing.
The result was tremendous. There was a stirring in
the mulberry trees all over Galilee. News of the
campaign reached Herod Antipas at Tiberias, his
capital. He had never seen Jesus, but he knew John
the Baptist only too well. Inquiry by Herod confirmed his superstitious fear that Jesus was after all
John the Baptist come to life again. He had agreed
to his death under pressure from his wife Herodias
(Mark 6:14–29) and still had qualms of conscience
over his surrender to the foolish oath to Salome, the
daughter of Herodias. The Twelve finally returned
to make a report to Jesus, apparently at Peter's
house in Capernaum. They told Jesus "all things,

whatsoever they had done, and whatsoever they had taught" (Mark 6:30). They were the first missionaries (apostles) who had gone on such a tour (state missions). It was their first independent preaching anywhere. We may be sure that Peter did his share of the talking, but he did not do it all. Jesus patiently listened to each one. The outcome revealed that they were weary and in need of rest after such a strenuous campaign and the Master himself was a bit worn. So he said, "Come ye yourselves apart into a desert place, and rest awhile" (Mark 6:31). How many fish did Peter catch this time? We can only speculate. But he was learning how to catch men alive for Jesus.

7. *Along with the Rest Peter Is Carried Away by Popular Enthusiasm for a Political Messiah.*—Jesus and the Twelve failed to find the needed rest because the people, when they saw the boat going across to the east, ran around the head of the lake to the region of Bethsaida Julias (Luke 9:10). So Jesus took pity on them, healed the sick, preached to them, and finally fed the 5000 men besides the women and children (Matt. 14:21). This nature miracle is given by all Four Gospels (the only one so given), and the apostles acted as waiters to distribute the food (bread and fish) to the orderly groups (Mark 6:40) that looked like "garden beds" (Mark reporting with Peter's eyes again) because of the varied colors of the oriental garments of the men on the green grass in the afternoon sun. It was a bountiful feast with twelve baskets full left over, the wallets car-

ried by every Jew "to avoid buying food from Gentiles" (Plummer). It was an unforgettable scene at the passover time (John 6:4), just one year before the final catastrophe at the next passover. The disciples had urged that Jesus send the great crowds away before night overtook them all (Mark 6:36), but now after this stupendous miracle no one wished to leave so that he "constrained his disciples to enter the boat, and to go before him unto the other side to Bethsaida (the one in Galilee), while he himself sendeth the multitude away" (Mark 6:45). McNeile skeptically doubts there being a Bethsaida of Galilee in spite of the express statement of John in 12:21 because "it is improbable that there were two Bethsaidas" (Comm. on Matt. 14:22). "Improbable" to McNeile, but in fact no more so than two Bethanys. It is a strong word (compelled) used here by Mark (and also Matt. 14:22) and shows that the disciples did not wish to leave the exciting crowds. "But at any rate Jesus found it necessary to make the disciples leave him; without them for some reason He could more easily persuade the crowds to disperse. The only reason that suggests itself is that their enthusiasm had been raised, and the presence of the disciples would increase rather than allay it" (McNeile on Matt. 14:22). John (6:14) makes it plain what this popular enthusiasm was. They were saying: "This is of a truth the prophet that cometh into the world," the one spoken of by Moses as like unto himself (Deut. 18:15), the Messiah of Jewish hope and promise. Undoubtedly the apostles already believed this and were overjoyed at the popular enthusiasm but Jesus saw the peril that the apostles did not see, namely that the people looked for a political Messiah who would throw off the Roman yoke. In a word, they wanted Jesus to lead a revolution against Rome and proclaim himself king in place of Cæsar. "This attempt to make Jesus a national king marks the climax of the popular enthusiasm for him. Since the beginning of the Ministry this has been on the increase" (Plummer). The disciples clearly sympathized with this movement to stampede Jesus into a political revolution. It was a dangerous crisis. So Jesus quietly sent the disciples off in the boat and then sent the multitudes away. "Jesus therefore, perceiving that they were about to come and take him by force, to make him king, withdrew again into the mountain alone" (John 6:15). No one understood him at this moment but the Father and he must talk to him in prayer (Mark 6:46). Peter was clearly swept off his feet like the rest who saw signs of place and power for each of them in such an earthly kingdom with Jesus as king. It was the temptation of the devil again with world power offered to Jesus from the people this time. *Vox populi* was certainly not *vox dei*, but *vox diaboli*. The safety of the apostles was in getting them quickly away from this wrong atmosphere. Evidently Peter and the rest had a long way to go before they could be entrusted with the message of Jesus to the world.

8. *Daring Impulsiveness on Peter's Part.*—It was

the fourth watch in the night (about 3 A.M. our time) that Jesus had not yet come to the disciples (John 6:17). They had apparently lingered awhile near the shore "watching the dispersion of the crowds, and wondering whether, after all, Christ would not require to be taken over in the boat" (Plummer on Matthew, p. 207). The lake is only seven or eight miles across and they are only half way across (John 6:19) when they behold Jesus "walking on the sea" (Mark 6:48; Matt. 14:25; John 6:19), not "by the sea" as some try to make it mean in order to get rid of the miracle of Jesus walking upon the water. The explanation is contradicted by the context in each of the three Gospels for he could not be "drawing nigh unto the boat" if he was four miles away on land. They had been facing a "contrary" ("great wind," John 6:18) wind and the sea was still rough. Jesus had seen them "distressed in rowing" (Mark 6:48) before he started towards them, but, when he came near, he seemed to wish to pass them by in order not to frighten them. They were already disturbed by the wind and the absence and the darkness of the night. It was daytime and they had had Jesus with them in the boat in the other storm on this lake. But the sight of one gliding along on the water at this time of night frightened them (John 6:19) for they supposed that they saw an apparition (Mark 6:49; Matt. 14:26) and screamed in terror. Then Jesus spoke: "Be of good cheer; it is I; be not afraid" (Mark 6:50; Matt. 14:27; John 6:20).

Here was a new role for Jesus who had just refused to be a national king and yet who is master over the elements of nature, even the force of gravitation. The reaction was great with them all, but greatest with Matthew who alone (14:28–31) gives the incident of Peter's walking on the water towards Jesus. "The miracle of Christ walking upon the sea is often spoken of as a legend. Goethe said it was one of the most beautiful of legends and a special favorite of his" (Plummer on Matt., p. 207). The episode about Peter is urged as further proof of its legendary character. But even McNeile (on Matt., p. 220) observes: "A strong point in favour of the story is its faithful reflexion of the apostle's character." For the consolation of those who consider it a legend McNeile suggests that it is "an acted parable of his proud impulsiveness," "his fall and repentance," and "his restoration." But why should such a story on Peter be told by Matthew with no basis in fact? It is true that Matthew does give Peter prominence in his Gospel (calling him "first" in 10:2) and it is noteworthy that Mark does not tell the incident. Clearly Peter was not in the habit of telling it himself, for it shows him in a not wholly favorable light. When joy at seeing Jesus dispelled the fear of an apparition, Peter's natural impulsiveness led him to make an almost boyish request to Jesus to prove his identity: "Lord, if it be thou, bid me come unto thee upon the waters" (not alongside the waters). Jesus gave the simple word "Come" and Peter quickly and gladly in full faith stepped down from the boat and did walk upon the waters like Jesus and actually came. It was a proud moment for Peter. But just then a sudden and severe gust of wind struck the waves and Peter, who, on seeing the wind, grew afraid, began to sink down into the sea right beside Jesus. What a parable is this for preachers and politicians who get their courage from the wind of popular favor. Poor Peter cried out to Jesus for help: "Lord, save me." The expression about seeing the wind is like seeing the voice in Revelation 1:12 by metonymy for the result of wind and voice. Jesus did at once reach out his hand, and take hold of him, but gave him a sharp rebuke, not for wanting to walk on the water, but for losing faith and courage while doing it at Christ's command and with Jesus right by his side: "O thou of little faith, wherefore didst thou doubt?" John (6:21) notes that now "they were willing therefore to receive him into the boat," a different account in no way inconsistent with the episode in Matthew, for until they recognized Jesus they had been unwilling to take him in. The wind ceased at once and the waves grew calm to the amazement of the disciples who had failed to see the full deity of Jesus in the miracle of the loaves and fishes because "their heart was hardened" (Mark 6:52), hardened by previous prejudices from a Pharisaic environment. But now with Jesus in the boat with them again, after all the wonders on land and sea, "they that were in the boat worshipped him, saying, Of a truth thou art the Son of God" (Matt. 14:33). There is no rea-

son for emptying the confessions and the act of
worship of their full significance. Plummer (on
Matt., p. 210) hesitates, "but perhaps even yet they
are not sure that he is the Messiah." But why not?
Andrew and Simon took him as Messiah at the first
in Bethany beyond Jordan. The Baptist had called
him the Son of God. Nathanael called him the Son of
God. The Samaritans termed him the Saviour of the
world (John 4:42). Jesus claimed to be Messiah in
the synagogue in Nazareth (Luke 4:21). Simon had
fallen at Jesus' feet in adoration after the miraculous draught of fishes (Luke 5:8). Jesus openly
claimed to be the Son of man (Mark 2:10; Matt.
9:6; Luke 5:24). In Jerusalem they heard Jesus
claim equality with God (John 5:18). The message
to the despondent Baptist claimed Messiahship in
fact (Matt. 11:2–6; Luke 7:18–22, from Q, the
Logia of Jesus). The disciples just the afternoon
before were carried away by the popular enthusiasm
for Jesus as the political Messiah (John 6:14 f.). To
be sure the apostles had not yet come to understand
that Jesus is a spiritual, not a political, Messiah.
But the facts in all the Gospels call for the accep-
tance of him as the Messiah with their understanding of the term long before this incident in the boat.
Humbly and with awed reverence they here worship
Jesus as the Son of God, according to Matthew,
please observe, not in John's Gospel. In particular
Simon Peter was moved to this act after his rescue
by Jesus from the angry wind and waves. Jesus had
not only walked firmly upon the sea, but had drawn

the sinking apostle up out of the water. Peter is learning, if slowly and with difficulty, "what manner of man" this is whom they have followed. He does not yet know the precise path along which he is leading the disciples. But Peter is still willing to follow on, the lesson that will have fresh meaning for him after his restoration to favor and fellowship, when Jesus will sum it all up for Peter by saying: "Keep on following me" (John 21:19). Each step that Peter takes brings him into fuller and richer truth about Jesus.

9. *The Lonely Loyalty of Peter.*—The same crowd that had shown such exuberant enthusiasm over the feeding of the five thousand turned up the next day in Capernaum, "seeking Jesus" (John 6:24) for another free feast, as he plainly pointed out, not for spiritual food. Some of them followed Jesus into the synagogue (6:59) where he gradually revealed himself as the true manna, the bread of God come down from heaven, which they must eat if they wished to live forever. This mystical appropriation of Christ's very flesh and blood mystified these superficial hearers who actually "strove with one another" (John 6:52) right in the synagogue as if Jesus took them to be cannibals! This language of Jesus is misunderstood by some today, who make it refer to the elements of the Lord's Supper either by anticipation or as the retrospect by the author of the Gospel who makes Jesus thus teach sacramentarianism and even thus to refute Gnosticism (so Bernard in his Comm.). Surely Westcott is right in

seeing here only the personal appropriation of Christ by the individual. But it was a test that broke the spell of Jesus for the Galilean crowd whose hero he was the day before. Now after they learn that he is in no sense a political Messiah and that he has no more loaves and fishes for them, but that he himself claims to be a kind of heavenly manna which they must eat, many of the nominal disciples in disgust desert him and leave the synagogue (6:60, 66). Henceforth there is no more wild enthusiasm in Galilee for Jesus. By degrees the crowded synagogue was emptied, for Jesus turned to the Twelve with the pointed personal query: "Would ye also go away?" It was a pertinent question and Simon Peter spoke up for the Twelve who had noticed the wholesale defection from Jesus with astonishment and despair. Not that they had themselves understood the almost strange discourse of Jesus which stood fast through the long years in the mind of the apostle John, the one spirit in the group with the spiritual temper to grasp and hold it till he should understand it. The reply of Peter shows that they had had whispered talk or understanding signs about the startling turn that things had taken. Jesus had driven his point in to the very quick when the crowd murmured at his words. "The words that I have spoken unto you are spirit and are life" (6:63). He had almost pushed away the unspiritual mob by saying that no man can come to him unless the Father draw him (6:44, 65). "Lord, to whom shall we go?" Peter said, as if they had meditated for a moment joining the crowd of deserters fleeing as in a panic from the now discredited leader. But Peter implied that there was no one to whom they could go for more light. No rabbi could help them at this juncture. They knew Pharisaïsm and Sadduceïsm. In sheer desperation they had to stay with Jesus. But Peter had more to say than this negative protest: "Thou hast the words of eternal life." Those very words that had driven the crowds away were, Peter means, "spirit and life" as Jesus claimed. Jesus had the only words that opened the way to eternal life. Then Peter adds his reason for this stanch conviction: "And we have believed and know that thou art the Holy One of God" (6:69). "The vital faith which grasps the new data of the higher life precedes the conscious intellectual appreciation of them" (Westcott). See the opposite order in I John 4:16. Curiously enough Peter uses the very language of the demoniacs to Jesus, "the Holy One of God" (Mark 1:24; Luke 4:34). Bernard insists that this confession of Peter is simply John's report of what is recorded in Matthew 16:13–20, a strange inability to understand the psychology of a man like Simon Peter with his varied moods. Westcott sees the thing rightly: "Here the confession points to the inward character in which the apostles found the assurance of life; there the confession was of the public office and theocratic Person of the Lord." Peter here reaches a climax to which he has been coming and makes this pledge of loyalty at a time when the tide was assuming strength against Jesus. It is a lonely loyalty, but strong and sincere all the same. Peter strikes a true note, but Jesus finds a disharmony in the Twelve of which they were not aware. Jesus had chosen them all, and yet one of them is already a devil. No one at the time knew to whom Jesus referred, perhaps not even Judas who, though already in the devil's grip, probably did not know it and fancied himself still loyal to Jesus in spite of his own selfish ambition. There is no hint here that Judas was a devil when Jesus chose him, but just the opposite. Jesus gave Judas his chance, but the devil captured him (17:12). The Master is grateful for the proof of the loyalty of the Twelve revealed in Peter's reply, but there is bitterness even in this cup of gladness and gratitude. But Peter shows up well on this occasion.

10. *Peter Uneasy Over Christ's Rebuke to the Pharisees.*—Jesus lingered yet awhile in Galilee and the Pharisees are bolder in their criticism of Jesus and the apostles because of the defection of the masses. The opposition in Judea was so keen that Christ remained away from the recent passover (John 6:4; 7:1). The Pharisees seem to have an organized conspiracy against Jesus with headquarters in Jerusalem. They now sent emissaries to Galilee to disturb the work of Christ (Mark 7:1; Matt. 15:1). They pick flaws with the disciples eating with unwashed hands and thus violating the punctilious ceremonial regulations of the rabbis. They cared naught about the sanitary aspects of the problem, but insisted on "the tradition of the elders." Jesus turns

on these spies and calls them "hypocrites" and quotes Isaiah 29:13 as rightly picturing their spirit. With keenest irony and biting sarcasm he adds: "Full well do ye reject the commandment of God, that ye may keep your tradition." Then he illustrates his charge by the shameful use of "Corban" by which one would refuse to help his mother under the pretext of the property belonging to God and then would use it for himself. The indictment literally cut to the bone. When it was all over, the disciples timidly said to Jesus: "Knowest thou that the Pharisees were offended, when they heard this saying?" (Matt. 15:12). Certainly Jesus had seen them wince under the lash of the whip of his words. But the Master cut deeper still: "They are blind guides. And if the blind guide the blind, both shall fall into a pit." Luke had already given this "parable" in his report of the Sermon on the Mount (6:39), but that was a long time ago and Jesus had taught many things since then, and repeated this proverb. But Peter's request for an explanation of the parable seems to refer to the words of Jesus just before about what defiles a man (Matt. 15:11) called a parable by Mark (7:17). This is what made the disciples call attention to the indignation of the Pharisees and Peter desires more light on the matter. "The contrast between the involuntary dullness of the disciples, and the self-satisfied blindness of the scribes is here very marked" (Plummer). Jesus rebukes the dullness, but removes it. "Are ye also even yet without understanding?" It is a sharp exposure of the fact that the disciples are still to some extent under the cloud of the Pharisaic blindness. So Jesus explains the importance of moral cleanness compared with ceremonial purification in words that virtually abrogate "the Levitical distinction between clean and unclean" (Bruce on Matt.). Mark (7:19) adds a clause (syntactical anacoluthon), "making all meats clean," pretty clearly a reminiscence of Peter's comment in the light of his experiences on the housetop in Joppa (Acts 10:14). Peter was amazed by this reply of Jesus and it was not till after the vision in Joppa that he comprehended the full meaning of Christ's revolutionary words. Mark here preserves Peter's own view as he later commented on the Master's reply to his own request for an explanation of "the parable." He got it with a rebuke for his dullness that he deserved. How slowly have men been able to see the worth of moral values in a world of ceremonies and rules and customs!

11. *Unwilling Like the Others to Be Bothered by a Gentile Woman.*—Mark (7:24–30) and Matthew (15:21–28) tell the beautiful story of the Syro-Phœnician woman who came to Jesus asking for mercy on her little daughter in the grip of a demon. At first Jesus answered her not a word (Matt. 15: 23) and the disciples begged him to send her away, "for she crieth after us." They were not willing to put up with a woman following and crying after them in public. It was a natural feeling that all the disciples shared. Peter may have been the spokes-

man, but it is not so stated. At any rate Jesus did
not here rebuke the disciples for not understanding
women and children, though that was true, because
a deeper issue was raised, the mission of Jesus to
Gentiles as well as to Jews. The plea was so straight-
forward, earnest, and skilful, taking up the very
words of Jesus about the little children and the little dogs and pleading for a little crumb for her
little girl. It was so bright and cheery and faithful
that Jesus healed her child "for this saying" (Mark
7:29). Mark tells the incident with vivid details as
he had heard Peter describe it.

12. *Helpless in a Great Emergency.*—There are
scholars who confuse the feeding of the four thousand with that of the five thousand though given
separately by both Mark (7:31–8:9) and Matthew
(15:29–38) and referred to by Jesus as separate incidents with careful distinction in the two words for
baskets ("wallets" for the five thousand, "hampers"
for the four thousand) in Mark 8:19–21 and Matthew 16:9 f. The objection is that the disciples could
not have failed to remember their experiences about
the five thousand when called by Jesus to him because of the hungry multitudes in the Decapolis
region (Mark 8:1–9; Matt. 15:32–38). But the
Gospels do not justify that conception of the apostles. Their propensity to forget and to fail to meet
an emergency is only too apparent. They are just as
helpless here as when on the green slopes near Bethsaida Julias with the same pessimistic wail of help-
lessness that nothing can be done. Those engaged in

Christian work today meet precisely this repeated plea that nothing can be done by us at this particular time. It has a familiar ring.

13. *Peter as Dull as the Rest about Christ's Parable of Warning.*—After feeding the four thousand Jesus crossed over again to Galilee after a prolonged absence because of the growing hostility of the Pharisees, the jealousy of Herod Antipas, the fanaticism of many of his followers, and to have a better opportunity to teach the apostles in the hills away from the heat more about himself. Apparently Magadan (Matt. 15:39) or Dalmanutha (Mark 8:10) was not far from Tiberias, but instantly on Christ's appearance in Galilee the Pharisees met him, now joined by the Sadducees (their ancient enemies and rivals) tempting him with a request for a sign from heaven. No wonder that Jesus "sighed deeply in his spirit" (Mark 8:12) at this reception which amply justified his long absence. Jesus left them and got in the boat with the disciples to cross over again to the region of Bethsaida Julias (Mark 8:22). The disciples forgot to take bread and Jesus said: "Take heed, beware of the leaven of the Pharisees and the leaven of Herod" (Mark 8:15) to which Matthew (16:6) adds "and Sadducees" in place of "and Herod." He probably said all three. They were near Tiberias where Herod Antipas, "that fox," lived. The Sadducees had just met him in company with the Pharisees. The opposition to Jesus is rapidly coming to a head, it is plain to see. The reasoning of the apostles among themselves is the acme

of stupidity. "We took no bread." As much as to say, What can the Master mean by such a warning as that when we have no bread at all? Jesus perceived their quandary and gave them the severest reprimand as their Teacher so far. If this was a test, they all got zero. Jesus asks a series of questions to wake up their sluggish mentality (mind, eyes, and ears), even memory being at fault. He appealed to the feeding of the five thousand and then to that of the four thousand to help them out. "Do ye not understand?" (Mark 8:21). He explained expressly that he was not talking about bread at all, but about "the teaching of the Pharisees and Sadducees" (Matt. 16:11 f). Then they understood. Peter was in this group, as dull as any of them, the very men who had once boasted that they understood parables (Matt. 13:51). Every teacher has pupils in a mood like this when it is a strain upon his patience and his hopefulness. Surely Simon is not much of a rock at this juncture. He was not catching many fish alive. But a better day always comes after a time like this.

14. *Peter Rising to the Occasion at Cæsarea Philippi.*—This is the fourth withdrawal from Galilee during the spring and summer months (to the region of Bethsaida Julias, to the region of Tyre and Sidon, to Decapolis, and now to Mount Hermon near Cæsarea Philippi), this time to Iturea ruled by Herod Philip as was true of Bethsaida Julias. Phœnicia and Decapolis (the ten Greek cities southeast of the Sea of Galilee) were also outside of the

land ruled by Herod Antipas (Galilee and Perea),
Phœnician and Greek regions. After the return to
Capernaum from near Bethsaida Julias Jesus had
made plain to the hungry crowds the spiritual nature
of his mission in that he was the true manna from
heaven. This revelation at first staggered the apostles, but they rallied and remained true to the Master as Peter nobly confessed for them all (John 6:
68 f.). Now after months spent in teaching the apostles about his person and mission, in what sense he
is the King Messiah in the Kingdom of God, he gives
them a pointed test concerning their apprehension
of it all. It has been probably two years since he
chose them as apostles. By this time they ought to
know their own minds. It is not a new problem with
these men. They had long ago made their own choice
to follow Jesus as the Messiah of Jewish prophecy
and hope. It is not now a question of how accurately
they understand the Messiahship of Jesus. The issue raised here by Jesus is to see clearly and sharply
how the apostles have reacted towards the fuller
revelation of himself and the corresponding defection of the masses. Are the apostles still loyal to
Jesus after all that they have heard from him and
after all that they have seen in the attitude of the
people towards him? Six months before this Jesus
was the popular hero of Galilee and they hoped by
force to make him the national king and throw off
the hated Roman yoke. But now he is in virtual hiding from his enemies and has been so for months. So
Jesus first raises a preliminary question to get

clearly before the apostles the issue. "Who do men say that I am?" (Mark 8:27). Luke (9:18) has "multitudes" for "men." Matthew (16:13) has "the Son of man" for "I," Christ's favorite phrase for himself and clear proof that here it cannot be merely the occasional Aramaic use of *barnasha* for "any man." That idea here is senseless. The apostles are quick with the answer that men differ in their opinion of Jesus, some thinking him the Baptist come to life again as Herod Antipas feared (Mark 6:14), some holding him to be Elijah as Herod also heard (Luke 9:8), some Jeremiah or another prophet come back (Mark 8:28; Matt. 16:14; Luke 9:19). All this variety of opinion about Jesus was common talk, known to Herod Antipas and to the apostles. Herod Antipas for long desired to see Jesus for himself (Luke 23:8).

It was no news to Jesus, this reply about the views of the people, but the answer prepares the way for the second and the vital point: "But who say ye that I am?" (Mark 8:29; Matt. 16:15; Luke 9:20). This is what Jesus cared for and wanted to know, their present attitude toward him after all their experiences with him. It was a pertinent and a crucial question for the Cross is only a little over six months ahead. The words are identical in each of the Synoptics with prolepsis of "ye" and emphasis on it in contrast with the populace: "But ye, who say ye that I am?" Jesus may have asked this question in Greek with the answer given in Greek also; but if he asked it in Aramaic, it is significant that the translation preserved in each Gospel is identical. This searching question by the Master probed each heart to the very bottom. Spitta thinks that Jesus really meant what had they been saying about him in their preaching. This time Peter speaks for the Twelve in words that must have gladdened the heart of Jesus. "The joy with which the Lord received St. Peter's answer shows the eagerness with which He must have asked the question" (McNeile on Matt.). "It was not the first time that Peter had expressed this belief" (Plummer on Matt.), but the point is that he still holds it firmly and unwaveringly even if not fully grasping all that is involved in the confession of faith in Jesus as the Messiah. The language of Peter is given directly and briefly in Mark 8:29: "Thou art the Christ," while Luke (9:20) has only "the Christ of God." (Cf. the phrase in Luke 2:26 "The Christ of the Lord"). All that Mark (8:30) and Luke (9:21) add is the command not to tell yet this fact that he is the Messiah. Jesus here accepts the appellation of Messiah (the Christ, the Anointed) as he had just called himself the Son of man. He is glad to know that the apostles are still firmly committed to this belief. It is no new claim for Jesus to make. He made it from the first, but popular misapprehension that the Messiah was to be a political king led Jesus to cease using the word to avoid issue with the Roman authority. This restraint will continue till the triumphal entry when Jesus boldly and publicly proclaims himself Messiah and takes the consequences. But Matthew (16:16) adds also to the confession the words "the Son of the living God" as involved in and belonging to "the Christ." In John 12:34 the people identify "the Christ" and "the Son of man" and in John 11:4 Jesus calls himself "the Son of God." In Matthew 26:63 Caiaphas identifies "the Christ" with "the Son of God" and Jesus on oath claims to be precisely that. But there is tremendous controversy concerning the remaining paragraph in Matthew 16:17–19 which is not in Mark or Luke. It can readily be seen why Peter would not speak of so personal an incident in his preaching and why Mark should not make use of it. Luke may not have had it in his sources or may have preferred to leave it out. Wendt (*Die Lehre Jesu*, I, p. 181) considers the paragraph either an addendum by the evangelist or introduced by a reviser for ecclesiastical reasons. But it is wholly improbable that we have here "invention" early or late (Plummer). Bruce (*Expositor's Greek Text*) thinks rightly that there is a hiatus in the report of Mark and Luke, that psychological reasons favor the authenticity of Matthew's narrative and that the high tension of Jesus at this critical moment demands and justifies his firm tone of conviction and thrill of satisfaction in Peter's reply: "The terms in which Jesus speaks of Peter are characteristic—warm, generous, unstinted. The style is not that of an ecclesiastical editor laying the foundation for Church power, and prelatic pretensions, but of a noble-minded Master eulogizing in impassioned terms a loyal disciple."

Accepting the words of Jesus here as genuine we face an almost endless dispute as to the meaning of Christ's words to Peter. They yield a proper evangelical sense if allowed to have their natural and obvious meaning. Jesus first felicitates Peter with a beatitude (Blessed) for his noble personal confession. He addresses him as "Simon Bar-Jonah" as when he first saw him (John 1:42, Simon, son of John) and in the notable interview by the Sea of Galilee (John 21:15–17). This conception of Jesus as the Messiah the Son of God Peter had received as a revelation from the Father in heaven. Jesus does not say or mean that it was a revelation just received by Peter. McNeile, in order to hold to this view, rejects the confession in Matthew 14:33 "Truly thou art the Son of God" and all those in John from 1:41 to 6:69. "The Lord emphatically declares that this confession of faith in his Messiahship is not the outcome of human instruction, but must be a revelation from God himself" (Plummer on Matt.). Peter has received it a number of times and will need fresh revelation on this very subject in the future, very soon in fact (Matt. 16:21), but is holding fast to his original conviction and has made progress. Then the Master has a further statement to make in response ("I also say unto thee") to what Peter has just said to him. "Thou art Peter," as Jesus had once predicted he would be (John 1:42). He is now living up to the name then given him. He is fulfilling that prophecy by this confession of loyalty. "And upon this rock," Jesus adds.

What does Jesus mean by the use of *petra* instead of *petros*? Plummer is sure that Jesus spoke in Aramaic and that there is no such distinction in *Cepha* which would occur in both places. He also thinks that *petra* (feminine) is impossible in both instances in the Greek, for Peter was a man and required a masculine form *Petros*. And *petros* would not do in both cases, because the meaning 'rock' was required rather than 'stone' " (Plummer). As a matter of fact *petros* can mean a large detached rock and not just a small stone for which *lithos* is common, though *petra* is the usual word for a ledge of rock on which a house is built (Matt. 7:24 f.). In I Peter 2:8 Peter says that the Jewish builders found Jesus both a *lithos* and a *petra*. But what is this *petra*? Some take it to be Jesus himself, some take it to be Peter, some consider it the confession of faith made by Peter. The context hardly suits Christ himself, though Jesus Christ is the foundation which no other can lay (I Cor. 3:11), the chief cornerstone in the kingdom (Eph. 2:20) as claimed by Christ himself (Mark 12:10 f.; Matt. 21:42; Luke 20:17), though rejected by the Pharisaic and Sadduceic experts. The choice seems to be between the other two or a combination of the two. There is a play on the name Peter (*Petros*) beyond a doubt.

The Roman Catholics and some Protestant scholars (John A. Broadus, for instance, in his great Commentary on Matthew) insist that the natural and obvious meaning is that Peter himself is the rock on which Jesus proposes to build his church.

But Origen long ago opposed that idea: "But if you suppose that upon one Peter only the whole Church is built by God, what would you say about John, the son of thunder, or each one of the apostles?" In Ephesians 2:20 all the fellow-citizens (Jews and Gentiles), members of the family of God, are said to be built upon the foundation of the apostles and prophets. Peter himself in I Peter 2:4 speaks of Christ as "a living stone" and all Christians "as living stones." There is no objection to applying the metaphor to individuals as Jesus did to Peter in John 1:42 and does also here. Certainly Peter is here living up to his name in making this good confession, but the question remains whether Jesus means to build his church on Peter himself or upon the kind of faith shown in Peter's confession. There are some cogent reasons for taking it to be the confession of faith by Peter. The recognition of Jesus as the Messiah is the very point in the question to Peter and the reply by him. The acknowledgment that Jesus is the Messiah is the point commended by him to Peter. The knowledge that Jesus is the Messiah is a revelation from God. The truth that he is the Messiah is what the apostles are warned not to tell as yet. The play on the word Peter (Cephas) is just as true in this sense as in the other, for he is playing the part of a rock in the confession. Jesus will shortly (Matt. 16:23) call Peter "Satan," not because he is Satan, but because he is acting like Satan. The personal and sincere acknowledgment of Jesus as the Messiah and Saviour is, in point of fact, what Jesus demands of every one who enters his kingdom. But, if the reference is to Peter personally, it must apply to the other apostles also, who have the same power of binding and loosening as Peter (Matt. 18:18), of getting sins forgiven (John 20: 23). The early disciples, including Peter himself, had no idea of any exclusive prerogatives bestowed by Jesus on Peter. Paul rebuked him to his face once as a hypocrite (Gal. 2:11–14). And, if Peter and the other apostles are the rock, there is no promise here that they have the power to pass on to others the keys of the kingdom in any sense not true of all Christians. The metaphor is kept of a building (I will build), applied to the church in the general sense like the kingdom, in the next verse. The use of "keys" shows that the same metaphor is carried on. The picture here is not that of a local or representative church, but Christ's church or kingdom in contrast to that in the Old Testament, Christ's Israel in place of the old Israel. Curiously enough all the important words in these verses appear in Psalm 89. The picture of the building here made to Peter by Jesus is reproduced in I Peter 2:5: "Ye are being built up a spiritual house," where Peter not only uses house, but the very verb build employed by Jesus. He is addressing the Christians in the five Roman regions mentioned in I Peter 1:1 so that the "spiritual house" is bound to be interpreted in the general sense like Paul's "temple" in Ephesians 2:21 f. The local sense of church is common in Acts and the Epistles, but the general idea recurs in Colossians 1:18; Ephesians 1:23; 5:27; Hebrews 12:23. Jesus promises that the gates of Hades shall not prevail against this church of the redeemed who are on the rock. There will always be true believers on earth, representatives of the kingdom of God. The keys of the kingdom which open the door of the kingdom to sinners are given to Peter, to the other apostles, and to every disciple of Jesus who knows how to show to any sinner the way to him. This interpretation of the great words of Jesus to Peter will not satisfy the high ecclesiastics who put ecclesiastical machinery and millinery between the sinner and Christ, but it is in accord with the New Testament as a whole. There is not a shred of evidence in the New Testament that Peter posed as a pope or was recognized as one by others. Every disciple has the privilege of binding and loosening the inquirer by declaring the terms of discipleship to Jesus Christ. Peter has honor enough in that Jesus took occasion on the basis of his noble confession, to say the great things here recorded as illustrated in him. There is no sort of infallibility conferred on Peter and dark days are ahead for him. He will not be able always to walk on this high level of insight and of privilege, but he is one of God's noblemen.

15. *Rebuked by Jesus for Presumption.*—Matthew (16:21) notes that the confession near Cæsarea Philippi marked an epoch not only in Peter's life, but in Christ's teaching about his approaching death. "From that time began Jesus to show to his disciples" how the Son of man must go to Jerusalem,

be rejected by the Sanhedrin, be killed, and the third day rise again. The time had come when they must be told if they were to be at all prepared for that coming catastrophe. After the event on Mount Hermon they ought to be ready for the full truth. The rising again on the third day was the silver lining to this cloud, but they did not see that promise at all. Jesus now makes plain that his Messiahship means suffering and death. Jesus himself saw it from the beginning of his ministry (John 2:20 f.). The opposition of the rulers made it plain (John 4:4; Mark 2:19 f.; John 5:18; Mark 3:6; Matt. 12:14). It is no surprise to Jesus, the inevitable outcome as he was facing his "hour." But now he began to speak openly and freely about it to the apostles (Mark 8:32). How many times Jesus did it during these days we do not know, but finally Peter took Jesus to himself, probably apart from the others, and "began to rebuke him," not from mere impulsiveness, but from deliberate conviction that Jesus was unduly discouraged, and with a new note of authority and officiousness (Plummer) towards him, perhaps of protection (McNeile).

The Sinaitic Syriac adds to Matthew 16:22 the words "as though pitying him." That pictures Peter patronizing Jesus. This tone Jesus would not endure from any one. "He did not get far." Peter was persuasive and consolatory: "Be it far from thee, Lord: this shall never be unto thee" (Matt. 16:22). As much as to say that he and the other apostles would never let it happen to the Master. "As soon as his meaning became apparent he encountered prompt, abrupt, peremptory contradiction" (Bruce). Jesus suddenly "turning about" faced Peter: "Get thee behind me, Satan" (Matt. 16:23). It is Peter, who had just recently made the noble confession, acting the part of Satan who once on the mount of temptation offered Jesus the kingdoms of the world and the glory of them. How is the mighty fallen, for here is Peter trying to turn Jesus back from the Cross. But Jesus drove the rebuke harder still, if possible, after calling Peter "Satan": "Thou art a stumbling block unto me." Peter was here a trap set to trap Jesus, a snare set by Satan who loves to set snares for preachers (I Tim. 3:7; II Tim. 2:26). That was a shock to Peter's self-esteem and sense of importance. It was like a bolt out of the blue and revealed tragically how little Peter understood the spiritual nature of Christ's mission even after his brave, if lonely, loyalty in the synagogue in Capernaum (John 6:69). Even after the noble confession near Cæsarea Philippi (Matt. 16:16) Peter still clung to the Pharisaic conception of a political kingdom with a living Messiah on the throne, not one who was to be lifted up on the Cross (John 12:34). It is a tragedy, this spiritual density on the part of the apostles about the death of Jesus. Later he will try again to bring them to understand about it, but with no better results. They were "exceeding sorry" (Matt. 17:23) to hear him talk thus, but "were afraid to ask him" (Mark 9:32) after this sharp rebuke to Peter. Jesus went on to show how true life consisted in bearing one's cross and following him, not in amassing money or gaining power. The shadow of Christ's own Cross is already over him.

CHAPTER V

ON THE MOUNT OF PRIVILEGE
(Mark 9:2–29; Matthew 17:1–20; Luke 9:28–43)

1. *The Reality of the Transfiguration of Jesus.*—
There are two extremes concerning this remarkable
incident, the Transfiguration of Jesus. Professional
spiritualists regard it as a séance with varying degrees of reality and humbug. Those who reject the
deity of Jesus and deny the supernatural elements
in his person and work treat it as mere legend, with
a minimum of fact, if any at all. This is not the place
to discuss the question of the deity of Jesus Christ
which is assumed and underlies all this discussion
about Simon Peter. But even so some who accept the
deity of Christ in a certain sense are ready to admit
that legends play a part in the Gospels as we have
them and are reluctant to admit the historical character of the narrative and of the event itself. To
these it is to be said that each of the Synoptics gives
the account of the Transfiguration with touches of
its own and in perfect good faith. Besides, there is a
direct reference to the event in II Peter 1:16–18
which is in accord with the Synoptics whether one
accepts the genuineness of Second Peter or not.
Plummer (on Matthew, p. 238) urges also "the im-
probability of invention" here, "its intrinsic suit-
ability to the crisis in the Ministry," and "the re-

markable injunction to silence" about it as reasons
that confirm the historical credibility of the Gospels
here. If Jesus is in fact the Son of God, the Messiah,
as Peter had testified (Matt. 16:16) and as Jesus
claimed to be, there is nothing inherently improbable
in the coming of Moses (the representative of the
law) and Elijah (the representative of the prophets)
to talk with Jesus about his "decease" (exodus, departure, Luke 9:31). The apostles had failed utterly and hopelessly to understand when he tried to
explain to them his approaching death in Jerusalem.
One can readily see how Jesus would desire comfort
by conversation with these choice spirits and how
there might be some preparation in the minds of
these three disciples for the culmination when it did
come.

2. *Peter's Opportunity.*—In spite of Peter's
dreadful lapse in his presumptuous rebuke to Jesus
for thinking and speaking of his approaching death
Jesus selects him along with James and John (so
Mark and Matthew, but Luke has John and James)
to go with him up into the mountain (probably
Hermon) to pray (Luke 9:28). Luke as usual mentions Christ's praying. The Master felt the need of
prayer in this crisis and he longed also for human
fellowship while he communed with the Father. It is
not clear whether Jesus was expecting what occurred on the mountain when he took these three
"apart by themselves" (Mark 9:2), though Plummer (on Matthew) thinks that he did for "the Lord
takes with him three witnesses," the same that were

with him when he raised the daughter of Jairus and
when he prayed in Gethsemane. Mount Hermon can
be reached in a week (Luke 9:28 "about eight days")
from Cæsarea Philippi (Plummer on Luke) and is
higher (9200 ft.) than Lebanon (8500) or Anti-
Lebanon (8700). Jesus exhibited the utmost confidence in Peter still by taking him along to see for
himself something of his heavenly glory which he left
(Phil. 2:6–8) when he came to earth. By this experience Peter might also get a new insight into the
meaning of Christ's death of which he had no clear
idea as yet. It is possible that Jesus was referring
to this anticipation of his glory which some of them
standing before him would see before they died
(Mark 9:1; Matt. 16:28; Luke 9:27). At any rate
once again Peter is in the inner circle of those who
are allowed to know something of the transcendent
dignity and glory of Jesus as the Son of God. There
is no evidence that either of these three disciples
had any premonitions of what was going to take
place. They were just up in the mountain while Jesus
prayed, a habit of his which clearly they did not
share.

3. *Peter Asleep in the Midst of Glory.*—Luke
alone (9:32) tells of the sleep of the three disciples
while Jesus prayed. They acted precisely in this manner in Gethsemane (Luke 22:45 "sleeping for sorrow"). There is some uncertainty as to the meaning
of the word used by Luke, "When they were fully
awake." Thayer takes it to mean "having remained
awake" in spite of being "heavy with sleep" ("bur-

dened with sleep") a possible meaning. But the Sinaitic Syriac has it "when they awoke" and this is
probably the idea here as Plummer and Easton
agree. This meaning of having become "thoroughly
awake" suits the context better also. It was only
then that "they saw his glory, and the two men that
stood with him" (Luke 9:32). "The celestial visi-
tants are supposed to arrive while the disciples are
asleep" (Bruce). "Luke does not say that the conversation ceased as soon as the disciples awoke, and
he implies rather that the listeners could overhear
the words" (Easton), though how much they heard
and understood is by no means clear. At any rate
Peter along with James and John had missed a great
opportunity, for they had certainly not heard all
that passed between Jesus and Moses and Elijah,
though apparently enough to know that the talk was
about the approaching death of Jesus and they saw
on awaking that the face of Jesus did shine as the
sun and his garments became "white as the light"
(Matt. 17:2), "glistening, exceeding white so as no
fuller on earth can whiten them" (Mark 9:3). Jesus
"was transfigured before them" (Mark 9:2; Matt.
17:2), the very word used by Paul of our spiritual
transfiguration (II Cor. 3:18).

4. *Peter's Impulsive Proposal.*—As Moses and
Elijah were parting from them (Luke 9:33) Peter
rallied and "answered" to Jesus (Mark 9:5), though
no word is reported from Jesus to Peter. He clearly
felt that the occasion called for comment, though
he did not exactly understand what it all meant.

Jesus calls it a vision (Matt. 17:9). That does not mean that it was unreal. "It was no optical illusion, but an appearance granted to three persons simultaneously. They were convinced that they had seen the glorified representatives of the Law and the Prophets conversing with the glorified Christ" (Plummer). Luke seems severe on Peter in saying that he spoke "not knowing what he said" (9:33). Mark (9:6) puts it more kindly (perhaps an echo of Peter's own explanation), "an apology for a proposal to keep the two celestials from returning to heaven" (Bruce), "For he wist not what to answer," while Matthew makes no comment at all. One may wonder why Peter ventured to speak if he did not know what he was saying or what to answer. But who of us has not had a like experience when out of sheer embarrassment one blurts out something without thinking before speaking? Peter had been in a deep sleep and is still dazzled by the brilliant light at night on the mountains, by the heavenly visitors, by the new aspect in which they see Jesus. He makes his suggestion in the ecstasy of the moment before the visitors had gone. Mark (9:5) and Luke (9:33) have it "Let us make" while Matthew (17:4) puts it "I will make." Easton thinks Peter's instinct is to help, the idea being that the presence of the three disciples opened the way for service. They could build the booths out of branches from the trees. It was apparently near the feast of tabernacles to which Jesus will soon go (John 7:2–14). Peter's proposal was in brief that they all celebrate the feast of tabernacles upon the mountain without going to Jerusalem. The visitors were already leaving, but perhaps they might stay a bit longer. Jesus made no answer to this blundering suggestion which was all impulse and sentiment, and yet with an element of tender eagerness and gracious hospitality that leads one to excuse and even to understand it. The suggestion answered itself by its sheer incompatibility with the facts amid which they lived. It is often so that men wish to keep up mountain-top experiences when the valley is calling loudly for them.

5. *The Voice Out of the Cloud.*—Both Matthew (17:5) and Luke (9:34) note that while Peter was yet speaking to Jesus a "cloud overshadowed them" (Matt. 17:5; Luke 9:34, called "bright" or "luminous" in Matt.) while Mark also (9:7) mentions the overshadowing cloud. It is the inchoative imperfect in Luke, "began to overshadow." In each instance the same verb is employed, the very verb used by the angel to Mary in announcing the birth of Jesus by the Holy Spirit: "The power of the Highest shall overshadow thee." Every one who has been on a high mountain is familiar with the clouds that suddenly sweep up and wrap the peaks in mist. But this cloud came so suddenly and overpoweringly that "they feared as they entered into the cloud" (Luke 9:34). Perhaps they were reminded of the glory like the Shechinah (Luke 9:31). Plummer observes that in Exodus 40:34 this very verb is used of the cloud overshadowing the tabernacle. "Light may be as blinding as darkness." "The very presence of this

cloud caused dread, as it revealed the presence of
God" (Easton). The "voice out of the cloud" (Mark
9:7) increased their dread. It was not thunder, but
articulate speech. There are four reports of this
voice (Mark 9:7; Matt. 17:5; Luke 9:35; II Peter
1:17), two of them from Simon Peter (Mark and
II Peter). They all vary slightly, though in sub-
stantial agreement. The order in Mark and Matthew is the same except that Matthew adds "in whom
I am well pleased" as in Matthew 3:17 (the voice of
the Father at the baptism of Jesus). The order is
different in II Peter 1:17 and we have "in whom I
am well pleased," practically the same as in Matthew, though II Peter does not have "Hear ye him"
as in the Synoptics. In Luke according to the best
manuscripts (Aleph B L) in place of "my beloved"
we have "my chosen," a recognized Messianic title
(Enoch 40:5) and the reading also of the Sinaitic
Syriac here. The voice is from the Father as at the
baptism though here coming out of the cloud and
the purpose is the same, the endorsement of Jesus
as the Son of God, then at the beginning and now
towards the close of the ministry. The immediate
command now to "hear" (heed) Jesus seems to re-
late particularly to the matter of his death, a point
on which Peter had dared to take issue with Jesus
shortly before (Mark 8:32) and which was the subject just discussed with Moses and Elijah (Luke 9:
31). "It was the first voice from heaven which the
apostles had heard" (Swete). Peter and the others
apparently took to heart this command for "they

fell on their face, and were sore afraid" (Matt. 17:
6). Then Jesus "came and touched them and said,
Arise and be not afraid" (17:7). They needed this
sympathetic word, for on lifting up their eyes again
(Matthew) and "suddenly looking round about, they
saw no one any more, save Jesus only with themselves" (Mark 9:8). The vision was over and Jesus
stood alone with Moses and Elijah gone.

6. *Forbidden to Tell the Vision As Yet.*—The
Transfiguration was at night and on the next day
(Luke 9:37) as they were coming down the mountain Jesus commanded them: "Tell the vision to no
man until the Son of man be risen from the dead"
(Matt. 17:9). This command was a further explanation of the Voice out of the cloud to hear God's Son
concerning his death. The concealment is for a
limited period. Meanwhile this experience should en-
lighten the three who would be able to comfort the
rest when Jesus is put to death, if only they can hold
it all firmly themselves. "They now know on additional authority of the highest order that the Messiah
must pass through death to glory, and hereafter this lesson would come home to them" (Plummer). Only we shall see that it did not come home
to them in the hour of darkness. Peter himself will
be in an eclipse of faith. But, meanwhile, Luke adds
(9:36), "they held their peace and told no man in
those days any of the things which they had seen."
They did not doubt the fact of the vision. "We are
not here concerned with a vision produced by natural causes, but with one sent directly by God," says

B. Weiss who adds: "Our narrative presents no stumbling block to those who believe in divine revelation." The silence of the Fourth Gospel throws no discredit on the incident as that book furnishes mainly new material to show the glory of Jesus as the Son of God. Mark (9:10) adds a significant word: "They kept the saying, questioning among themselves what the rising again from the dead should mean." Clearly they were not yet able to connect the death of the Messiah (now vaguely accepted by these three after the experience on the mountain) with the resurrection. It is possible that it was this "questioning among themselves" as they were coming down the mountain that led the Master to give the prohibition. But this talk seems to have done no harm and to have ended with themselves. They will need the coming of the Holy Spirit to make the things of Christ plain to them (John 16: 13 f.). Then Peter will be able to interpret the death and the resurrection of Jesus (Acts 2:23 f., 31 f.).

7. *The Coming of Elijah and of Christ.*—But there is one problem that they do not keep to themselves as they go on down the mountain, but bring it to Jesus. One theological discussion led to another as often with preachers. The discussion "has revived and given point to an old perplexity. How was Elijah's appearance at the Transfiguration to be reconciled with the official doctrine of his return?" (Swete). The teaching of the scribes grew out of Malachi 3:1 f.–4:5. These disciples had accepted Jesus as the Messiah before Elijah appeared on the

mountain. It seemed a knotty theological puzzle till
Jesus deftly untangled it. Elijah in the sense meant
by Malachi (Elijah in spirit and the forerunner of
the Messiah) had indeed come, though the scribes
knew him not (Matt. 17:12), but they (the scribes
and Herod and Herodias) did to this Elijah what
they wished. That is to say, they had him put to
death. (See the treatment of Elijah by Ahab and
Jezebel, I Kings 19:2–10). The disciples then perceived that Jesus meant John the Baptist as the
Elijah foretold by Malachi. The Baptist himself had
denied to the committee from the Sanhedrin that he
was Elijah returned in person as the Jews expected
(John 1:21). He was not the Elijah in person just
seen on the mount of Transfiguration. The Baptist
is the Elijah in spirit promised by Malachi. Jesus
had already before this stated that John the Baptist
was Elijah that was to come (Matt. 11:14). "A
suffering forerunner is to be followed by a suffering
Messiah" (Plummer). We do not know whether Peter
and the others were satisfied with this explanation
by Jesus or not. They probably were saddened afresh
by his prophecy about himself. "Even so shall the
Son of man also suffer of them." But their minds
and hearts were too full for further argument.

8. *The Failure of the Nine at the Foot of the
Mountain.*—Finally Jesus and the three disciples
reach the bottom of the mountain and were confronted by a great multitude (Mark 9:14; Matt.
17:14; Luke 9:37) surrounding the nine disciples
and "scribes questioning with them" (according to

Mark who is fuller here). "The scribes were probably rabbis attached to the local synagogues, but as ready as the rest of their class to seize an opportunity of discrediting the disciples of Jesus before the people" (Swete). Apparently the nine disciples were getting the worst of the dispute. Raphael in his great painting on the Transfiguration places the picture of this crowd at the foot of the mountain in a line below the scene on the mountain. He has been criticised for this license, but it emphasizes the contrast between the glory of Jesus on the mountain and the failure of the nine disciples in the valley below. The crowd in amazement ran up to Jesus and saluted him, and he asked them what they were questioning the nine disciples about. Then a man stepped out from the crowd and told his pitiful story, how he had brought his epileptic boy to the nine for a cure, but "they could not cure him" (Matt. 17:16). The boy had dreadful symptoms at times. Jesus said: "Bring him unto me." Even then the demon hurled the poor boy to the ground where he wallowed foaming. In desperation the father said to Jesus: "If thou canst do anything, have compassion on us, and help us." The father's faith was very slight after the failure of the nine disciples who had so signally failed. Jesus picks up the father's words "If thou canst," and reassures him that "all things 'can' to the one believing." The father pathetically pleads: "I believe; help thou mine unbelief." It was a glorious victory. Such is life, from the mountain top of glory to the depth of human misery and need.

Needless to say, the nine were deeply moved. They had cast out demons when on the tour of Galilee. So when they had gone into the house they asked Jesus privately (Mark 9:28 f.), "Why could we not cast it out?" Two answers are given. One is by Mark: "This kind can come out by nothing save by prayer." The nine were so confident of success that they had neglected by prayer to get in touch with God, as many a preacher has done in preaching and so failed. Matthew (17:20) says: "Because of your little faith." They had self-confidence, but lacked the reliance on God which comes by prayer. Their failure was not due to the absence of Jesus on the mountain nor to the taunts of the scribes. "The fault lay in themselves" (Swete). Their faith in the healing power of Jesus had dwindled. They no longer had faith "as a grain of mustard seed" that will remove "this mountain" of difficulty (one of Christ's many parabolic metaphors). It is always "this mountain" right before us that makes us quail and fail.

Simon has been on the mount of privilege with Jesus and then he saw Jesus at work in the valley of sin and suffering. It all goes to the making of a rock and a fisher of men out of this man. But there is more to come before he is really equipped for effective service for Christ.

CHAPTER VI

RIVALRY FOR THE PRIMACY

(Mark 9:33–37; Matthew 18:1–5; Luke 9:46–48; Mark 10:35–45; Matthew 20:20–28; Luke 22:24–30)

1. *No Leader at First Save Jesus.*—The notion that Jesus appointed Simon Peter the leader of the Twelve when he chose the apostles has no foundation in the Gospels nor in fact. Jesus himself remained the Lord and the Teacher of them all as they gladly and fully recognized (John 13:13). A slave is not greater than his lord nor an apostle than the one who sent him forth, as Jesus reminds the disciples (John 13:16). With this clearly in mind we may consider how early Peter came to be acknowledged as the leader of the group that Jesus had gathered around him. The repeated disputes among them (on three occasions that are recorded) prove that no one was recognized by the Twelve themselves as above the others in merit or in rank. Jesus repeatedly reminds the Twelve that he chose them, not they him, as in John 6:70, 15:16, 17:18, etc. This is such an obvious fact as to call for no further comment.

2. *The Early Prominence of Peter.*—We have already had several instances where Simon Peter is the voluntary spokesman for the Twelve, as when Peter made a protest to Jesus about his desire to know who had touched him (Luke 8:45), in the con-

fession of loyalty in the synagogue in Capernaum
(John 6:68 f.), in the request for an explanation of
the parable when the Pharisees stumbled so (Matt.
15:15), in the great confession near Cæsarea Philippi (Matt. 16:16), in the rebuke to Jesus for
telling about his death (Mark 8:32), and in his
proposal for three tabernacles on the Mount of
Transfiguration (Mark 9:5). It was Peter also who
dared to ask for the privilege of walking on the
water to Jesus (Matt. 14:28). And then Peter was
one of the three selected to go with Jesus into the
death-chamber in the home of Jairus (Mark 5:37)
and to go with him to the mount of Transfiguration
(Mark 9:2). We do not know whether this fact on
this occasion excited the jealousy of the nine other
disciples or not. Peter will continue his rôle as
spokesman for the rest, not by appointment, but
by temperament. He was, so to speak, eager and
impulsive and sometimes spoke prematurely, but the
others did not try to anticipate him in his talk.

It is interesting to note that the tax collectors
came to Peter for information about Christ's paying the temple tax (Matt. 17:24). Of itself this
proves nothing, for the Greeks approached Philip
for an introduction to Jesus (John 12:21). Peter
wants to know about the personal application of the
parable of the waiting servants (Luke 12:41). Peter
speaks up to tell Jesus of the sacrifices made by
the Twelve (Mark 10:28). It is Peter who calls
attention to the withered fig tree (Mark 10:21).
Peter is the leader of the group of four (Peter,

James, John, Andrew) who ask Jesus the meaning
of his startling words about the temple (Mark 13:3)
and Peter is the one who objects to Christ's washing
his feet (John 13:8 f.). Peter is the one who asks
the Beloved Disciple to find out from Jesus the
name of the traitor (John 13:24). It is Peter who
loudly protests his fidelity to Jesus to which they
all agreed (Mark 14:29–31). To all this can be
added the choice of Peter with John to arrange for
the last passover meal (Luke 22:8), his choice along
with James and John to watch in Gethsemane while
Jesus prayed (Mark 14:33), his drawing his sword
to fight for Jesus (John 18:10). But then came the
sad denials of Jesus by Peter (Mark 14:54, 66–72;
Matt. 26:58, 69–75; Luke 22:54–62; John 18:15–
18, 25–27), the special message of the Risen Christ
to Peter (Mark 16:7), his running with John to the
tomb (John 20:2–10), the appearance of Jesus to
Peter (Luke 24:33–35; I Cor. 15:5), the restoration of Peter by Jesus at the Sea of Galilee (John
21:1–23). These instances give Peter a place of
undoubted prominence whatever the explanation may
be.

3. *The Disciples Disputing Who Is the Greatest.*
—The Synoptics all give this incident (Mark 9:33–
37; Matt. 18:1–5; Luke 9:46–48). It was apparently in Peter's house in Capernaum ("in the house"
Mark 9:33), "a kind of home for Jesus" (Bruce on
Mark), that Jesus asks the disciples what they had
been disputing about "in the way" to the house
from the neighborhood of Cæsarea Philippi. "Pos-

sibly the preference shown to Peter, James and John
at the Transfiguration had led to this dispute; or
Peter's forwardness on that occasion may have led
the three to dispute whether he had any right to
precedence" (Plummer on Matt.). Matthew says
nothing about the "dispute" or "reasoning" (Luke
9:46). It was more than mere thoughts, but words
were undoubtedly spoken by them. "He went before,
thinking his deep thoughts, they followed thinking
their vain thoughts" (Bruce on Mark). Jesus saw the
"reasoning of their heart" (Luke 9:47) and asked:
"What were ye reasoning in the way?" (Mark 9:33).
He had read their hearts, seen the angry emotions
on their faces, heard some of their words. The question hushed them to silence for "they hold their
peace" for a while. They were guilty, as they now
know that Jesus knows, of jealous rivalry towards
each other. Matthew (18:1) merely says that the
disciples brought the academic question to Jesus:
"Who then is greatest in the kingdom of heaven?"
But the use of "then" points back to the brooding
dispute of Luke (9:46) "which of them should be
greatest." That is to say if and when Jesus should
set up his political kingdom. They are evidently
concerned about the place which each of them will
have in this kingdom. The experience of the three
on the Mount of Transfiguration had not removed
the deep-rooted expectation of a political Messiah
shown by the populace in John 6:14 f. The Master,
Mark says (9:35 f.), "sat down and called the
twelve" and gave them the philosophy of humility:

"If any man would be first, he shall be last of all,
and minister of all." Then "he took a little child
(Peter's child? A late tradition suggests Ignatius)
and set him in the midst of them" (Mark 9:36),
"by his side," Luke says (9:47), the place of honor.
Then "taking him in his arms" Jesus gave the apostles a profound object lesson in humility as if they
were a kindergarten class: "Whosoever shall humble
himself as this little child, the same is the greatest
in the kingdom of heaven" (Matt. 18:4), "for he
that is least among you all, the same is great" (Luke
9:48). Surely there was never a more needed lesson
than this one, but it is a lesson that will have to
be repeated both in Mark 10:43 (Matt. 20:26) and
later in Luke 22:24–30 and John 13:1–20. It is sad
to see these first ministers of Jesus the victims of
ecclesiastical jealousy and rivalry. This serpent has
left its trail through the centuries. But it is beyond
dispute that at this stage of Christ's ministry no
one of the Twelve was acknowledged as the leader.

4. *The Ambition of James and John.*—The telling rebuke of selfish promotion did not last perma-
nently. The months pass rapidly by. The disciples
have seen Jesus raise Lazarus from the dead (John
11), have received another rebuke from Jesus for
trying to prevent some mothers from bringing their
children to Jesus for his blessing (Mark 10:13–16),
have been amazed at the hard conditions of discipleship laid down by Jesus to the rich young ruler
(Mark 10:24), when Peter wanted to know what
they would get after leaving all for Jesus (Matt.

19:27). Jesus is in Perea on his last journey to Jerusalem with a large caravan going up to the passover. The Master is conscious of his approaching death and showed it in his countenance. "Jesus was going on before them: and they were amazed; and they that followed were afraid" (Mark 10:32). Repeatedly before this Jesus had foretold his death: once at the first passover in Jerusalem by a parabolic picture (John 2:19), once by the parable of the bridegroom taken away (Mark 2:20; Matt. 9:15; Luke 5:35), once by the metaphors of fire and baptism (Luke 12:49 f.); thrice in plain language (Mark 8:31 f.; Matt. 16:21 f.; Luke 9:22; Mark 9:9; Matt. 17:9–12; Mark 9:31 f.; Matt. 17:22 f.; Luke 9:44 f.), once by implication (Luke 13:33–35). Now again in plain terms Jesus vividly says: "We are going up to Jerusalem" (Mark 10:33; Matt. 20:18; Luke 18:31). He repeats the previous plain prediction and adds the word "crucify" (Matt. 20:19). It is all according to what the prophets wrote (Luke 18:31) and the resurrection "on the third day" (Matt. 20:19; Luke 18:33) "after three days" (Mark 10:34) is also repeated, but to no effect in spite of the previous explanation (Mark 9:10 f.). "They understood none of these things; and this saying was hid from them, and they perceived not the things that were said" (Luke 18:34).

But this is not the worst of the incident. "Then" (at that time), says Matthew (20:20), with the amazing look and tragic words of Jesus before them, the mother of James and John along with her two sons comes to Jesus "worshipping him and asking a certain thing of him." It seems strange and almost incredible that these three should have been unable to turn their minds from thoughts of personal ambition even while Jesus had been speaking sorrowfully of his death just ahead of him. Plummer (on Matt.) thinks that the apostles, in spite of Christ's rebuke to Peter (Matt. 16:22 f.), had been confirmed in their hopes of political preferment in the Messianic Kingdom by Christ's promise of their sitting on twelve thrones (Matt. 19:28), a promise of a spiritual reign in heaven, not on earth. At any rate here they come, the Beloved Disciple (the most spiritual of all of them) included, with a request of sheer earthly ambition. They all three seem to feel that this caravan procession to the passover in Jerusalem means that Jesus on his arrival will set up the Messianic Kingdom with the great opportunities open for preferment and power. So they bluntly ask for the two best places for James and John, one on the right hand, the other on the left hand, of Jesus "in thy glory" (Mark 10:37), the two places of honor by the throne of the King (Josephus, *Ant.* vi, 11, 9). "Both the homage offered and the terms of the petition (cf. 6:23) suggest that the Lord is approached in the character of a King, and so can gratify the desires of His subjects without limitation" (Swete). Once more Swete thinks that "the petition was a bold attempt to raise afresh the question *tis meizōn* (9:34), which the Lord had already dismissed." The reply of Jesus is considerate. "Ye

know not what ye ask." They were really as ignorant as Peter on the Mount of Transfiguration and
far more selfish. They exhibit also a bland self-
confidence in saying that they are able to drink this
cup that Jesus is to drink and to be baptized with
this baptism of blood that he was to receive. This
cup and this baptism they will get, James first of all
the apostles (Acts 12:2), while John will be the
last to receive the baptism of suffering in Patmos
(Rev. 1:9). Jesus does not question their courage
or blame it (Plummer). But rewards are in the
Father's hands. "Perhaps the Ten had expected that
Christ would reprove the ambition of the sons of
Zebedee more severely; but the attempt to gain an
advantage by private solicitation was enough to
provoke their indignation against James and John"
(Plummer). This emulation and strife (Matt. 18:1
f.) had already been rebuked, but was still alive.
James and John did not recognize the primacy of
Peter or any others of the Twelve who were indignant at them for their presumptuous ambition. To
see the disciples acting like heathen (Mark 10:42)
at the very moment when Jesus had been speaking
about his death (Mark 10:33 f.) is surely a pitiful
spectacle. So Jesus "called them to him" once more
and said: "Whosoever would become great among
you, shall be your minister: and whosoever would
be first among you, shall be servant of all" (Mark
10:43 f.; Matt. 20:26 f.). And then the Master in a
final word, as if to shame them, appealed to his own
mission to men: "For verily the Son of Man came

not to be ministered unto, but to minister, and to give his life a ransom for many." And yet, in spite of these words, there are some who deny that Jesus foresaw the Cross or had it in his plan for the redemption of men. This language implies the pre-existence of the Son before the Incarnation and places the Cross in the centre.

5. *The Position of Judas.*—Almost certainly Judas Iscariot, because he carried the bag or was treasurer of the group (John 12:6), considered himself equal to any of the Twelve in importance. He was not suspected of being a thief till later. Apparently no one else in the group held any official position. Doctor A. Wright in the *Journal of Theological Studies* (Oct. 1916, pp. 32–4) argues for the primacy of Judas on the basis of a possible rendering of Mark 14:10 as "the first" like "the first day of the week" in Luke 24:1. It is certainly a possible translation (see "The Primacy of Judas Iscariot," pp. 127–137, in my *The Christ of the Logia*). But the most likely meaning in Mark 14:10 is that he is "the notorious one," not "the first in rank." The dispute among the Twelve and the selfish ambition of James and John deny official and recognized primacy to Judas Iscariot just as completely as to Simon Peter. There is no doubt at all about the ambition for leadership on the part of Judas. He probably aspired to be treasurer in the political Kingdom of Jesus. No doubt this rankling aspiration of disappointed ambition was one of the stings that spurred him at the last to treason. But it is impos-

sible to see any ground for thinking that the Twelve were led by Judas Iscariot.

6. *The Contention at the Last Passover Meal.*—As Jesus moved on from Jericho up towards Jerusalem the caravan grew in number and in excitement, because "they supposed that the Kingdom of God was immediately to appear" (Luke 19:11). Jesus sought to calm the intensity of the expectation by the parable of the pounds and then "went on before, going up to Jerusalem" (Luke 19:28). In Jerusalem just before the passover the populace wondered if Jesus would dare to come since the Sanhedrin had given orders that, if any one should see Jesus, he should report it (John 11:56 f.). At Bethany, when Jesus came, crowds came to see Lazarus as well as Jesus so that the chief priests decided to kill them both. Perhaps Lazurus might stay dead this time. The triumphal entry was a public proclamation by deed that Jesus was the Messiah and the people so hailed him in exultant jubilation (Mark 11:10; Matt. 21:9; Luke 19:38) to the dismay and disgust of the Pharisees (John 12:19; Luke 19:39 f.). That evening, when Jesus returned to Bethany (Mark 11:11; Matt. 21:17), the apostles no doubt felt that Jesus had at last burned all the bridges behind him. He had said to the complaining Pharisees: "I tell you that, if these shall hold their peace, the stones will cry out" (Luke 19:40). Each apostle sees the fulfilment of his own hopes of preferment as near at hand, Peter among the rest. The agitation of Jesus over the request of the Greeks and his talk

about being "lifted up" (John 12:33 f.) no doubt
disturbed the apostles no little as well as the timidity of some believing Pharisees (John 12:42 f.).
But Jesus was the master of debate in the temple
and the press of the people who flocked early to the
temple to hear him revealed his praise. "The common people heard him gladly" (Mark 12:37) when
the Sanhedrin tried in vain to loosen his grip upon
the masses who "hung upon him listening" (Luke
19:48). Peter was puzzled over the withered fig tree
(Mark 11:21), but still more when Jesus swept the
temple clear of his enemies with withering sarcasm
and terrible exposure of the hypocrisy of the Scribes
and Pharisees who posed as lights and leaders of
the people (Matt. 23). He did this "while the Pharisees were gathered together" (Matt. 22:41) and in
the hearing of the disciples (Matt. 23:1). The effect
on the apostles of this breach between Jesus and
the rulers (Matt. 21:45) was to create astonishment
and pessimism so that Peter and these others came
to Jesus at the Mount of Olives for an explanation
of his words on leaving the temple (Mark 13:3). It
began to look, if the temple was to be destroyed, as
if they might not realize their ambition for place and
power after all. That evening in the house of Simon
the leper a feast was given in honor of Jesus with
the Twelve present and the Bethany family (Martha,
Mary, Lazarus). At this feast Judas made strong
protest against the waste of money by Mary on the
ointment for the anointing of Jesus, a deed defended
by Jesus as showing insight into his death (Mark

14:8), a subject that the Twelve had failed completely to understand. And all the other apostles agreed with the point made by Judas, "some" (Mark 14:4), "the disciples" (Matt. 26:8). Judas was so incensed with the rebuke by Jesus (added to his growing discontent and the increasing power of the devil over him) that he slipped out and went on to the secret meeting of the chief priests and offered to betray Jesus during the feast (Luke 22:6). Jesus went on with the preparation for the passover meal, sending Peter and John to make proper arrangements (Luke 22:8).

So Jesus and the Twelve meet at the regular hour for the passover meal on Thursday evening after sunset (beginning of Jewish Friday). There is no real disagreement between the Synoptics and the Fourth Gospel properly understood as to the time of this last passover meal (at the regular time, beginning of 15th of Nisan). Judas is on hand with his usual bland suavity just as if he had not made a bargain with hell and the Sanhedrin. Jesus himself looked forward to this last passover meal with eagerness: "with desire I have desired to eat this passover with you before I suffer" (Luke 22:15), and perhaps also with some uneasiness about the Twelve who had been so slow to comprehend him and his mission. He had not long to wait for trouble. "And there arose also a contention among them, which of them is accounted to be greatest" (Luke 22:24). The occasion for this dispute grew out of the sensitiveness of the Twelve about precedence at the table. Each wanted the place in accord with his rank or his self-esteem. Etiquette at such a time is proper and often the hostess prevents embarrassment by having the names of the guests at each plate. This third manifestation of selfish ambition at such a time and place as this cut Jesus to the very quick. They were again acting like heathens. "But ye are they which have continued with me in my temptations" and yet you are acting as if ye were strangers to me and my spirit (Luke 22:28). The contention continued after they had all reclined. The post of honor was the centre of the table and that Jesus had. The next was to the left of Jesus, behind him as each reclined on his left side, and this apparently Peter held (Westcott), while the Beloved Disciple John had the place to the right of Jesus so that his head (lying obliquely) lay on the bosom of Jesus. Leonardo da Vinci's great painting pictures them all seated, not reclining, which is an anachronism, though it is a marvellous painting. It is plain that the strife went on after the meal began because "during supper" (John 13:2) Jesus rises, takes a towel, girds himself, pours water into a basin, and begins to wash the disciples' feet. He may have begun with Simon Peter. At any rate at first Peter demurs vehemently against this menial act by Jesus and then characteristically says: "not my feet only, but also my hands and my head" (John 13:9). After the service was over with them all, Jesus reclined again and interpreted to them this object lesson (an acted parable) in humility for the apostles, "an example" (13:15), to show that "an apostle" is not greater than the one who sent him (13:16). The Master and Teacher (13:13) did not here introduce a church ordinance, but he did try once to teach these preachers the lesson of humility that they might be free from jealousy and rivalry even on so solemn an occasion as this last passover meal with their Lord. This is abundant proof that no one of the Twelve was as yet acknowledged to be first.

7. *The Beloved Disciple.*—John is the only other one of the Twelve for whom a serious claim for leadership can be made, though James is associated with his brother in the plea for the two first places in the Kingdom (Mark 10:35; Matt. 20:20) and is mentioned before John as is usually the case. No doubt the mother according to Matthew is the chief incentive in this request. John is the one who sought praise from Jesus for his effort to prevent one outside of their circle from casting out demons in the name of Jesus (Mark 9:38 f.; Luke 9:49 f.), but who received rebuke instead of praise. But James and John prove themselves true to the nickname, Boanerges (sons of thunder), given to them by Jesus as explained by Mark (3:17), when they wish lightning to fall on the Samaritan village that refused to receive them because their faces were set to go to Jerusalem (Luke 9:54), a spirit that again met a prompt rebuke from Jesus. John and James both belong to the inner circle of three along with Peter, but it is John who is sent with Peter to arrange for the last passover meal (Luke 22:8) and John runs

with Peter to the tomb on receiving Mary Magdalene's report of the empty tomb (John 20:2 ff.).
John is associated with Peter also by the sea of
Galilee (John 21:7, 20–23) and in the work after
pentecost in Jerusalem (Acts 3:1). But the chief
claim of John for precedence is his identity with the
Beloved Disciple whose head rested on the bosom of
Jesus (John 13:23). Here he is plainly indicated to
be one of the apostles at the last passover (Luke
22:14). But even this intimate fellowship with Jesus
of which the author (John 21:24) of the Fourth
Gospel has pardonable pride, as shown by the so frequent use of this title (21:7, 20), does not prove
actual leadership of the Twelve. At the last passover
it is probable that Peter had the post of honor next
to Jesus and John ranked next to Peter. Clearly
John cares more for his close bond of love with
Jesus than for any titular leadership. The mention
of Philip and Andrew in John 6:5–8 (feeding the
5,000) and in John 12:20–22 (request of the
Greeks) does not justify any special claim for leadership in their cases. The case seems to be closed. Up
to the time of Christ's death on the Cross no one of
the Twelve is accepted as the leader. Even Peter by
his denials is in disgrace.

8. *Peter the First at Last.*—Matthew expressly
calls Peter "the first" in his list of the Twelve
(10:2), and all the four lists name Peter first, but
this is from the standpoint of a later time after he
came to be so recognized. As the apostles and others
waited in the upper room for the promise of the

Father it is Peter, now back in the fold, who strengthens the brethren, as Jesus said he should (Luke 22:32), and suggests a successor to Judas Iscariot (Acts 1:13–26). Then, after the Holy Spirit did come in power upon the disciples, Peter is the one who rises to explain the conduct of the disciples and to give the first interpretation of the life, death, and resurrection of Jesus, under the influence of the Holy Spirit (Acts 2:14–47). Peter like the others had gained faith and hope, but now he has insight and power as Jesus had promised. The Holy Spirit is teaching him to comprehend the spiritual nature of the Kingdom and the Messiahship of Jesus, a thing which they did not understand as Jesus ascended on high (Acts 1:6). Now he has power from on high and defies the Sanhedrin with amazing boldness and skill even when imprisoned and threatened with death. In Acts 1 to 12 Peter is the outstanding leader of the disciples in Jerusalem. When Paul is converted and returns to Jerusalem, he makes a visit to Cephas (Gal. 1:18). In the conference in Jerusalem Paul recognizes Cephas as intrusted with the gospel of the circumcision as he is with that of the uncircumcision (Gal. 2:7 f.). There is no manner of doubt of the leadership of Simon Peter among the Jewish Christians after the coming of the Holy Spirit at pentecost. In Jerusalem itself, due largely to Peter's absence on his preaching tours, James (the brother of Jesus) comes to the fore as the local leader, but he does not displace Peter as the leader of Jewish Christians in general. This aspect of Peter's wide leadership appears in the countries addressed in I Peter 1:1 and II Peter 3:1. Whether or not Peter visited Rome, established the church there, became the first pope are all matters for future discussion (see Chapter XIX). In the Gospels, therefore, Peter is not the acknowledged leader of the Twelve as he undoubtedly is in the opening chapters of the Acts. This eager impulsiveness was humbled into rich service for Christ under the guidance of the Holy Spirit.

CHAPTER VII

CONFIDENT BOASTING THOUGH WARNED BY CHRIST
(John 6:70; Luke 22:21–34; John 13:21–30)

1. *Bitterness Long in Christ's Cup.*—A year ago in the synagogue in Capernaum when Peter spoke up bravely and loyally for the Twelve after the crowd had all left Jesus, the Master poignantly said: "Did not I choose you the twelve? And yet one of you is a devil" (John 6:70). How long before he said this Jesus had known the treachery in the heart of Judas we do not know. But for the past year at least he knew all the time what was in the destiny of this one whom he had chosen. And yet Jesus went on working with this man who had let the devil come into his heart till he became a very devil himself. Several times appears that vivid and dreadful statement about Judas (Luke 22:3; John 13:2, 27; Mark 14:18–31; Matt. 26:21–35; Luke 22:21–38; John 13:18–38). There was other bitterness also in the cup that Jesus was to drink (Mark 14:36), but there was undoubtedly this gall of treachery by Judas, one of the Twelve.

2. *Definite Warning after Washing the Disciples' Feet.*—Hitherto Jesus had carried his sorrow in secret (Westcott) save for the one piercing word about Judas in John 6:70 which the apostles did not

111

seem to take seriously, not even Judas himself. But now Jesus pointedly says that he knows the kind of men (Bernard) that he chose as apostles, little as they seem to know the traitor. Jesus does not mean by quoting Psalm 41:9 that he consciously chose Judas that he might betray him, but simply that the faithlessness of Judas is no surprise to him, though it was to others. Jesus was to realize in his own experience, like David and Jeremiah, the falsity of a close friend. Eating one's bread is in all countries a sign, and in the orient (Arabs today) a pledge, of friendship. "To eat bread at the table of a superior was to offer a pledge of loyalty (II Sam. 9:7, 13; I Kings 18:19; II Kings 25:29); and to betray one with whom bread had been eaten, one's 'mess-mate,' was a gross breach of the traditions of hospitality" (Bernard). Judas' eating Christ's bread on this very night, after making the compact with the Sanhedrin to betray Jesus, aggravated the crime. But even so the apostles do not yet exhibit any particular agitation on this revelation by Jesus, though he himself "was troubled in spirit" (John 13:21). "This it was which troubled his spirit, that one of the Twelve whom he had so cherished should turn traitor, using the familiarity and knowledge of intimacy to betray him" (Dods).

3. *The Sudden Shock to the Apostles.*—It was only when Jesus proceeded to say bluntly, probably with a sweeping gesture, "One of you shall betray me" (Mark 14:18; Matt. 26:21; John 13:21, put picturesquely by Luke in 22:21 "But behold the

hand of him that betrayeth me is with me on the
table") that "they began to be sorrowful" (Mark
14:19), "exceeding sorrowful" (Matt. 26:22). There
was no escaping the Master's meaning now. No pre-
occupied thoughts or selfish ambitions availed them
at this juncture. The betrayer was in this group of
apostles reclining with their Lord and Master at
this last passover meal. Who was he?

4. *The Mournful Suspicious Look.*—It is John
(13:22) who says: "The disciples looked one on another, doubting of whom he spake." The Beloved
Apostle was there and vividly recalls over the long
years that tragic moment, when each glanced at the
others to see if he could see any signs of guilt in
any face. "The first effect of the Lord's words was
silent amazement and perplexity" (Westcott). They
were really bewildered, perplexed, distressed, each
conscious of his own innocence, each save Judas
Iscariot, who was determined to bluff the thing out
and "did not suggest by his demeanor that he was the
guilty one" (Bernard). The contention about precedence at the beginning of the meal "may have ac-
centuated the perplexity which they felt" (Bernard).
It is a natural piece of psychology for each at
such a time to look at the others. Luke adds that
"they began to question among themselves, which
of them it was that should do this thing." Perhaps,
in whispers and suspicions of surprise and wonder.

5. *The Sorrowful Question.*—Finally the disciples
turn to Jesus with a personal question: "Is it I,
Lord?" (Mark 14:19; Matt. 26:22). They had be-

gun to look into their own hearts and to wonder if, after all, treachery had found a place there. This they did "one by one." Even Judas had to ask it, though he now knew that Jesus knew his purpose to betray him. Matthew alone (26:25) singles out the question of Judas, last of all: "Is it I, Rabbi?" Jesus admitted that it was, but the rest seem not to have grasped this affirmative answer of Jesus. The rest did not suspect him and this "new horror" (McNeile) settled on their hearts like a pall of gloom. "Each looks into his own heart, and each of the eleven hopes that he may acquit himself" (Plummer). The form of the question expresses the negative answer in a rather vigorous way. "Yet surely it cannot be I" (Swete).

6. *Peter's Appeal to John.*—With characteristic eagerness and initiative Peter, reclining behind Jesus, beckons or nods to the Beloved Disciple reclining in front of Jesus with his head on his bosom, to tell whom Jesus had in mind, thinking that he had already told John "in an undertone the name of the false apostle" (Westcott). Perhaps, as Westcott suggests, Peter was able to do this "as the eyes of the disciples were turned in surprise from one to another." But John had not been told by Jesus. So he leaned back on the bosom of Jesus and asked "Lord, who is it?"

7. *The Sign Given.*—Swete thinks that the reply of Jesus to John's inquiry was spoken in a low voice and so was heard by very few. At any rate it was quite ambiguous (McNeile), for they all dipped

with Jesus in the dish, possibly a dish of "sauce composed of fruits, spices, and vinegar, into which the food was dipped" (McNeile). It is not said in the Synoptics (Mark 14:20; Matt. 26:23) that it was the next one who dipped in the dish who was to betray Jesus. "There was probably only one dish, into which all the company dipped, and therefore all had dipped in the dish with Christ" (Plummer). Plummer suggests that the hand of Jesus may have touched that of Judas in the act of dipping so that he would understand the sign while the rest did not. In John 13:26 the sign is more minutely explained as the "sop" or "tit-bit" which an oriental host often gives to a guest as a mark of special honor. (So Boaz to Ruth, Ruth 2:14.) John's account, clearly his own recollection of the answer of Jesus to his inquiry, renders it even more difficult to understand the failure of Peter, after asking the favor of John, to see the answer of Jesus by act as well as by word. "So when he had dipped the sop, he taketh it and giveth it to Judas, the son of Simon Iscariot" (John 13:26). Bernard thinks that Judas, not Peter, reclined next to Jesus on the left and so it was easy for Judas to receive the sop without any noticing it except John who heard it. They all were so excited over what Jesus had said and done. Hence when Judas took the sop the devil entered into him afresh and Jesus said what he understood, but the others did not: "What thou doest, do quickly" (John 13:27). Some even supposed that Judas, because he had the bag, was urged to buy what they needed for the feast (not for this meal) or for the poor. There was some vague suspicion, but it did not centre on Judas, unless in the case of the Beloved Disciple who had heard and seen it all. Judas understood perfectly, but was in no wise restrained from his diabolical enterprise. John adds that, when Judas went out, "it was night," probably meaning that darkness had now come, no longer twilight, and it was, forsooth, blackness of darkness for all the world and particularly in the heart of Judas. Jesus had pronounced the terrible woe on the betrayer before he left his hearing: "Good were it for that man if he had not been born" (Mark 14:21; Matt. 26:24). Those who try to excuse Judas on the ground that it was predestined for him to betray Jesus may ponder the solemn doom pronounced on him here by Jesus for his responsibility and for his guilt.

8. *Christ's Special Prayer for Peter.*—With Judas gone on his hellish mission Jesus exhibits great concern for the rest. He speaks of his coming death as "being glorified" (John 13:31 f.) and urges the apostles to love one another as proof to the world that they are his disciples. He then predicts that they will be scattered like sheep without a shepherd by his death and makes an appointment with them in Galilee after his resurrection. Jesus turns to Peter with much concern: "Simon, Simon, behold Satan asked to have you, that he might sift you as wheat" (Luke 22:31). One thinks of Satan's demand about Job. Satan has already gotten Judas "the son of perdition" (John 17:12), but he wants the whole

group ("you" plural). Satan had tempted Jesus and
will attack any preacher and in particular preachers. We need not split hairs about divine sovereignty
and human free agency when the lives of men are at
stake. Jesus, of course, prayed for all of these men,
but in particular for Peter ("for thee," singular),
that his faith "fail not." It was a gracious blessing
and help to Peter for which he should have been
profoundly grateful. But instead of such gratitude
Peter took it as a reflection on his loyalty that
Jesus considered him in dire peril of deserting him
and his cause. Peter probably did not yet know the
truth about Judas, but he had been so prominent in
his confessions of devotion and loyalty that he took
it ill that Jesus should feel uneasy about him.

9. *Peter's Vehement Protest.*—Jesus, Peter felt,
had better make special prayer for the others. As
for him, though all should stumble, "yet will not I"
(Mark 14:29; Matt. 26:33). Luke (22:33) puts it
vividly and dramatically: "Lord, with thee I am
ready to go both to prison and to death." Surely
that was positive enough, but it did not satisfy Jesus
who calmly said to him: "Thou today, even this
night, before the cock crow twice shalt deny me
thrice" (Mark 14:30; Matt. 26:34; Luke 22:34;
John 13:38). All the Gospels give this dire prediction, but Mark alone mentions the cock crowing
"twice." That usually happens when one cock crows,
either he crows again or others join him in crowing.
Peter becomes greatly stirred and "spake exceeding
vehemently, If I must die with thee, I will not deny

thee" (Mark 14:31; Matt. 26:35). "Unconsciously,
no doubt, yet in point of fact, as Origen says, he
gave the lie to the Master" (Swete). He may have
repeated it in his passion. Thomas had spoken once
of sharing Christ's death in his pessimistic mood
(John 11:16). But Peter's words have more the air
of grand-stand heroics. "He claims to be stronger
than the other disciples; and he relies on his own
strength" (Plummer). Peter has thus repudiated
Christ's special prediction about himself, but he was
followed in this by the other ten apostles: "And in
like manner also said they all" (Mark 14:31; Matt.
26:35). Peter had done most of the loud boasting,
but they all chimed in with him just as they had all
agreed with Judas in his criticism of Mary of Bethany's "waste" of the ointment. There is no further
reply of Jesus to Peter recorded or to the other
boastful disciples. It was Peter who was in immi-
nent peril without knowing it. Pride goes before a
fall.

10. *New Charge to Peter.*—"And do thou, when
once thou hast turned again, stablish thy brethren"
(Luke 22:32). This rainbow of promise that Peter
would "turn again" apparently made no impression
on Peter, so indignant was he at the prediction that
he would deny his Lord and for the time being fall
a victim to Satan's devices. The special prayer of
Jesus would bring Peter back in due time. How many
a mother has won back a wayward son by the prayers
over the years! Jesus gives Peter a charge to
strengthen his brethren when once he has turned

back to him. This promise and this charge will be clearer to Peter when he stands before the Risen Christ by the Sea of Galilee (John 21). But now Peter is full of self-confidence and feels no need of the prayers of Jesus for the strength against Satan. It is just at this point that many a disciple has fallen. Paul could teach Peter a lesson here—he said: "For when I am weak, then am I strong" (II Cor. 12:10), weak in myself, but strong in Christ. Jesus warns the apostles, however, to be prepared for trouble and peril, a warning that they took literally about two swords, but Jesus rather weariedly said: "It is enough" (Luke 22:38) and refrained from further explanation.

CHAPTER VIII

THE CRISIS IN THE GARDEN

(Mark 14:26–42; Matthew 26:30–46; Luke 22:39–46;
John 18:1)

1. *The Institution of the Lord's Supper.*—According to the record in Mark (14:22–25) and Matthew (26:26–29) Jesus instituted the Memorial Supper after pointing out Judas as the traitor (Mark 14:18–21; Matt. 26:21–25) and his departure (John 13:27), though Luke (22:17–23) reverses this order of events. John does not mention the origin of the supper. The Synoptics also give the warning of the apostles by Jesus after the supper. The chronology of events here is not perfectly clear, but at any rate the words of Jesus concerning the bread and wine as memorials of his death left their impress on the minds of the disciples. From the point of view of psychology the spirit of self-confident boasting on the part of Peter and the rest falls in better before the institution of the Supper than afterwards, because here Jesus treats his death as a solemn certainty near at hand and gives directions for the observance of the memorial on the basis of it as a fact. The order in the Gospels (Christ's prayer in the Garden of Gethsemane just after the boastfulness of Peter) Plummer calls "a tragic irony." At any rate here is one more great experi-

ence in Peter's life during these crowded hours so full of the deepest significance. One fears that the sharp rebuke received by Peter for his rather loud boasting left him in a poor frame of mind for the meaning of the death of Christ in fact or in symbol.

2. *The Farewell Talk and Prayer.*—It is one of the blessings from the Fourth Gospel that we have preserved through the alembic of John's long rich spiritual experience the words of Jesus in the Upper Room and on the way to Gethsemane with the Intercessory Prayer. There are few critics who will say that the writer made up these high and holy words and that they do not really represent the heart of Christ towards the apostles on this climacteric night. Jesus has gone on to carry out his full purpose and the heart of the Master yearns for these eleven who are left in the world that they may not be of the world, but may go into the world, sanctified in the truth, and transform it. They will miss him, but he will come back for them, in death at any rate, and take them home to heaven with the Father when they will be with Jesus forever. That is the noblest picture of heaven given to man, the one drawn by Jesus in John 14, at home with Jesus. Thomas stumbled over it as many of a sceptical turn of mind do now, not perceiving that Jesus is the way to the Father. Philip is puzzled about seeing the Father, not knowing that the Father is revealed in Jesus. Judas (not Iscariot) wonders how Jesus will manifest himself to the disciples and not to the world, precisely what we see today for the world at large does not see Jesus

who dwells in all who will let him do so. Peter had
become silent before the others interrupted Jesus by
their inquiries. As usual, he spoke up first and
wanted to know "whither" Jesus was going and
"why" he could not go with him "even now" (John
13:36 f.). "I will lay down my life for thee." The
pointed prediction of denial by Peter this very night
finally silenced him and left him possibly in somewhat glum humor. But now all the apostles become
still, that is they cease questioning Jesus, though
some (Peter probably among them) began whisper-
ing to one another what he means by "a little while"
they would not see him and then again "a little
while" and they would see him (John 16:17). Jesus
noted it and chided them for not asking him about
it. He had promised them the Holy Spirit as another
Paraclete (comforter) to take his place with them
as teacher and interpreter of him and his words and
works. They seem to understand Jesus a bit better
when he drops the parabolic proverbs (16:29). Jesus
again foretells their desertion of him (16:32), but
proclaims his victory as he faces death. "But be of
good cheer; I have overcome the world." He was
probably no longer in the Upper Room (14:31), but
on the way to Gethsemane, when he lifted up his
eyes to heaven and prayed, first for himself (17:
1-5) in a prayer of thanksgiving at the prospect of
returning to the glory of heaven, then for these
eleven men (6-19) that they may be kept and used
of the Father, and also for all believers in all time
(20-26) that they be one in spirit and love so as to

convince the world that Jesus is in fact the Messiah, the Son of God. So they went into Gethsemane under the hush and awe of these words of gold, the very heart of Christ opened to these men. He had chosen them, had taught them, had shown them his spirit and his hopes, and now he was to leave them. The future of the Kingdom of God turns largely on how these men bear themselves when Jesus is gone from them in person. Will they submit to the will and guidance of the new Paraclete? For the moment there are no bickerings and no jealous words. But how much do they comprehend what the Master has been saying to them? Fortunately the Holy Spirit will remind them and will interpret it to them by degrees.

3. *The Chosen Three on Guard in Gethsemane.*— After the prayer in John 17 Jesus "went forth with his disciples over the Brook Kidron, where was a garden" (John 18:1). The name of the garden is not given by John or by Luke, but is called in Mark (14:32) and Matthew (26:36) Gethsemane (oil press or olive-vat). Swete thinks that the enclosure now known as the Latin Gethsemane is the right location. It had been an olive orchard or garden according to John and "was probably fenced in as a private plot" (McNeile). Josephus (*Wars* VI. 1.1.) observes that private gardens were numerous around Jerusalem. There is no reason to think, however, that the old gnarled olive trees now on the place were there when Jesus was there. The Kidron was only a winter torrent. Jesus was in the habit of going to

this garden at night to pray when in or near Jerusalem, a fact that Judas recalled and used for his nefarious purpose (John 18:2). It was by catching Jesus here off guard and alone that he hoped to help the Sanhedrin seize him without waiting till after the feast when the crowd would be gone (Mark 14:2, 11; Luke 22:6). It is not certain that the other disciples knew whither the Master was now going, though they should have known. Once inside the enclosure Jesus said to the disciples: "Sit ye here while I go yonder and pray" (Matt. 26:36). He had just finished the Intercessory Prayer of John 17, but the Master feels the need of more communion with his Father. "The apostles are so sure of their own strength that they will not allow the possibility of failure, even when they are forewarned of it by Christ. The Son of Man is so conscious of the weakness of his humanity that He prays to the Father that He may be spared the approaching trial" (Plummer). He feels also the need of fellowship and sympathy while he prays. Often he preferred to pray alone (Matt. 14:23) according to his own direction (Matt. 6:6). But now he wants fellowship and freedom from interruption by Judas and his band of confederates. So he takes with him Peter and the two sons of Zebedee (Mark 14:33; Matt. 26:37) a little farther into the garden ("yonder"). The eight remain near the gate of the garden while the same three intimate disciples that were with Jesus on the Mount of Transfiguration when he went there to pray (Luke 9:28) now go with him.

Mark (14:33) gives a startling item (probably from Peter's vivid telling) about Jesus himself who "began to be greatly amazed, and sore troubled." Celsus sneered that Jesus went to Gethsemane to hide! Swete explains it thus: "The shadow of death begins to fall upon him as he passes with the three into the depths of the olive grove." Mark's word is stronger than that in Matthew (26:37) and means amazed. The other word is in Matthew also and nowhere else in the New Testament save in Philippians 2:26. The idea may be that of terrified surprise. But most probably the meaning is to be away from home, to be homesick. This idea suits Epaphroditus in Philippians 2:26 and it suits the longing of Jesus to return home to his Father (John 17:5). So patent is his anguish of soul "even unto death" that he confesses it to the three disciples (Mark 14:34; Matt. 26:38) and warns them to pray not to enter into temptation (Luke 22:40). Clearly Satan was now pressing Jesus hard again as at the beginning of his ministry, pressing him now to draw back from the Cross for which he had come to earth and not to give his life a ransom for many (Mark 10:45; Matt. 20:28). So he bids them to wait here while he goes a stone's throw farther on (Luke 22:41) and falls on his face on the ground and prays: "Abba, Father, all things are possible unto thee; remove this cup from me" (Mark 14:36; Matt. 26:39; Luke 22:42; Heb. 5:7). This outcry came "in the days of his flesh" with all the tenderness of a loving son to his Father, using both the Aramaic and the Greek

words for Father (*Abba, Pater*) as Paul does in
Galatians 4:6 and Romans 8:15.

We need not speculate about this sorrow and this
agony of soul by Jesus. Origen explained that it was
only for the woes and the sins of men. It was caused
by the sins of men, of course, but "his human soul
shrank from the Cross, and the fact adds to our
sense of the greatness of his sacrifice" (Swete). Paul
(II Cor. 5:21) throws some light on this aspect of
Christ's suffering: "The one who knew no sin he
made (treated as) sin for us." It was not lack of
courage in facing death, but Jesus literally staggered under the burden of the sin of the world (John
1:29). But the cry was only momentary and instantly
came the resignation to the Father's will: "Howbeit,
not what I will, but what thou wilt" (Mark 14:36;
Matt. 26:39; Luke 22:42). Jesus won the victory
over the tempter in this surrender to the Father. He
learned from what he suffered (Heb. 5:8), though
God's only begotten Son. With this victory over his
human weakness attacked by Satan Jesus is able to
go on to Calvary. Luke (22:43) adds that at this
juncture an angel appeared unto Jesus strengthening him. Some manuscripts do not have this verse or
verse 44, though both verses are probably genuine.
Mark (1:13) and Matthew (4:11) record that angels came and ministered unto Jesus after his victory over Satan in the first temptations. This was a
more severe temptation than those. But the agony
of Christ continued and so did his praying. "His
sweat became as it were great drops of blood falling

down upon the ground." Satan will not confess defeat till he has tested Jesus to the bottom and to the limit.

4. *Christ's Disappointment in Peter.*—The plea of Jesus to the three was: "Watch with me" (Matt. 26:38). The word for "Watch" means to stay awake. Jesus, feeling afresh the need for human sympathy in his terrific struggle, comes back to the three disciples "and finds them sleeping" (Mark 14:37; Matt. 26:40; Luke 22:45), "for sorrow" Luke adds. Here was tragedy indeed. The chosen three are asleep while the Son of man has been agonizing because of the sin of the world. Jesus wakes up Peter with the pathetic words: "Simon, sleepest thou? Couldst thou not watch one hour?" The word translated "couldst" means to have strength. Plainly Peter did not have it, in spite of all that he had gone through, perhaps because of all this his flesh was weak, though his spirit was willing (Mark 14:38). So Jesus excused him for this failure and went back to his praying in agony. Luke does not give this return to prayer, but only the repeated warning to pray not to enter into temptation (22:40, 46). Mark (14:39) says that Jesus "prayed, saying the same words," while Matthew (26:42) gives the words. Once more Jesus came to the three disciples for sympathy in his agony and found them sleeping again, "for their eyes were very heavy" (Mark 14:40; Matthew 26:43), "weighed down" according to Mark, in a state of stupor according to Matthew. Mark adds (Peter's reaction) that "they wist not what to

answer him" for very shame. Had they offered an excuse the first time? So Jesus left them and prayed a third time and says on his return: "Sleep on now" (Mark 14:41; Matthew 26:45), "uninterrupted by further calls to prayer" (McNeile) in pathetic and mournful irony. That is he has won his victory over Satan without their help or sympathy. But the hour has come. The betrayer is at hand. "Arise, let us be going" to meet this peril, not to flee from it. Alas, that so often those on whom our Lord depends for help in a crisis fail him now. But Jesus is ready for Judas, even if Peter has only been asleep. Is Peter ready for his part in this great drama, this tragedy of the ages? Just being asleep at his post is poor preparation of his own soul for the temptation that now confronts him and that he so little comprehends. But Judas is coming like the train that comes on while the switchman is asleep at his post. The sleeping disciples arise and rub their eyes in time to see Judas and his great band of helpers coming.

5. *Peter's Rash Act.*—While Jesus was speaking and urging the three disciples to arise and go with him, he sees Judas, "one of the twelve" as all the Synoptics have it, the very phrase used by Jesus when pointing out the traitor (Mark 14:20). In Mark 14:10 we have "the one of the twelve" to do this horrible deed, "the literary reflection of the chronic horror of the Apostolic Church that such a thing should be possible" (Bruce). Jesus may have stepped outside the entrance in the movement to meet Judas (McNeile). There is Judas at the head

of a band (John 18:3) from the garrison in the
tower of Antonia under the command of a tribune
(John 18:12), according to John (18:3, 12). Mc-
Neile thinks that John's account is only "symbolic"
of an official arrest, not the way the actual arrest of
Jesus occurred in the Synoptics, for since no criminal charges had been made and the arrest was to be
as secret as possible "the Sanhedrin could not ask
for the services of soldiers." But that view overlooks
the desire of these ecclesiastics by the use of money
to secure a small detachment of soldiers for an un-
named purpose. Luke (22:47) merely mentions the
multitude or mob while Mark (14:43) and Matthew
(26:47) say that the crowd were "from the chief
priests and the scribes and the elders," that is from
the Sanhedrin, while John says that "officers" or
some of the temple police were sent by the Sanhedrin.
Possibly some members of the high priest's family
came also, certainly one did (Malchus). These were
armed also with swords, staves, lanterns, torches.
Judas was evidently afraid of armed opposition after
Christ's exposure of him as the traitor. The lights
would come in handy if they had to search under the
olive trees or behind the shadow of walls. It was the
time of the full moon, but it may have been cloudy.
But Jesus boldly stepped forth to meet Judas and
his motley crew of Roman soldiers and temple police,
"knowing all the things that were coming upon him"
(John 18:4). John alone tells the dramatic episode
of the falling back to the ground of this armed band
as Jesus faced them fearlessly. He made them and

Judas feel his power before he surrendered voluntarily. Probably at this juncture Judas mustered up his courage to betray Jesus with a kiss, the sign agreed on to indicate to the soldiers and police who Jesus was, but not needed now. But Judas stood before him. "Judas, betrayest thou the Son of man with a kiss?" (Luke 22:48). He had stooped that low in his infamy. The sign or concerted signal (Mark 14:44) agreed upon was the kiss, "the customary mode of saluting a rabbi" (Swete). "Nothing that has been told of Judas has so excited the horror of Christendom as this demonstrative and atrociously offensive kiss" (Plummer). It cannot be an invention of special blackness for Judas, for the Gospels show much restraint in their treatment of Judas. The meaning of Matthew 26:50 is uncertain, because of the relative clause, "for which thou art come." In the *Koiné* the relative is sometimes used as an interrogative. That is possible here as an ironical question to Judas just as he approaches before the kiss. But when Judas had thus by the kiss indicated Jesus, the soldiers and police laid hands on him and took him prisoner. Then the disciples said: "Lord, shall we smite with the sword?" (Luke 22:49). They did have two swords (Luke 22:38). Before Jesus could answer, Peter drew one of these swords and aimed to cut off the head of Malchus (told by John with Peter's name in 18:10 after Peter's death) who dodged so that Peter cut off his right ear (Luke 22:50; John 18:10). The Synoptics for prudential reasons do not mention Peter's

name, a slight incidental argument for dating the
Synoptic Gospels before Peter's death. This was
a foolish act on Peter's part in view of the number of soldiers and police all armed, but it is thoroughly characteristic of him now that he is really
awake and sees the dastardly deed of Judas with
whom they had fellowshipped. Jesus calmly touched
the ear of Malchus and healed it, a miracle of surgery mentioned only by Luke (Luke 22:51). But
Jesus told Peter to put up his sword in its sheath,
"for all they that take the sword shall perish with
the sword" (Matt. 26:52), a good text for the bene-
fit of warlike nations and individuals. Jesus reminds
Peter that even now he could call for twelve legions
of angels to fight for him if he had wanted to offer
resistance. Jesus had fought the devil at every step,
but now makes a voluntary surrender to Judas and
the Cross. There would be no value in the death of
Christ on the Cross if it had not been voluntary. He
said himself that he laid down his life of himself and
he took it again (John 10:17). "The cup which the
Father hath given me, shall I not drink it?" (John
18:11). The Master then made a dignified protest
against the manner of his arrest, by armed soldiers
and police as if he were a robber. Why had they not
arrested him while he was teaching daily in the temple? "Ye stretched not forth your hands against
me" (Luke 22:53). But the Scriptures, he added,
must be fulfilled (Mark 14:49; Matt. 26:56), and he
fully recognized that his hour had come: "But this
is your hour and the power of darkness." In Colos-

sians 1:13 we have this same vivid phrase, "the power of darkness." Lightfoot there observes that power here may be unrestrained, tyrannical or delegated power. Difficult as it is for us to understand, Satan is "prince of this world" (John 14:30), only by God's permission and a limit is set to his diabolical rule.

6. *The Flight of the Apostles.*—"Then all the disciples left him and fled" (Matt. 26:56). Jesus had said that they would all stumble this very night and be scattered as sheep without a shepherd (Mark 14:27; Matt. 26:31) as Zechariah had foretold (13:7). They had reason enough for their flight according to their thinking. Jesus refused to resist his arrest. He made Peter put up his sword when he attempted to fight. Peter's conduct in trying to cut off the head of a servant of the high priest Caiaphas exposed him to arrest also. When Judas and his mob came, Jesus had made a plea for their freedom (John 18:8), but no promise of immunity for them had been given. If Jesus could be taken a prisoner by the Sanhedrin, there was no safety for them save in flight. But what about their vows of loyalty to the death made some hours before on this very night? And in particular what about Peter's boast that he would go with Jesus both to prison and to death? (Mark 14:31; Matt. 26:35; Luke 22:33; John 13:37). Circumstances alter cases, to be sure, and they were caught all of a sudden, so to speak. So Peter's flight follows his fight. The disciples are in a panic, a rout, and they run for their lives. Mark (14:51 f.)

preserves a glimpse of the panic, how a young man had come to the garden with only a linen cloth around, perhaps his night covering on the bed. When the mob laid hold on this linen cloth, he left it and fled home naked. The early Christian writers took this young man to be John Mark, the son of Mary of Acts 12:12. That is quite possible if Jesus had eaten the passover in the upper room in this same house (Luke 22:8–12). The young man could very well have followed the crowd or even the disciples into the garden after noticing the departure of Jesus. But the incident is a graphic picture of the excitement attending the arrest of Jesus.

7. *Peter's Rallying and Following Afar Off.*—Apparently John, the Beloved Disciple, rallied first, for he had gone into the court of the high priest's house before Peter came up. But Westcott argues that Peter rallied first because of the singular verb in John 18:15 and stopped at the door while John went on in. Both "followed." Peter "followed afar off" as all the Synoptics say (Mark 14:54; Matt. 26:58; Luke 22:54). That was apparently more than any of the other disciples except John did, when the officers led Jesus away "bound" (John 18:12). Peter did not wish to be discovered by the band with Judas and yet he wanted to see what they did with Jesus. This conduct is quite in keeping with Peter's character. So he followed on, "fearful, yet drawn on by love and curiosity" (Bruce), till Jesus had been led "into the court of the high priest; but Peter was standing at the door without" (John 18:15 f.). Pos-

sibly he might not have gotten inside at all but for
the fact that the Beloved Disciple was known unto
the high priest. So when he saw Peter standing there
at the door, John went out and spake to the portress
and brought him in. John then went on into the room
where the trial was going on. What will Peter do
now that he is in the court?

CHAPTER IX

THE COWARD IN THE COURT
(Mark 14:53–15:1; Matthew 26:57–27:1; Luke 22:54–71; John 18:24–27)

1. *The Stages in the Jewish Trial.*—The Jewish trial of Jesus by the Sanhedrin came first and then the Roman trial by Pontius Pilate. There were three stages in the Jewish trial, first the informal examination by Annas, the ex-high priest and father-in-law of Caiaphas, while the Sanhedrin was gathering (John 18:12–23), then the hurried trial before the Sanhedrin while still night (Mark 14:53–65; Matt. 26:57–68; Luke 22:54–65; John 18:24), then the ratification of the condemnation by the Sanhedrin after dawn (Mark 15:1; Matt. 27:1; Luke 22:66–71). The scene of the Jewish trial was the residence of Caiaphas the high priest. It was during the Jewish trial that the denials by Peter took place, though we are not able to locate them precisely. John, indeed, mentions one of the denials (18:15–18) before Christ's appearance before Annas (18:19–23) and the other two (18:25–27) after Jesus was sent bound to Caiaphas (18:24). Annas apparently occupied one wing of the palace of Caiaphas so that the three denials may very well have extended through all the stages of the Jewish trial before Jesus was sent to Pontius Pilate.

2. *The Order of the Three Denials.*—All the Gospels tell this sad story of Peter's downfall with much

detail (Mark 14:66–72; Matt. 26:69–75; Luke 22:55–62; John 18:15–18, 25–27). Each seems to be independent of the other (Matthew more like Mark) with fresh items that are not contradictory when properly understood. Each gives three denials by Peter just as Jesus had foretold (Mark 14:30; Matt. 26:34; Luke 22:34; John 13:38). It is not clear that each Gospel gives them in the same order, though that is entirely possible when we consider that probably each time more than one joined in the accusation against Peter that he was a disciple of Jesus. All mention a maid as the one who was the first to observe to Peter her suspicion about him. The next time Mark and Matthew mention another maid while Luke mentions a man while John says "they spoke" to Peter. The third time Mark and Matthew have "they that stood by," Luke has "another man," while John mentions "one of the servants of the high priest." There is no essential incongruity in these various details. It is patent that each time others joined in the general talk and made it very uncomfortable for Peter. It is worth observing that there is no effort on Mark's part to gloss over the conduct of Simon Peter, though he wrote so much under Peter's influence. We may follow Mark's order of the denials with reasonable confidence in his chronology.

3. *Peter Warming Himself by the Fire.*—John seems to locate the first attack on Peter by the portress soon after John got Peter into the court, though he does picture him soon as "standing and

warming himself." It was not far from the door to
the centre of the open court where the fire of char-
coal was, possibly in a brazier. The word here (John
18:18) is the one from which our "anthracite"
comes, but no true coal was known in Palestine till
the nineteenth century (Bernard). It was cold at
night in Jerusalem in the early spring, for it was
up in the mountains 2400 feet high. All Four Gospels mention this maid as the one who began the
attack on Peter. "It was not Pilate, nor any of the
Sanhedrin nor a mob of soldiers, but a single wait-
ing-maid, who frightened the self-confident apostle
into denying his Master" (Plummer). The Roman
soldiers had apparently returned to the barracks in
the Tower of Antonia. The temple police, who had
effected the arrest of Jesus, were still in charge of
their prisoner. So Peter stealthily made his way
(Bruce) from the door up to the fire where these
officers were and took a seat with them "to see the
end" (Matt. 26:58). "St. John meanwhile (it must
be supposed) had pressed on into the audience chamber, so that St. Peter was alone. St. John, who remained closest to the Lord, was unmolested: St.
Peter, who mingled with the indifferent crowd, fell"
(Westcott). John indeed states that the officers were
standing by the fire warming themselves (18:18) and
pictures Peter standing with them, while the Synoptics say that the officers and Peter were sitting.
Forsooth, both statements may be true at different
moments. Certainly Peter was restless and uneasy
enough to be now up and now down. He was hoping

to conceal his identity in this crowd of temple police, household servants, and others who had straggled in. He was sitting "beneath in the court," Mark says (14:66), while Matthew (26:69) has only "without in the court." It was outside the audience-chamber where the trial before Caiaphas was going on, but below the level of the audience-chamber. He did not have the courage of the Beloved Disciple to go on into the trial chamber nor was he willing to remain in the street outside. So here he is in a place of compromise like many modern Christians who mingle with the enemies of Christ and seek to hide their identity. It is always a place of peril.

4. *Recognized as a Disciple of Jesus and a Sudden Disclaimer.*—As Peter was warming himself, he apparently overlooked "the light of the fire" (Mark 14:67; Luke 22:56) which shone into his face. The maid (the portress) looked at Peter's face, gazed intently, Luke says. "She sees at once that he is a stranger, going closer to him, and looking sharply into his face in the dim fire-light, she comes at once to her conclusion" (Bruce). She may have seen Peter with Jesus in the temple or on the street: "Thou also wast with the Nazarene, Jesus" (Mark 14:67). Matthew (26:69) says "Jesus the Galilean." Luke (22:56) makes it a comment about Peter, not to him: "This man also was with him." John (18:17) makes it a question to Peter: "Art thou also one of this man's disciples?" All of these terms may have come rapidly from the mouth of the maid. The point is the same even if she said it only once. The answer

to this sudden recognition when he was hiding his identity had different touches in each report. John's is blunt and short: "I am not." Luke's report adds the word "Woman" and disclaims acquaintance with Jesus: "Woman, I know him not." Matthew mentions Peter's ignorance, "I know not what thou sayest." Mark has the fullest form of the denial: "I neither know nor understand what thou sayest." "Then again Peter may very well have said all these things in his vehemence by repetition, after he had been surprised into the first lie" (Plummer). Plummer thinks that "had he been arrested by the Temple-guard and taken before the high priest, he would probably have answered with courage and truthfulness." Perhaps so, though one cannot feel sure. At any rate, he did not take refuge in flight just yet, though Mark (14:68) does say that "he went out into the porch." It is clearly too hot now for Peter by the fire. He was perhaps afraid of expulsion from the court or of arrest by the temple officers with whom he sat. Plummer adds in Peter's defense that "he found out that it may be more difficult to act rightly in small things than to brace oneself for an act of heroism." But it was not a small thing to deny the Lord Jesus to whom he had a few hours before vowed loyalty to prison and to death. Mark notes also that "the cock crew" at this juncture. He alone mentions that Jesus spoke of the cock crowing twice (14:30) and he notes the fulfilment of this item also (14:72). This incident should have brought Peter back to his senses, but it did not.

5. *Another Denial Out in the Porch.*—Peter felt
the need of fresh air. Luke says that the second
denial (22:58) was "after a little while." "He slunk
away from the fire into the forecourt" (Bruce). The
portress who had recognized Peter by the fire soon
returned to her post at the door "and began to say
to them that stood by, This is one of them" (Mark
14:69). This was all quite natural. She was carrying on her comment to Peter by the fire, only now
to the bystanders, justifying her identification of
Peter as a disciple of Jesus, the prisoner then on
trial before the Sanhedrin. Luke (22:58) says that
another man, taking up the remarks of the maid,
turned to Peter and said: "Thou also art one
of them." John (18:25) uses the question again, but
says that "they said therefore unto him," that is,
the officers at the fire, apparently before Peter moved
out into the porch. It is plain that more than one
person joined in this attack on Peter. It had become
no less general in the group. Peter's denial this time
is blunt: "Man, I am not" (Luke), while Matthew
adds that he spoke to the maid: "Again he denied with
an oath, I know not the man." The others mitigate
Peter's offense this time by not giving the oath, but
it is still a lie like the first. That is one trouble about
lying. One lie is certain to call for another to cover
up the first. Peter's descent, once he started on his
toboggan slide down hill, is "quite normal" (Plummer), yes, but none the less deplorable and despica-
ble. "The falsehood was of a glaring character denying that he had any knowledge of him whose most

trusted disciple he had long been, and whom he himself had recognized as 'the Messiah' and the 'Son of
the living God' " (Plummer).

6. *The Third Denial an Hour Later.*—Mark (14:
70) and Matthew (26:73) place the third denial
"after a little while," but Luke (22:59) locates it
"after the space of about one hour." It is not clear
what Peter did during this interval of an hour. He
may have gone out beyond the porch or he may have
remained there for a while. It was plain to Peter now
that he was recognized as a follower of Jesus, the
very thing that he was trying to avoid and that had
led him to deny twice any knowledge of Jesus. But
he finally returned inside by the fire. "Peter in the
course of that time would begin to think that no
further annoyance was to be looked for" (Bruce).
Westcott thinks that at this juncture Jesus was
brought from the presence of Annas before the whole
Sanhedrin and that this incident started up afresh
the talk about Peter. Finally another man in the
group of bystanders, after observing Peter closely,
remarked to the crowd: "Of a truth this man also
was with him; for he is a Galilean" (Luke 22:59).
The talk about Peter became general and "they that
stood by" said directly to Peter: "Of a truth thou
also art one of them; for thy speech bewrayeth thee"
(Mark 14:70; Matt. 26:73). They had commented
on Peter's accent which "confirmed the suspicions of
the bystanders" (Swete). The precise peculiarities
of the Galilean pronunciation of Aramaic are not
known, though Dalman, Neubauer and Schürer indi-

cate some of them with probability (difficulties about the gutturals, for one thing). But Peter's repeated denials had themselves revealed that he was a Galilean Jew. This was embarrassment enough, for the coils were tightening around Peter. At this point John (18:26), "whose acquaintance with the High Priest gave him special opportunities of knowing the fact" (Swete), reports that a "kinsman of him whose ear Peter cut off saith, Did not I see thee in the garden with him?" Here was confirmation of Peter's worst fears. This man was also a servant of the high priest and he probably saw Peter when he tried to slay Malchus. In spite of his denials Peter saw himself in grave peril of arrest and possible death. He had little time to think, but he went on down the declivity of denial as before. This time, to add emphasis to his denial, "he began to curse and to swear" (both Mark and Matthew report), though Matthew says that "he denied with an oath" in the second denial. Evidently this time he proceeded "to call down curses on himself in case he was telling lies" (Bruce). He is "growing desperate as he sees the meshes closing round him" (Swete).

7. *The Cock Crowing.*—But, alas, even while Peter was cursing and swearing so confidently about his ignorance of Jesus, the cock crew (Luke 22:60), the second time it had happened according to Mark (14:72). Not much is said about the crowing of the cock, but it played a real part in the conviction of Peter.

8. *The Look of Jesus.*—Easton thinks that Jesus

was standing close enough to hear these terrible
words of Peter, but Plummer doubts it. At any rate
he turned quickly and "looked on Peter." Jesus could
see Peter through an open window or door. He spoke
not a word, but gave him a look of sorrow and sympathy, an indescribable look that cut Peter to the
heart. "In this touch, given by him alone, Luke the
Artist is at his highest. He has put the sublimest
pathos into the simplest words" (Ragg). There was
no need for Jesus to say anything. The mist and fog
in which Peter had enveloped himself blew away from
around him before this piercing look. No one has
equalled Mrs. Browning's sonnet, *The Meaning of
the Look:*

> "I think that look of Christ might seem to say—
> 'Thou Peter! art thou then a common stone
> Which I at last must break my heart upon,
> For all God's charge to his high angels may
> Guard my foot better? Did I yesterday
> Wash *thy* feet, my beloved, that they should run
> Quick to deny me 'neath the morning sun?
> And do thy kisses, like the rest, betray?
> The cock crows coldly.— Go, and manifest
> A late contrition, but no bootless fear!
> For when thy final need is dreariest,
> Thou shalt not be denied, as I am here;
> My voice to God and angels shall attest,
> *Because I* KNOW *this man, let him be clear.'* "

"He called to mind the word, how that Jesus had
said unto him" (Mark 14:72), to prepare him and to
warn him against this very deed (Mark 14:30). John
omits this recollection by Peter because the Syn-

optics all give it. The shock of the look of Jesus made vivid the whole dreadful scene through which he had just passed, a psychological reaction quite understandable. Mark adds a comment, "when he thought thereon," that has puzzled scholars through the ages. The Western text substitutes "began" while Theophylact made it to mean "covering the head." But the English rendering is probably correct, for a papyrus example exists which means "to set to." The more Peter put his mind on the word of Jesus recalled by his look the less he could bear it, without an emotional explosion.

9. *Peter Weeping Bitterly.*—So "he went out and wept bitterly." "He burst into tears" (Matt. and Luke), "he began to weep" (Mark). He could stand it no longer in the court by the fire with the mockers and scorners and in his humiliation he could not face his Master after that look. So he went outside with his "bitter" tears (Matt. and Luke). From this time on through the rest of the trial of Jesus (both ecclesiastical and civil) Peter drops out of the picture, a desolate deserter, groping in the dark with his sins and his sorrow. All his boasting rushed back into his mind and added bitterness to his salty tears. All his ambitious schemes for leadership have come to naught. All his high moments of insight and confession made his present degradation seem deeper. And there was no one to whom he could open his heart. The Beloved Disciple was on the inside with Jesus. Judas was too contemptible to think of. Peter at least had not sunk that low, he had not actually

betrayed his Lord, though he had renounced him and denied him. The other nine had, indeed, fled, but they had not committed his sin. The women would despise him for his cowardice. Surely Peter is a pitiful figure as the hours of this night of destiny wore on. He was now afraid of a shadow, especially his own shadow. The story of Peter's downfall is told with sheer simplicity and graphic power in the Four Gospels. There is no effort to cover up his sin nor to justify it. Mark, who wrote under Peter's influence, puts the dreadful fact as sharply and clearly as the rest. Peter has no defense to make for his denials. The look of Jesus melted his heart and broke it. There was only one word of hope that he could recall. Jesus had said, when he foretold his fall: "And do thou, when once thou hast turned again, stablish thy brethren" (Luke 22:32). Jesus, then, did have faith in his recovery and did hold out work for him to do after that. We do not know whether Peter was able at this time to recall this word of hope or not. He was at the very bottom of the abyss of exposure and humiliation. He was caught by the Master redhanded in his sin. He was unworthy of anything at the hands of Jesus whom he had disowned and disgraced. He had no wish to see the other apostles whose leader he hoped to be, whose ambitions rivalled his own. All his confidence was now fled from him. He had now only dead hopes on which to brood in his abject despair. So we leave Peter out in the night whither Judas had gone. Judas will come to the Sanhedrin and confess his sin, fling down the accursed money at their feet, and then go out and hang himself. Did Peter come close to the verge of that abyss of despair? Jesus had made special prayer for Peter and he was held back from the worst.

CHAPTER X

THE HUMBLED PENITENT
(Mark 16:7; Luke 24:12, 34; I Corinthians 15:5; John 21:1–23)

1. *Peter's Desolation.*—It seems plain that Peter did not hang around in the crowd before Pilate's palace while Jesus was on trial there. The dreadful story moved on to its culmination. Pilate in disgust and fear of the Jews agreed to the crucifixion of Jesus whom he had pronounced an innocent man. The crucifixion was witnessed by a group of faithful women who dared the confusion of the public execution to be with their Lord to the end. Even the Mother of Jesus stood beside the Cross as the sword of which old Simeon had prophesied pierced her heart. She had believed the words of the angel Gabriel and now this. It was more than she could understand or stand. The Beloved Disciple, alone of the apostles, was there. The dying Saviour committed his mother to John's care who at once took her to his Jerusalem home and returned to the Cross in time to see the Lord's body pierced by the Roman soldiers and to see water and blood come out (John 19:31–37), proof against the Docetic denial that Jesus had an actual human body, proof that he literally died of a broken heart for the sin of the world. Peter had no share in the burial of Jesus' body which fell to the brave and loving care of two timid believers, members of the Sanhedrin, who now in the

147

darkest hour rose to the height of courage (Nicodemus the timorous Pharisee and Joseph of Arimathea the wealthy councillor). They buried with tender love the body of Jesus on Friday afternoon before sunset in Joseph's new tomb outside the city walls. The women from Galilee (God bless the brave and loyal women) "followed after, and beheld the tomb, and how his body was laid" (Luke 23:55). See them then "sitting over against the sepulchre" (Matt. 27:61) with brooding melancholy and holy memories and blighted hopes. These women had never disputed, as the apostles had done, over place and primacy. They found their joy in ministering of their substance to the wants of the Master whom they loved and served (Luke 8:3). And now it had come to this. Luke (23:56) states that the women rested on the Sabbath with chastened hearts and dead faith. Curiously neither they nor the apostles recalled Christ's promise of resurrection on the third day which he had repeatedly made during the previous six months, not even Peter and the two sons of Zebedee who had a special commission on this subject as they came down from the Mount of Transfiguration. The eclipse of faith was complete. It was night without a star of hope. Only the Pharisees, fearing Jesus though dead, recalled his prediction of rising on the third day (Matt. 27:62–66) and had the Roman seal placed on the stone at the mouth of the tomb with a guard of Roman soldiers to protect it from grave robbers. Only the women among the disciples take further interest in the tomb of Jesus.

They prepared spices Friday afternoon on their return before the Sabbath (Luke 23:56). Late on the Sabbath before sundown (when the Sabbath closed) two of them (Mary Magdalene and the other Mary) made a visit to the tomb, but did not come close enough to see the guard or the seal on the stone (Matt. 28:1). After the Sabbath was past (after sundown) several of the women bought more spices (Mark 16:1) that they might anoint the body of Jesus. But this is not discussing Peter's desolation? No, but in the conduct of the lonely and loving women we can get some idea of the heartaches of the disciples during this long and dreadful Sabbath with the body of Jesus in the tomb. The Beloved Disciple is with the Mother of Jesus, but there was little that he could say to her now that the end had come to her glorious hope and to his. John knew that Jesus loved him and his own Mother. There was comfort in that, but the King was dead and His kingdom had vanished into thin air. Who can fathom the woe in Mary's heart during this long Sabbath? The other apostles (ten besides John, for Judas is dead) do not appear in the picture. Peter, we may imagine, was alone, unless in sheer desperation he sought fellowship with the other disconsolate nine. Why did he not recall the very rebuke of Jesus to him when he doubted his words about his rising from the dead? Jesus called him "Satan" then and surely he had been acting like the devil in three times denying his Lord and Master. But Peter, perhaps most of all, was in the depths of gloom and of despair. His own conduct was an impenetrable fog that prevented his seeing his way out for himself or for others.

2. *The Message of Mary Magdalene to Peter and John.*—Somehow Peter lived through Friday and Saturday, the Days of Darkness for the kingdom of God. He saw the first day of the new week come (our Sunday). Mary Magdalene left the other women at the tomb (the plural, "we know," shows that Mary was not alone) on that morning at sunrise (Mark 16:2). She sees the stone taken away and at once fears a grave robbery or at least removal to an unknown place. Without waiting to investigate further than to see that the tomb is empty she runs away to find Peter and John (John 20:2). As she sees it, there is need of a man to prevent desecration of the Lord's body: "They have taken away the Lord out of the tomb, and we know not where they have laid him." "The rapid boldness of the conclusion is characteristic of a woman's eager nature" (Westcott). Latham thinks that it was the other women who looked into the tomb who reported to Mary that it was empty, whereupon she at once ran off to tell Peter and John, but Westcott thinks that Mary reached the tomb first and fled before the other women came up. In all probability Mary did not know that Peter had denied the Lord, if indeed any of the disciples knew it at this time, unless the Beloved Disciple had overheard him, which is unlikely. The presence of Peter here with John shows that he was not regarded by him as a renegade. It shows also that Peter had at last sought the fellowship of John

in his desolation and desperation. It would seem that
Mary knew where to find them, probably in separate
places (Bengel, because of the repetition of *pros*)
or possibly at John's Jerusalem home. We are not
to think of Mary Magdalene as being Mary of Bethany, in spite of the effort of Bernard and others to
identify them. Peter acted first, impulsive as always,
and "went forth," and "they went on toward the
tomb." A vivid picture drawn by John who ran this
race with Peter. "The two were running together."
Bernard calls attention to a remarkable picture of
this race between Peter and John by E. Burnaud in
the Musée du Luxembourg in Paris. Peter had
started first, but "the other disciple outran Peter."
It was a rivalry of eager love. So the other disciple "came first to the tomb." So he stoops and
looks in and sees the linen cloths lying therein, but
did not go on inside. But Simon Peter, when he came
up, went on boldly into the tomb. Peter sees also the
linen cloths and the napkin that had been on Christ's
head "not lying with the linen cloths, but rolled up
in a place by itself." Peter's quick eye saw all this
at once. He was startled by it. Chrysostom notes
that, if Mary's inference were correct, the grave-
clothes would have been removed with the body. Then
it was that the Beloved Disciple mustered up courage to go in also after Simon Peter. He saw what
Peter had already seen, but he saw into the facts as
Peter had not done. He saw the meaning of the orderly arrangement of the grave-clothes left behind.
It was no grave robbery, it was no mere removal of

the body to another resting place. It could only mean one thing. Jesus is now risen from the dead (Bernard). Westcott hesitates to go that far and can only say that the absolute sense of "believed" here ("he saw and believed") means to "imply that St. John believed in some way that the Lord was alive." That is entirely too cautious a statement. John does not mean to say that he had a vision of the Lord Jesus in the tomb or that he at that moment understood all that he came afterwards to know about the Risen Christ. As an old man, John looks back upon his conduct on this momentous occasion as the one who "came first to the tomb and he saw, and believed." Dods puts it clearly; "Standing and gazing at the folded napkin, John saw the truth. Jesus has himself risen, and disencumbered himself of these wrappings." It was enough for John who may have begun to recall dimly and vaguely the predictions of Jesus about rising from the dead on the third day, though certainly he did not understand them nor the Scriptures on that subject (John 20:9) like Psalm 16:10 (cf. Acts 2:24 f.; I Cor. 15:3 f.). In saying this, "John is thinking of his readers, who may be surprised that Peter and the Beloved Disciple were not more quick to recognise what had happened" (Bernard). John does not say that he tried to convince Peter of his new faith and hope. "So the disciples went away again into their own home" (John 20:10). The Greek idiom is like the French *chez eux* "to themselves," probably John's home (John 19:27). It was fit and proper that they should go and tell Mary the Mother of Jesus what they had seen at the tomb. She was entitled to the wonderful new hope now in John's heart. Luke (24: 12) does not mention John as going with Peter in the visit to the tomb of Jesus, though he does say (24:24) that several brethren did go to the tomb after the women made their report. He says that Peter "departed to his home" (using the same idiom as in John 20:10), "went off to himself," as if Peter did not go to John's home. But that is not clear. He went "wondering at that which had come to pass." That would seem to mean that Peter was more perplexed than John who had already believed that Jesus was risen, before he saw him. That is John's crown of glory. Renan pictures both Peter and John as going to their home *dans un trouble extrême*. It is not true of either of them, least of all of John. Peter and John did not see the angels that the women had seen and that Mary Magdalene saw. "Such manifestations necessarily follow the laws of a spiritual economy" (Westcott). That is true, but it does not explain why women, not men, saw the angels. Some things we can best leave unexplained. It is to be observed that Mary Magdalene did not reach the tomb again (John 20:11–18) until after Peter and John were gone. She was hopelessly out of the race with them.

3. *The Idle Talk of the Other Women.*—The group of women, left at the tomb by Mary Magdalene when she ran to see Peter and John, saw the empty tomb and the two angels, received the mes-

sage from them about the Risen Christ and from him
for the disciples to meet him in Galilee. The angels
reminded the women of Christ's words while in Galilee about rising again on the third day. "And they
remembered his words" (Luke 24:8). So these women
are the first of the disciples to recall Christ's own
blessed promise. In fear and astonishment they fled
to tell the disciples this message from the Risen
Christ through the angels (Matt. 28:8), though
speaking to no one else (Mark 16:8). They "returned from the tomb, and told all these things to
the eleven, and to all the rest" (Luke 24:9). Here
was good news at last, a ray of hope in the gloom.
How did the apostles receive the wonderful story?
"And these words appeared in their sight as idle
talk; and they disbelieved them" (Luke 24:11). The
word *lēros* Hobart finds "applied in medical language to the wild talk of the sick in delirium." It
was all "nonsense," to the eleven apostles. There is
no comfort here for those who claim that the disciples started the story of the resurrection of Jesus,
because they wanted to carry on his work. The apostles themselves are the disbelievers, the sceptics, who
have to be convinced. And they were not convinced
by the words of Mary Magdalene and the other
women; they looked on the reports of the women as
"nonsense," the words of nervous, excitable women,
not to be credited by sensible men like themselves. It
must be confessed that the new faith of the Beloved
Disciple suffers a slight eclipse in the reports in
Luke and Mark, if he was present when the women

made their reports. The word "eleven" need not be pressed to mean that each one was there. Did the women use their fresh recollection of the words of Jesus about rising on the third day? At this stage one must think that neither Mary Magdalene nor the other women had as yet seen the Risen Christ. It is all, as yet, the story of the empty tomb, of the angels and their message to the women. The brethren who went to the tomb found it empty, but they did not see the Risen Christ (Luke 24:23). It was so far too much mere angels and women for the men among the disciples. "They had seen him dead, and women's talk about angels who said that he was alive did not cancel that" (Plummer). Why did not Peter tell what he had seen about the orderly arrangement of the clothes? Why did not John tell his own convictions which were in accord with the story of the women? Were they restrained by the contemptuous reception given the words of the women? We do not know the reason for their silence, if they were present at the time of their report. It does seem a bit queer for the women to be left alone in their championship of the fact of the Risen Christ, when Peter and John had at least some confirmation to offer. On the whole one may conjecture that Peter and John were not present when the women delivered their message, for they two went straight from the tomb to John's home to tell the Mother of Jesus. They were probably there when the meeting was held.

4. *The Special Message to Peter.*—Strangely enough there is no mention of the actual delivery of

the special message of Jesus to Peter (Mark 16:7).
If he was absent from the meeting of the disciples
when the women made their report, as has just been
conjectured, then it may have been delivered to him
privately and personally. This was probably the
case. One can easily imagine how Peter would be
touched by this proof of the Master's love for him
after all that he had said and done to dishonor Jesus.
"But go, tell his disciples and Peter," in particular,
not because of Peter's primacy and superior dignity,
but because of the Master's pity and love as shown
already by the look of considerate compassion (Luke
22:61). This personal proof of Christ's interest in
him should have done something to bring him to
John's belief that Jesus was indeed risen from the
dead and to believe the story of the women about
the angels at the tomb, though he and John did not
see the angels. One may be allowed to hope that
Peter and John did not join in the scornful disbelief
of the testimony of the women shown by the other
apostles. If, as is likely, they were absent, they are
not included in Luke's statement on that subject. It
is not easy, some say impossible, to weave together
into one consistent narrative the various independent
items mentioned in the Four Gospels about the resurrection and appearances of the Lord Jesus Christ.
This very independence in details strengthens their
undoubted agreement on the great essential fact of
the actual resurrection of the body of Jesus. The
empty tomb proves that the body of Jesus was not
there when the women and Peter and John went to

the tomb. It is sheer incredulity to say that the
story of the empty tomb was invented by the apostles to strengthen belief in their story of the Risen
Christ. The evidence, if the Gospels can be credited
at all, is precisely the other way round. The two
outstanding facts are the empty tomb and the unbelief of the apostles save the Beloved Disciple who
plays no important part in the testimony. His fine
spiritual insight first convinced himself by the obvious facts, but he apparently made no effort to
rally others to this new hope, not till more convinc-
ing evidence came. Events moved rapidly on this day.
Up to this point no one has actually seen Jesus
himself risen from the grave. There was, of course,
much talk and wonder.

5. *The Appearance to Simon Peter.*—This crucial event is told by Luke (24:34) and Paul (I Cor.
15:5). Paul, indeed, mentions it first in his list of
six appearances given as proof of the fact of Christ's
resurrection from the dead. Paul does not say that
it is a complete list, but only a conclusive one to
prove the incontestable fact. The last one is to Paul
himself, and this statement in an undoubted Epistle
by Paul furnishes a splendid historical starting point
to sustain the fact of Christ's resurrection as the
corner-stone of his claims to be the Son of God.
Paul also mentions the appearance of the Risen
Jesus to James (I Cor. 15:7), the Lord's brother, a
fact not stated in the Gospels, but which explains his
being with the disciples in Acts 1:14. Paul mentions
two appearances of Jesus to the apostles (in Jeru-

salem apparently) and one to above 500 most of whom were still alive (the mountain in Galilee). He passes by five other appearances (to Mary Magdalene, to the other women, to Cleopas and his companion on the way to Emmaus, to the seven by the Sea of Galilee). Paul's list casts no discredit on the narratives in the Gospels that describe these five appearances. Some argue that, since Paul mentions the appearance to Peter first in his list, therefore it was first in point of time to the discredit of Mary Magdalene and the other women. It is argued further that, since Peter was in such a highly wrought state, he was in a fit frame for subjective visions which mystics have often experienced and that Peter actually projected his subjective vision of the Risen Christ into objective fact and told it so. Then it is seriously presented, as the result of this "historical and scientific method," that from this modicum of fact (Peter's subjective vision) all the others have developed to make more objective Peter's vision. So comes the story of the empty tomb which was not empty, the appearances to the women and the apostles and others which never occurred. So out of faith in Peter's subjective vision as objective fact Christianity came to life again and Peter indeed proved himself to be the rock that Jesus had foretold and became in fact the foundation stone in Christ's church. It is to laugh, if not to weep, to see how unbelieving criticism can swallow its own fine-spun cobwebs while denying the simple facts told us in the Gospels.

Luke (24:34) also mentions the appearance of the Lord to Peter as a crucial event, but makes it purely confirmatory of what had already taken place, not as the starting point of myths and legends. The two disciples on the way to Emmaus had walked and talked with the Risen Christ without knowing who it was while he was opening to them the Scriptures about his suffering (24:25–32) though their hearts did burn within them as he did so. In an ecstasy of faith and joy they return to Jerusalem to tell their story which confirms that of the women and the angels (24:22–24), but, before they can open their mouths, they are told by the assembled and happy believers: "The Lord is risen indeed and hath appeared unto Simon." The appearance of Jesus to Simon is the explanation of the use of the adverb "indeed" (really). So then Mary Magdalene and the other women were right at the start. They had added to their story of the empty tomb and the message of the angels. Mary Magdalene herself was the first to see the Risen Master (John 20:11–18; Mark 16:9–11. Mary Magdalene probably went first to the Beloved Disciple and told him her wonderful story: "I have seen the Lord" (John 20:18). If so, John was predisposed to believe her. But she went and told the others "as they mourned and wept" (Mark 16:10) in spite of the story of the women and the angels. "And they, when they heard that he was alive, and had been seen of her, disbelieved" (Mark 16:10 f.). Perhaps some even ridiculed or pitied Mary as having the seven demons back again.

These verses belong to the addition to Mark (16:9–20) and cannot be used as on a par with the rest of the Gospel, but it is probably a true narrative and confirms the narrative in Luke about the disbelief of the apostles (except John and Peter) concerning the testimony of the women. The other women also had met Jesus and worshipped him and received the message to meet him in Galilee (Matt. 28:9 f.). Meanwhile the Sanhedrin were busy in paying the Roman guard at the tomb of Jesus now empty to say that the disciples of Jesus stole his body while they slept (Matt. 28:11–15), an "Irish bull" indeed. But it was the appearance of Jesus to Simon Peter that threw a new light on all that the women had said. Mary Magdalene and the other women had actually seen Jesus risen from the grave. So had Peter. Now, forsooth, the men finally admit that the women were right at first, as they usually are. It is a glorious time of joy. The two from Emmaus add their witness to that of Peter, Mary Magdalene and the other women. It is a matter of curiosity to note that Peter seems not to have preserved in any form this interview with the Risen Christ. Perhaps little was said or could be said with profit before the searching of heart by the Sea of Galilee (John 21). But Mark does not even mention this appearance to Peter. In the nature of the case Peter could not in his preaching say much about his first personal experiences with the Risen Lord in view of his own base denials. Evidently Peter was present at this gathering and had told the brotherhood the glorious fact of his

seeing Christ. Plummer thinks it happened after the
two had started back to Emmaus and so they did
not hear of it till their return. Ragg marvels that
the Gospels do not record an appearance of Jesus to
his mother. It is by no means certain that Jesus did
appear alone to his mother in spite of church tradition and ecclesiastical art. The shock would be great
to her, perhaps too great alone. We see her gathered with the 120 disciples in Acts 1:14 full of
unspeakable joy and glory. She had probably seen
Jesus ascend in the clouds (Acts 1:8–12). But it
is clear that Peter was the first of the apostles to
see the Risen Lord. The apostle "most in need of
comfort was the first to receive it" (Lange).

It was already evening (John 20:19) when the
two from Emmaus (Luke 24:29) arrived with their
glad tidings. It was while they were rehearsing to
the group of happy disciples (men and women) their
experiences on the road with Jesus that "he himself
stood in the midst of them, and saith unto them,
Peace be unto you" (Luke 24:36). Peter was still
present, of course, all in fact but Thomas (John
20:24). The narrative in the addition to Mark's
Gospel (16:14) has the eleven reclining at meat. At
any rate "they were terrified and affrighted, and
supposed that they beheld a spirit" (Luke 24:37).
One may wonder a bit at Peter's previous confidence to the disciples. But psychology is a curious
thing. The apostles had taken Jesus to be a ghost
when they saw him walking on the water toward
them (Matt. 14:26) as they do now. This is pre-

cisely what some modern scholars hold, the vision of the living Christ (his spirit), but without his body. But this is exactly what Jesus chided them for believing and proceeded to show the prints of the nails in his hands and his feet (Luke 24:40; John 20:20). "While they still disbelieved for joy and wondered" (Luke 24:41), he took a piece of broiled fish and ate it. Many ancient manuscripts add "and a honeycomb." Then the disciples were glad (John 20:20). They tried to convince Thomas who was absent and made an abject failure of it. Thomas was still where they had been before Peter saw the Lord and before they had all seen him. Slowly Peter is learning again the power of Christ. He is now accepted in the fellowship of the disciples in spite of his denials of Jesus. The special message and the special appearance have shown Christ's confidence in him. Peter will be with the group of disciples the next Sunday evening when even Thomas is convinced by seeing for himself the Risen Christ (John 20:26–29). If Thomas was slow in believing in the Risen Lord, he believed whole-heartedly and hailed Jesus as "My Lord and My God." This testimony Peter heard and seems to refer to Christ's rebuke of Thomas in I Peter 1:8 "whom not seeing ye love."

6. *Peter Back at His Fishing.*—Certainly now the disciples have faith and hope. Jesus had appeared to them in Jerusalem five times on the first Sunday (to Mary Magdalene, to the other women, to Peter, to the two on the way to Emmaus, to the group of disciples) and once on the succeeding Sunday eve-

ning to all of them including Thomas. There was an appearance to James, either in Jerusalem or in Galilee. The Ascension was from Olivet, but two appearances came in Galilee. One was to be on a mountain in Galilee by prearranged appointment. That time has not yet come. Meanwhile during the forty days until the Lord's Ascension (Acts 1:3) the disciples are in Galilee. They will return to Jerusalem for the Ascension (Luke 24:44–53; Acts 1:3–12; Mark 16:19 f.). Some scholars seem troubled over some of the appearances of the Risen Christ being in Jerusalem and some in Galilee and insist on the genuineness of only one place for them, though why one fails to see. Paul does not tell where those were that he mentions and Luke mentions only those in Jerusalem, but Matthew and John have some in Jerusalem and some in Galilee. The effort to confound the incident in John 21:1–14 with that in Luke 5:1–11 has failed of success. There are a few items of similarity, but the differences are too many, as to time, place, details. The one in Luke is early in Christ's ministry, this one in John is after his resurrection. We must not think that these seven apostles have abandoned their work for the Risen Christ. Not at all. They are simply waiting for the appointment with Christ on the mountain in Galilee. Meanwhile they are beside "the beloved lake" rich with so many hallowed memories with Jesus their Master and Lord. The names of five (Peter, Thomas, Nathanael or Bartholomew, the sons of Zebedee or James and John) of the seven are given. If one may hazard a guess as to the names of the other two, one would say Andrew and Philip (Andrew as Peter's brother, Philip as the one who brought Nathanael to Jesus). This is the only time in the Fourth Gospel that the sons of Zebedee are named. Elsewhere John alludes to himself only as "the disciple whom Jesus loved." As usual, Peter takes the initiative when he feels again the call to try his luck at fishing once more, his old calling which he gave up to follow Jesus. So Peter can stand it no longer and says: "I go a fishing." The other six instantly respond: "We also come with thee." Every true fisherman understands the feeling of these old fishermen. But, alas, they had fisherman's luck as once before on this lake (Luke 5:1–11) and caught nothing. Day was breaking and a stranger stood on the bank and said: "Children, have ye aught to eat?" They had to say, "No." The stranger said: "Cast the net on the right side of the boat, and ye shall find." It was a hint from a stranger and could do no harm. They could not possibly have worse luck than they had already had. So they risked one more throw of the net with the result that they could not draw in the net for the multitude of fishes in it. It is John whose quick insight recognizes that only Jesus could repeat a miracle like that of long ago (Luke 5:1–11). So John exclaims: "It is the Lord." The hint was all that Peter needed. He quickly slipped on his outer garment and leaped into the shallow sea (they were near the land). Peter helped John and the others to draw the net ashore, full of a hundred and fifty-three large fish (evidently counted). There was already a fire on shore which Jesus had made. He had also bread and now soon they had broiled fish fresh out of the water. Is there anything to eat that is daintier in the early morning? The Master invited them all to this novel and delightful breakfast. The seven all know who it is who is the host on this occasion. They do not have to wait for the mountain engagement though that will come in due time (Matt. 28:16–20; I Cor. 15:6; Mark 16:15–18). This is the third time that Jesus has appeared to groups of his disciples, John explains (21:14).

7. *The Probing of Peter's Heart and His Restoration.*—It is a bit curious that in the Synoptic Gospels the denials of Jesus by Peter are given in full, but only in John do we have the story of his forgiveness and rehabilitation to apostolic fellowship (Bernard). It is even suggested that Chapter 21 is added as a postcript after the Fourth Gospel was finished (John 20:30 f.) in order to make plain that Peter was now in a stable position and also to correct the erroneous view that Jesus had promised that John should live till the second coming of Christ. If this beautiful chapter is an afterthought, it can be said for it that it is written in the same style and tone as the previous chapters and forms a fitting climax to the greatest of all books. The first and second generations of disciples would be glad to know precisely how Peter was treated by Jesus and how Peter himself behaved towards the Master so that full fellowship was restored. John was present

and it is eminently proper that he should tell the facts, for he alone knew them when he writes at the close of the first century. But the first thing of importance is the probing of Peter's heart by Jesus himself who is the searcher of hearts like the Father. Jesus is here piercing to the joints and marrow of Peter's inner life to see and remove the pus of sin, doubt, pride, boasting, cowardice, whatever may be lurking there unseen even by Peter. The very hour was propitious for such spiritual surgery. "Therefore he lets Peter settle down, he lets him breakfast, and then takes him at the coolest hour of the day" (Dods). All of a sudden Jesus turns to Peter and says: "Simon, son of John, lovest thou me more than these?" The question revived a flood of memories of times when the apostles disputed which of them was greatest, of Peter's sure claims about himself, in particular of his boast of loyalty even to prison and to death, though all men should forsake him. It is idle and puerile to take "than these" to refer to the fish. The dreadful night when Jesus had warned Peter before his boasting and in which he had so shamefully denied his Lord and Master flashed back upon him. He had been trying to let this sore heal up, but now it was opened afresh and the pus revealed. What can Peter now say to his Lord, in full view of his past and in the presence of his brethren who know the story of his downfall? In Mark's (14:28) and Matthew's (26:32) report of Christ's warning to the apostles the promise to meet them in Galilee is given. That fact "gives peculiar force

to the question" (Westcott). Peter cannot evade this
direct thrust and shows no desire to do so. He re-
affirms his love, but leaves off the proud boast: "Yea,
Lord; thou knowest that I love thee." Little as it
seems so, Peter feels certain that Jesus understands
his real love for him. Jesus did not ask about his
faith, for he had prayed for Peter's faith (Luke
22:32), but his love at this present time. "It will be
noticed that the foundation of the apostolic office is
laid in love and not in belief" (Westcott), for love
includes faith and is greater (I Cor. 13:13). This
is what matters. It is interesting to note that Peter
in his reply uses *phileō* to love as a friend (*philos*)
while Jesus employed *agapaō* to love in the highest
sense. These two words are here kept distinct, though
that is by no means always true. In Aristotle, Lu-
cian, and the Septuagint both words are used
for both kinds of love. In the Fourth Gospel
Bernard shows that both verbs are used of God's
love for man (*agapaō* in 3:16, *phileō* in 16:27),
both occur of the Father's love for the Son (*agapaō*
3:35, *phileō* 5:20), both appear for Jesus' love for
men (*agapaō* 11:5, *phileō* 11:3), both are used of
the love of men for other men (*agapaō* 13:34, *phileō*
15:19), both occur for the love of men for Jesus
(*agapaō* 8:42, *phileō* 16:27). So then they are in
John's usage practically synonymous, though ety-
mologically different. *Agapaō* is "more dignified and
restrained" (Bernard), while *phileō* has a bit more
warmth and personal attachment. It seems clear that
Peter here purposely prefers the word *phileō* as ex-

pressing all that he dared to claim on this occasion. Jesus has a charge for Peter, consonant with that given when he was warned: "And do thou, when once thou hast turned again, stablish thy brethren" (Luke 22:32). So he says now: "Feed my lambs." The verb is used for feeding swine (Matt. 8:30) in the Synoptic Gospels, but for feeding sheep in the Septuagint. *Arnion* (lamb) occurs elsewhere in the New Testament only in the Apocalypse for the Lamb of God (twenty-nine times). Peter is here treated, not as a rock or as a fisherman, but as a shepherd by the Great Shepherd of the sheep (Heb. 13:20), a title that Jesus loved to apply to himself (John 10:11) and that Peter will apply to Jesus as "the Shepherd and Bishop of your souls" (I Peter 2:25) and as "the Chief Shepherd" (I Peter 5:4). Peter will remember this charge and will urge ministers to be models for the flock (I Peter 5:3).

But Jesus has not finished with Peter. A second time he questions him without the comparison but with the same verb *agapaō:* "Simon, son of John, lovest thou me?" Peter's reply is identical with his first one, word for word. "He still shrinks from taking to himself the loftier word" (Westcott). Jesus accepts this reassurance of his love and reinforces the shepherd charge with a new turn: "Tend my sheep." The true shepherd does more than just feed the sheep, as Jesus shows in John 10:1-18. Peter employs this verb in his charge to the elders (I Peter 5:2): "Shepherd the flock of God among you," probably with conscious recollection of the Master's use

self. After the keen and searching examination through which he had just gone at the hands of Jesus with the promise of a martyr's death before him, one might suppose that Peter would be near a nervous collapse with little life left in him. But the lively rebound of his nature asserts itself when he turned round and saw John the Beloved Disciple following (the very word used by Jesus to Peter) them. Peter's quick mind at once wanted to know the fate of John. He had just heard his own from Jesus. "Lord, and what shall this man do?" Literally, "Lord, but this one, what?" Latham (in *The Risen Master*, p. 265) calls this "a peculiar kind of curiosity, which we find in people of very active minds." But after all, it was very natural, when we consider the intimacy between Peter and John. But Jesus rebuked Peter rather sharply. "Peter, in seeking even to know the future of another disciple, was stepping beyond his province" (Dods). "If I will that he tarry till I come, what is that to thee?" It is a condition of the third class with possibility of being determined, but Jesus did not say, as John proceeds to show, that he was to live on till the Master came again. "While I am coming" the idiom means (indicative, not subjunctive). That saying went abroad, but it was not what Jesus said or meant. The Beloved Disciple lingered on till near the close of the first century and took pains to correct this erroneous view before he died. He and the others hoped for the coming of Jesus at any time, but no one set a time for that glorious and blessed event. Jesus had one word for Peter. He repeats his previous command before Peter made this superfluous and somewhat impetuous inquiry about John: "Do thou me keep on following" with the emphasis on "thou" side by side with "me." "Your business is to follow me, not to intermeddle with others" (Dods). "These intricate matters will become hopelessly entangled in your hands. Let God unwind them in his own time, and he will keep them clear" (W. M. Taylor). With these words the story of Simon Peter in the Four Gospels closes save that we know that he was with the disciples (more than 500) on the mountain in Galilee when Jesus gave them what we call the Great Commission to capture the world for Christ (Matt. 28:16–20; I Cor. 15:6; Mark 16:15–18). He was also back in Jerusalem with the other apostles and disciples when Jesus took them out on Olivet, "opened their minds" (Luke 24:45), gave them the promise from the Father (the Holy Spirit) for they were still looking for a political kingdom (Acts 1:6), and ascended on high as they worshipped him. They returned to Jerusalem with great joy (Luke 24:44–53; Acts 1:1–12).

CHAPTER XI

THE DYNAMO IN ACTION
(Acts 1 and 2)

1. *The Promise of Power.*—The resurrection of Jesus had revived faith and hope in the disciples. It was a slow process with some of them, first the women, then the apostles, finally even Thomas, then a group of 500 on the mountain in Galilee though even then "some doubted" (Matt. 28:17). There was no stampede to believe in the fact of the Risen Christ, least of all a conspiracy to create belief in such a tremendous fact. The darkness and gloom of the death of Jesus had obliterated all recollection of his promise to rise again, till he was actually seen by one after another. On the mountain in Galilee the Risen Christ had charged the disciples (over 500) to go forth and take the world for him. It was a majestic moment, for Jesus, though risen from the dead, seemed to have little that men called power. He had no government, no army, no money, no prestige in the world, little organization (only a small band of apostles with an unknown number of disciples), and these disciples not men and women of culture and of the schools, but standing outside of the ecclesiastical machinery, followers of one who had been condemned as a criminal (rebel against Rome) at the demand of the Sanhedrin, and members of a despised race with little chance to carry on propaganda

among the Gentiles for the spread of the kingdom of God. It is true that Jesus, before he ascended to the Father, gave the disciples a promise of power from on high by the coming of the Holy Spirit which he termed "the promise of the Father" (Luke 24:48 f.). The Holy Spirit would "endue" them (like putting on a new suit of clothes) with power that they did not have both for knowledge and for service. Jesus had promised in the talk in the Upper Room and on the way to Gethsemane (John 14–16) to send another Paraclete or Comforter (the Holy Spirit) who would refresh their memory concerning his teachings and lead them into the understanding of the meaning of the words of Jesus. They clearly needed this new teacher who would take of the things of Christ and make them theirs. Even as Jesus was about to ascend on high from Olivet, the apostles in fear and apprehension of losing their places in the kingdom said: "Lord, dost thou at this time restore the kingdom to Israel?" (Acts 1:6), the political kingdom that they were still expecting and that they did not know how to carry on with the king gone and with the offices still unassigned to the various aspirants among the apostles. Suppose in point of fact, that the disciples (apostles and all the 500) had undertaken to carry out the Magna Charta of missions (Matt. 28:18–20), what sort of a propaganda would they have begun? Clearly one for a world empire, a mixture of the political and the spiritual such as was set up in Rome in later centuries, such as Satan had offered to Jesus on the mount of temptation. Peter still had his share of this misapprehension of the kind of kingdom that Jesus was establishing on earth in the hearts of men. Progress in spiritual knowledge is gradual even when we have a clear revelation of truth. The new truth has to be accepted and to be assimilated. Jesus had told the apostles that he could not tell them all that they needed (John 16:12 f.). They had received more than they could bear already.

2. *Waiting for the Promise.*—Jesus definitely commanded them to "wait for the promise of the Father" (Acts 1:4), little as they understood what that promise involved or meant. They had received this "promise of the Father" from Jesus. There was nothing to do but to wait for the coming of the Holy Spirit in power which was to be "not many days hence" (Acts 1:5). Jesus had come to earth from the Father, he had lived his life as the Incarnate Son of God and the Son of man, he had taught men the truth about the reign (kingdom) of God in the hearts of men here and now, he had given his life on the Cross as a ransom for many (Mark 10:45) in accordance with the Father's redemptive plan of love (John 3:16), he had risen from the dead on the third day as he had predicted in proof of his claim to be the Messiah and Saviour from sin, he had appeared to many of the disciples during the forty days before he ascended on high to return to the Father, he had left them the promise of his continual presence all the days through the Holy Spirit who was to carry on his work, and he had promised

to return in person in due time to consummate the redemptive work. This promise two angels confirmed as the disciples gazed after the Ascended Lord (Acts 1:11). Meanwhile the disciples were to wait for the dispensation of the Holy Spirit, the new era in the revival of Christianity soon to begin. The story of the waiting is briefly told in Acts 1. The disciples were to be "witnesses" (Acts 1:8), but they must understand the message before they began to deliver it. So the dazed and yet jubilant disciples returned from Olivet with worshipful hearts to the upper room in Jerusalem, evidently a well-known room in some private home, possibly Mary's, the mother of John Mark (Acts 12:12), and probably also the same as that in which Jesus appeared on the two Sunday evenings (John 20:19, 26), if not also the one where the last passover meal was celebrated (Luke 22:11 f.). This "upper room" was not necessarily the roof as in Acts 10:9. The Jews often set apart an upper room or the loft for retirement and prayer (Knowling). If this same large upper room is meant, it already was hallowed by blessed memories of Jesus. There were about a hundred and twenty (Acts 1:15) so that it was a room of considerable size, though certainly not a room in the temple. The names of the eleven apostles are given with Peter first as always and with the significant addition of "the women and Mary, the Mother of Jesus, and his brethren." The names of the brothers (half-brothers strictly) of Jesus are not given here, though they occur in Mark 6:3 (James, Joses, Judas, Simon).

These brothers had once (John 7:5) been sceptical towards the claims of Jesus, but they are now here as followers of the Risen Lord, due to the appearance of Jesus to James (I Cor. 15:7). And were the sisters of Jesus (Mark 6:3) here also with the other women? That would mean that all the family of Jesus are now his "brothers" and "sisters" in the full spiritual sense (Mark 3:34 f.). But to no one did this gathering in the upper room mean so much as to Mary the Mother of Jesus. She had stood by the Cross with a broken heart and now with joy unspeakable and full of glory she can await the fulfilment of the wondrous Son's promise of power from on high. Now she knows that the angel Gabriel and the shepherds were right and even Simeon for the sword no longer pierces her heart. This last appearance of the Mother of Jesus in the New Testament leaves her in the company of the choice spirits who understand and appreciate her nobility and her courageous faith. We are told very little about the manner of the waiting in the upper room save that they all "with one accord continued steadfastly in prayer." The record does not say whether it was audible or silent prayer, perhaps some of both, or whether each individual remained in the upper room night and day for the ten days of waiting. There was probably coming and going, though a solid body was on hand all the time. There is no manifestation of impatience, though there were no premonitions or preparatory indications of the nearness of the realization of the promise. But all signs of jealousy and rivalry are gone, hushed by the solemn events through which they had passed. No chiding of Simon Peter for his denials was indulged in, for each felt his own unworthiness of their common and glorified Lord. They had all received the great command to go into all the world and no one felt equal to the task. Their present duty was prayer and patience.

3. *A Proposal from Peter.*—At some point during the days of waiting Peter rises up in the gathering and makes his first talk since the Master had left them, possibly the first talk of any during those days of waiting. Peter makes a number of speeches in the early chapters of Acts. It is common to say that Luke composed these addresses as Herodotus and Thucydides, Sallust, and Livy did. That literary device was common enough with ancient writers, but there is a curious appropriateness in these speeches by Peter, Stephen, James and Paul to the special occasion and the case of Peter, James, and Paul. We have their epistles (save Stephen) with which the speeches may be compared. There is a striking similarity in minute points of language between the speeches and the epistles as has often been pointed out. Furneaux argues that Luke at any rate condensed the speeches as he did those of James and he wonders how he obtained data for some of them when he was obviously not present, as when Peter spoke on this occasion. Peter may have spoken in Aramaic or in Greek. John Mark was probably present, but had hardly begun to take notes of Peter's speeches thus early. Verses 18 and 20 seem to be a

parenthesis of Luke (about Judas' death) in the midst of Peter's talk, and it is so printed by Westcott and Hort and in the Revised Version. Peter does not allude to his own downfall (an inconceivable omission according to Furneaux), but he makes two main points (two necessities, vss. 16, 21 f.). He first shows how "it was needful" for Judas to fulfil the scripture (Psalms 41:9) in betraying Jesus, but he does not mean to absolve him from responsibility for his treachery for he went to his own place (vs. 25). Then Peter urges the present necessity in verses 21 and 22 of choosing a man to take the place of Judas among the Twelve, a man who had followed Jesus from the baptism of John till the Ascension to the Father. It is claimed by some that Peter makes this suggestion on his own impulsive initiative, for the Holy Spirit had not yet been bestowed. But the appeal was made to God to decide by lot between the two names proposed (Joseph Barsabas Justus and Matthias). The choice of Matthias was accepted, though he is not mentioned by name again in the Acts, but that is true of all the Twelve except Peter and John. No argument can be made for technical apostolic succession from the choice of Matthias, for after the first century there would be none who could fulfil the condition laid down here of continual personal fellowship with Jesus and a personal witness to his resurrection. But it is interesting to see that Peter's restless energy has returned, and that he is accepted by the disciples in good standing and his proposal carries, although made by one who was once in disgrace who now dares to interpret the fate of Judas Iscariot.

4. *The Sudden and Stupendous Happenings.*— Luke is looking back upon the great event with the eyes of the historian who is trying to see it all from the standpoint of the participants who were anxiously waiting for the promise of the Father. We ourselves have recently passed the nineteen hundredth anniversary of this great day. The disciples did not know that the fulfilment would come on the day of Pentecost (fiftieth day from the recent passover feast day when Jesus was crucified on Calvary). He ascended to heaven forty days after his crucifixion so that they had been waiting ten days when "the day of Pentecost was now come" (Acts 2:1). Probably some of the number had hopes that this feast day, completing the period of harvest, would be the day of their hopes. Luke describes the day as going on. The Jewish day began at sunset and lasted till sunset. So we place it early in the morning before the third hour, Jewish time, that is before nine A.M. (Acts 2:15). Rackham thinks that the disciples went to the temple early that morning and then returned to the place of prayer. Pentecost was more widely attended by Jews of the dispersion than the Passover because sea travel was safer by that time. At any rate the whole 120 disciples were together in the same place (the upper room) when three strange phenomena suddenly manifested themselves (the sound as of a mighty wind, tongues as of fire distributed upon each of the 120, speaking with other tongues

than those known by each one). Whether these phenomena appeared in quick succession or practically at the same time is not made clear and is not very material. The sound some would today call a sudden squall of wind, but that explanation helps not at all if one is trying to get rid of the supernatural element on this occasion. The tongues as if of fire were not cloven, but distributed either simultaneously or running from one to another. No natural electrical display was ever like this. The tongues symbolized speech which was at once present. Then it is expressly stated that "the Spirit gave them utterance" (kept on giving them power to speak). It was eager, impassioned utterance which the speaker did not understand (foreign, different tongues) but which others did who knew the particular language spoken. It was not jargon or mere ecstatic rhapsody with no intelligent meaning. This gift of tongues is repeated in Cæsarea with Peter (Acts 10:45 "on the Gentiles also") and interpreted by Peter as like the outpouring in Jerusalem (Acts 11:15 "as also upon us in the beginning") and in Ephesus with Paul (Acts 19:6). Furneaux admits all this, but insists that Paul's language in I Corinthians 14 "is wholly inconsistent with the idea that the gift lay in the power to speak foreign languages." But that position misses the real point of difference between Corinth and Jerusalem. In Jerusalem Luke expressly explains that there were at this Pentecost Jews from every nation under heaven (Acts 2:5), some of whom could understand any language spoken in the Roman

Empire and even beyond (Parthians, Medes, Edomites). The speakers were mainly Jewish Christians from Galilee who understood and spoke only Aramaic and the Greek *Koiné*. These simple men and women spoke different tongues understood by one or another in the great crowds attracted by the noise made as the disciples were now in the open street. In Corinth interpreters were needed because at an ordinary meeting of the church no such variety existed. By chance a foreigner might be present. If not, one speaking in a tongue would sound like a barbarian to others unless the Holy Spirit inspired one to interpret the tongue. This is the crux of the difference and shows plainly the merit of Paul's contention that the gift of tongues caused wonder, as at Pentecost, but not edification unless understood. The gift was inferior to prophecy and was not meant as a means of spreading the gospel. The use of Greek almost everywhere made that unnecessary anyhow. The gift was temporary and belonged to the opening phase of the dispensation of the Holy Spirit. There is no justification whatever in the modern imitations of this supernatural demonstration of the Holy Spirit's power at the beginning such as one sees in Irvingites, the "Holy-Rollers," etc. One must sharply distinguish between the gift of the Holy Spirit and these initial supernatural phenomena (the wind, the tongues of fire, speaking with tongues). The baptism of the Holy Spirit has two meanings. One is the beginning of the new era when the Paraclete takes up the work of Christ and carries it on. We are now in that era. In this sense the baptism of the Holy Spirit cannot be repeated. But there is another sense of the phrase which is individual. No single individual Christian is endued with this power from on high who does not submit himself to the will of God and who does not place himself at the service of the Holy Spirit by full surrender to him. It is just here that most Christians fail. They are saved by grace but are useless as witnesses for Christ because they do not continue in vital contact with God in Christ through the Holy Spirit. Christ is the dynamo (the power house) for the Christian and that fact explains Paul's strong language in Philippians 4:13: "I have strength for all things in the one who keeps on pouring power into me." Now Peter was in this group of 120 disciples who felt the inrush of this fresh "power" of the Holy Spirit as Jesus had promised (Luke 24:49; Acts 1:8). What "tongue" Peter spoke in as they were giving utterance to their new joy we do not know and apparently he did not know himself.

5. *Peter's Interpretation of the Phenomena.*—The crowds were amazed ("stood out of themselves") and perplexed (entirely at a loss), not knowing what to think. Some took it seriously: "What meaneth this?" Others flippantly scoffed: "They are filled with new wine." Here was a call for defense and explanation, the whole group of apostles arose as Peter stepped forward with the first message in the new dispensation of the Holy Spirit. He lifted up his voice to quiet the confusion of voices (even of unkind voices

on whom Paul urged silence in I Cor. 14:28), and "spoke forth." Every speaker should speak so as to be heard if possible, but deaf, or partly deaf, people should not make unreasonable demands of the preacher. Now at last Peter's opportunity for leadership had come. He had shown great agility in speaking up for and to Jesus in the olden days before his downfall. He has been restored to fellowship and he, along with the others, has been clothed with power from on high and is eager to be "a witness" for Christ to remove misapprehension by rightly interpreting these events in relation to the life and mission of Jesus Christ. Now Simon is the Rock (*Petros*) as Jesus had predicted. Now he is the Fisher of men (catching men alive). Now he can feed and shepherd Christ's flock as Jesus had charged him to do. Now, since he has turned and is filled with the Holy Spirit, he can strengthen his brethren. From every point of view it is fitting that Peter should be the spokesman on this great occasion. He rises to it with sublime mastery, possible only to one led by the Spirit of God, in one of the great sermons of all time. Peter first appeals for attention (2:14): "Give your ears to my words." He then flatly denies that these people are drunk (2:15); if for no other reason, it is too soon in the day (nine A.M.).

Peter proceeds first to explain the phenomena that have caused the disturbance (2:16–21). "This is that," he says. This phenomenon is the event foretold by Joel (2:28–32) long ago. This quotation is full of imagery picturing the pouring out of God's

Spirit upon all flesh, upon their sons and daughters, upon all men, even upon slaves, with wonders
and signs, blood and fire and vapor of smoke. Some
of these images cannot be taken literally, like the
sun turned into darkness and the moon into blood,
apocalyptic language for spiritual events. There is
a wholesome lesson for us all here in Peter's interpretation of these symbolic portents in terms of the
spiritual events on the great day of Pentecost.

Then Peter proceeds to interpret to the crowd of
listeners the meaning of the life of Jesus because of
whom these things have come to pass (2:22–36).
This is the first interpretation of Christ since the
Holy Spirit came. Gone now from Peter are the stupidity, the timidity, the selfish personal ambition for
political preferment. He boldly asserts that God has
set the seal of his approval on Jesus by his mighty
works and wonders and signs. He claims that he
and all the 120 disciples are witnesses (2:32) of the
Risen Christ, whom "ye by the hands of lawless men
did crucify and slay" (2:23), but "whom God raised
up" (2:24, 32). The Exalted Jesus at the right hand
of God, having given the promise of the Holy Spirit,
has poured out this which ye see and hear (2:33).
Jesus is in charge of the new kingdom of grace. The
Holy Spirit is here as the Interpreter of Christ.

The conclusion drives the wedge in: "God hath
made him both Lord and Christ, this Jesus whom ye
crucified" (2:36). No doubt Luke has given only a
condensed account of this discourse. This is the man
who once tried to hide himself from the Sanhedrin

by the fire and who in terror denied his Lord. Now he boldly defies both Jews and Sanhedrin. What has happened to Peter is typical of the new era that has come to these men and women who are to take the world for Christ. It is not certain whether Peter spoke in Aramaic or Greek *Koiné*. He knew the Aramaic best, but the presence of such a mixed multitude from all over the world argues for the *Koiné* as the language in which he spoke on this occasion.

6. *The Immediate Effect of the Sermon.*—The eager listeners "were pricked in their heart," just as if a sharp knife had stuck into their hearts as Peter relentlessly and mercilessly drove home on them the responsibility for the death of the Son of God. Peter aimed at conviction of their sin. He preached his sermon for a verdict from the jury (the audience right before him). He won his verdict. Smitten by his words under the power of the Holy Spirit those Jews, convicted of their share of guilt in the death of Jesus which they had so lightly called down on their heads and the heads of their children, cried out to Peter and to the rest of the apostles: "Brethren, what shall we do?" "They felt the sting of his words" (Page), and wanted the pain removed. By "brethren" the people meant "Jews," not "Christians," not yet. Peter had not spoken in vain. God's word, rightly spoken, is sharper than any two-edged sword (Heb. 4:12). It had cut into the very joints and marrow of the minds and hearts of these people. They were convicted of sin by the Holy Spirit. There is no conversion without it.

7. Peter's Message for Inquirers.—Peter was ready for the application of his sermon to these broken-hearted inquirers. At once he took up the word of John the Baptist and of Jesus and said: "Turn ye, and let each one of you be baptized in the name of Jesus Christ on the basis of forgiveness of your sins, and ye shall receive the gift of the Holy Spirit; for to you is the promise and to your children and to all those who are afar off whomsoever the Lord our God calls" (Acts 2:38 f.). Nearly every word in this practical turn to this address has been in dispute. The first word is for "repent" and it means to change one's mind and life. Unfortunately this great word used by the Baptist and by Jesus has been rendered by a Latin word *repoenitet* which means to be sorry again, an idea not in the Greek word at all. Paul draws a sharp distinction between the words to change and to be sorry (used of Judas in Matt. 27:3) in II Corinthians 7:8–10. This stupendous blunder in translation is now ingrained in our language and theology. But this "change" comes first. Peter then uses the third person singular (not plural) imperative of *baptizō*, making it a separate act following the turning (repenting). The act is in the name of (on the authority of) Jesus Christ. The name of Jesus Christ stands for the Trinity (Matt. 28:19 where the full formula is given) and is sufficient and alone occurs in the Acts about baptism. Peter is not here giving a formula, but the authority for the act. The use of *eis* with "the remission of your sins" can be understood in either of two ways. One way is to take it to mean purpose or design. That is an undoubted usage of *eis* as in Matthew 26:28 "My blood of the covenant which is shed for (*eis*) the forgiveness of sins" where undoubtedly *eis* conveys the idea of purpose. But in Matthew 10:41 "in the name of a prophet" *eis* cannot mean purpose, but only basis or ground. So in Matthew 12:41: "They repented at (*eis*) the preaching of Jonah." There it is impossible to take *eis* as other than the basis or the occasion of the repenting. Mere grammar cannot settle this dispute of the centuries between the sacramentalists and the evangelicals. The tone of the New Testament is salvation by grace, not by rite or ceremony whether circumcision or baptism. The promise is to the Jews who do thus turn and to their children who do so and to Gentiles (those afar off) who do so, to all whomsoever God calls. Peter's horizon is expanding surely from the merely political kingdom of the Pharisees. But it will take the vision on the housetop in Joppa and the experience with Cornelius in Cæsarea before Peter will clearly understand that the Gentiles are not also to become Jews as well as Christians. But he has made a pungent application of his great message. Peter kept on exhorting the seekers: "Be ye saved from this crooked generation" (Acts 2:40). That is always the personal problem, to be saved in time.

8. *A Picture of Happy Church Life.*—Some did accept Peter's word, turned, and were baptized. On that one day (2:41) there were added together about

3000 souls, surely a marvellous revival, wonderful
results from one sermon plus the power of the Holy
Spirit. Small objections have been made to Luke's
report here that so many people could not be baptized in one day. Doctor J. E. Clough himself baptized 2222 Telugus in one day at the Baptist mission. There were plenty to lend a hand on this occasion and Jerusalem always had plenty of pools with
abundance of water. Probably Peter superintended
the task. The word *ekklēsia* (church) is not genuine
in verse 41, but the thing is here in reality, though
no pastors or elders (Acts 11:30) or deacons (6:
1-6) are mentioned as yet. But the work of grace
went on daily (vs. 47) as new conversions continued
to be added by the Lord. Fear continued on all as
miracles multiplied. The visitors from afar remained
and their wants were supplied from a common fund
as one after another held his property at the service
of actual need (2:44-46). This was not modern com-
munism but a way to meet the special emergency in
Jerusalem, one that was not called for elsewhere so
far as known. Apparently the Lord's Supper was
periodically observed also. They prayed, preached,
and praised with gladness and singleness of heart.
No wonder that they had favor with the people.
What a picture of ideal church life do we have here
when evangelism is normal and continual for they
were all full of power from on high! The promise of
the Father had become their power in daily life. The
gospel stream was running at full tide. Will it keep
on?

CHAPTER XII

THE PRISONER FOR CHRIST
(Acts 3 to 5, 12)

1. *Worshipping in the Temple.*—The picture of Peter and John going up into the temple to pray at the ninth hour (3 P.M. Jewish time) is vivid. Doctor W. M. Taylor likens the relation of Judaism to expanding Christianity to that between the bud and the flower. At this stage probably Peter and John (together again in their work and worship) had no idea of a formal breach with Judaism, though Peter in his Pentecostal sermon had charged the Sanhedrin and the Jewish people with the death of Jesus. The Master had preached in the Jewish synagogues and in the temple courts. "They differed from other Jews in the fact that they believed in the Messiahship of Jesus of Nazareth, and were knit to each other in the bonds of a brotherhood which had its origin in a common experience of the great salvation; but they kept up also a strict observance of the Mosaic law" (Taylor).

2. *Healing the Lame Man.*—This (Acts 3:2–10) is the first of many miracles recorded in the Acts by Luke, the great physician and historian. Men differ today in their opinion of Luke's qualities both as physician and historian. It is often forgotten that the ancient Greeks developed genuinely scientific

medicine that really surpassed the medical art in the middle ages. Men like Dioscorides, Galen, and Hippocrates were not charlatans and Aristotle is the father of modern biological science. Sir William Osler spoke of "the glories of Greek science" and contended that "Hippocrates is a living force to-day." Harnack has argued ably and successfully to prove that Luke is the author of both Gospel and Acts, yet he is willing to admit the use of legends by him in the early chapters of Acts. Furneaux wonders whether in the earlier chapters of Acts "the miraculous element may not have received a degree of legendary embellishment." Per contra, Sir W. M. Ramsay dares to place Luke on a par with, if not superior to, Thucydides as a historian. In simple truth, it is mere prejudice to refuse to believe in the possibility of miracles in the New Testament because we do not see them happen now. They may happen now more often than we know, for all real healing is done by nature, as every scientific physician knows, which is only another way of saying that God does the healing after all. Paul wrought miracles and had Luke as his beloved physician. Doctors and medicine are merely agents for God's works. It is a vivid story that Luke here records, how the lame beggar had his stand at the door of the temple called Beautiful. On the top of the "Mountain of the House" (Kidron on the east, Ophel on the south, the Tyropœon on the west) stood the temple area as built by Herod the Great. There was first a vast court of nearly 1000 feet square, the court of the

Gentiles. The tower of Antonia stood on an eminence to the north of the temple and here in this castle the Roman garrison resided, overlooking the temple courts. There were cloisters or pillars surrounding the open court of the Gentiles and here Jesus preached to the crowds and the Greeks heard him. The cloisters on the east rested on the foundations of Solomon's temple and were called Solomon's Porch (Acts 3:11). The tables for the money-changers were in the court of the Gentiles. The sacred inclosure or the court of Israel was to the north by a flight of fourteen steps upward. A barrier was erected here to keep Gentiles out and at intervals appeared marble tablets which forbade Gentiles to go farther on pain of death. One of these tablets was discovered in 1871 by M. Clermont Ganneau and is now in Constantinople. Around the top of the steps to the court of Israel ran another wall with nine gates or doors (four on the south, four on the north). The ninth was in the eastern wall and was of bronze and was the Beautiful Gate of Acts 3:2, 10 (Rackham). At this door or gate the lame beggar had his seat. As was his habit, he asked alms of Peter and John. Peter fastened his eyes on the man and asked him to look on him and John. That look raised great expectations of money, not of healing, "expecting to receive something from them." Peter spoke again, and dashed to the ground the poor man's hopes by saying: "Silver and gold have I none." He did offer healing to him "in the name of Jesus Christ of Nazareth." We do not know what the lame man knew about Jesus. Clearly Peter was unknown to him. Apparently the man did not walk, for that he could not do. So Peter seized him by the right hand and raised him up and at once the man felt strength in his unused ankle bones and feet. He leaped, he stood, he began to walk. The unexpected had happened. He got no money, but he no longer had to sit as a beggar. Peter and John passed on into the court of Israel to worship. The joyful healed man went on with them "walking and leaping and praising God." He was trying out his legs and feet. He had been a well-known beggar and the people wondered as they began to recognize that he was no longer lame, if forsooth he ever had been! They were filled with astonishment and amazement while the man in apparent terror of the crowd held on to Peter and John as the men responsible for his new condition. We see Peter here in a new rôle. No doubt, when the Twelve were sent out by Jesus, Peter cast out demons like the rest, but here he appears in an unexpected situation. He called on Jesus to heal this man, and the Master did it.

3. *Peter Explaining the Miracle to the Crowd.*— Peter was quick to see the situation and apparently some were asking Peter about it for he "answered unto the people" (3:12–26) in an address (his third in Acts) along the same line and on a par with the great one at Pentecost. The people had been "gazing at" (same word in 1:10 and 3:4) Peter as a wonder worker in his own power or godliness. Peter would not pose as "some great one" like Simon

Magus in Cæsarea or like the medical and religious fakirs so common then and now. The explanation is very simple. God has glorified his servant Jesus by healing this man. It is faith in the name of Jesus that has made this man strong (3:16), the very Jesus whom ye denied and in whose place ye asked for a murderer. Ye "killed the Prince of life; whom God raised from the dead; whereof we are witnesses" (3:15). We here see Peter at his best. He has the same note of courage and power so manifest at Pentecost. He uses this incident as the occasion for proclaiming Jesus as Messiah and Saviour from sin. "None can fail to see that in Chapter III the Messianic idea becomes richer and fuller. Jesus is the prophet greater than Moses: Jesus is the fulfilment of the Abrahamic covenant, through which the blessing of Abraham is to extend to all the earth (Matt. 8:11)" (Knowling). Peter drives home with tremendous power (3:17–26) the peril in which the Jewish people, those very people before him, find themselves because of the treatment of Jesus, God's Son whom they refused to accept (John 1:11). They acted in ignorance and so there is a chance for them, but they must change their mental attitude and their conduct that their sins may be blotted out (obliterated) by the blood of Jesus as he later explains (I Peter 1:18 f.), that seasons of refreshing may come from the face of the Lord. It all turns on man's attitude toward Jesus Christ. He is the prophet foretold by Moses and the one to whom all the prophets from Samuel on bore witness. They

were the sons of the covenant with Abraham who
will through Christ bless the world. The Jew is first
in privilege, but that comes to little if the Jews fail
to accept Jesus as the Messiah and do not turn
away from their sins. Here are the boldness of John
the Baptist and the skill of Paul. Jesus has come
as a blessing to them.

4. *Arrested by the Sadducees for Preaching the
Resurrection of Jesus.*—While Peter was speaking
the chief priests and other Sadducees came together
with the captain of the temple area (the second in
dignity to the high priest himself, who was in charge
of the priests and Levites and the temple police).
These came upon Peter suddenly and interrupted
Peter's address. "The Sadducees were at the helm,
and the office of the high-priest was in Sadducean
hands, and the Sadducees predominated in the high-
priestly families" (Weizsäcker). The Sadducees were
a wealthy and aristocratic oligarchy and the captain of the temple felt responsible for order in the
temple precincts. They were annoyed or vexed (the
word used of Paul about the girl who followed him
in Philippi, Acts 16:18) at the uproar and at the
"inflammatory language" (Rackham) of Peter (3:
15, 17) when he mentioned "your rulers." The Sadducees took a leading part with their opponents, the
Pharisees, in the death of Jesus. The point mentioned by Luke is their displeasure that Peter and
John "proclaimed in Jesus the resurrection from
the dead." Furneaux agrees with Spitta that Luke
gives the wrong reason here for Peter's arrest on

the ground that the Sadducees "were political ecclesiastics, not intolerant dogmatists." But that
misses the point. The Sadducees did work with the
Pharisees in the Sanhedrin, though they disagreed
on the doctrine of the resurrection. Peter had spe-
cifically stated (3:15) that God raised Jesus from
the dead, of which fact we are witnesses. Here was
a concrete case, and concerning the very one
whom the Sadducees had helped the Pharisees put to
death. They may also have been irritated over the
presumption of Peter and John daring to teach the
people in the temple precincts as if they were acknowledged rabbis. So they laid hold on them and
put them in prison as it was now towards evening,
to await trial on the morrow. The captain of the
temple probably arrested them in person. There was
ample cause for alarm at the rapid growth of Christianity in Jerusalem. Already the number of men
(as distinct from women, 4:4) was about 5000. If
the women were added, the number would be easily
doubled or trebled. Peter is surely now catching men
alive for Christ. God's word was not bound, even
if Peter and John were in prison.

5. *Before the Sanhedrin as Jesus Had Been.*—
Peter and John had been together once before in
the house of Caiaphas when Jesus was on trial (John
18:16) and when John went on into the inner room
where Jesus was while Peter stayed in the outer court
by the fire and denied his Lord. Jesus had said that
the apostles would be brought before rulers and
had promised "mouth and wisdom" to them. Here is

a regular meeting of the Sanhedrin with the various elements (Sadducees and Pharisees) and the two
high priests present. Annas had been high priest
and was the father-in-law of Caiaphas then high
priest. The Jews had never acquiesced in the removal of Annas in A.D. 14 by the Romans. The Sanhedrin no longer had the power to impose death,
but they still had a great deal of authority. They
sat in a semicircle with Peter and John in the
midst of the arc with the lame man as chief witness. No formal charge was made, but by a series of
questions the rulers sought to entrap Peter and
John into admitting that the miracle, which they
did not deny, was not wrought by God, as they
charged Jesus with doing his works by the power
of Beelzebub (Matt. 9:34. Cf. Lev. 20:27; Deut.
13:1). They ignored what Peter had said about the
death and resurrection of Jesus (their real griev-
ance). Peter, filled with the Holy Spirit, spoke in
reply, as usual, his fourth address in the Acts, and
made a skilful turn to the "examination" "concerning a good deed done to an impotent man," a phrase
that at once put the Sanhedrin in the wrong by
telling the truth. They had asked for the "power"
and the "name" and Peter gives both, the name and
the power of Jesus "whom ye crucified, whom God
raised from the dead" (4:10). He had said this to
the crowd at Pentecost (2:23 f.) and to the crowd
at Solomon's Porch the day before (3:15), but here
he boldly speaks these words to the Sanhedrin when
on trial himself and points to the healed man in

proof of his claims about Jesus. Peter then dares to repeat to a gathering of the Sanhedrin in the Gentile court of the temple the very argument and Scripture used by Jesus, that he is himself the head of the corner of God's temple, though rejected by the Jewish experts (Psalms 118:22 f.; Mark 12:10 f.; Matt. 21:42; Luke 20:17), as he will quote it again some thirty years later for the same point (I Peter 2:6–8). Then Peter said that they must be saved by the name and power of Jesus, if saved at all (4:12). Here is real courage, for Peter risked his own life in this defiance of the same men who had compassed the death of the Lord Jesus.

In truth the Sanhedrin were taken aback by the boldness of Peter and John who clearly endorsed Peter's daring words. They perceived at once that they were unlearned or unschooled (unlettered) and unprofessional or private men (not rabbis or priests). Gradually they recognized them as men that they had seen with Jesus, possibly in this very hall where they are now assembled (John inside, Peter in the outer court). But they also recognized a likeness in Peter's boldness of speech and that of Jesus who spoke as never man spake (John 7:46). "They perceived a likeness between their courage and dignity and the bearing of their Master" (Furneaux). They had once sneered at Christ as one who did not know letters (John 7:15). But their contempt for Jesus as for Peter and John had some restraint. Here was the healed man right before them. It was useless to deny a patent fact, for no one would believe the lie.

So they decided to threaten Peter and John to teach no more in the name of Jesus (4:18), saying nothing about the miracle now. They called the name of Jesus this time, though in verse 17, they sneeringly said, "in the name" as the Talmud will refer to Jesus "Peloni" (so and so). This prohibition put it squarely up to Peter and John who flatly refuse to obey such a command in heroic words worthy of martyrs in all ages who hazard their lives to be true to Christ: "We are not able not to go on speaking what we saw and heard" (4:20). The Sanhedrin renewed their threats, but did not punish Peter and John because the people glorified God for the healing of this man. It was, indeed, a notable triumph over the Sanhedrin, but the end is not yet.

6. *The Fear of the Disciples.*—Peter and John, once set free, at once "went to their own company" (the very phrase used of the people of Jesus, the Jews in John 1:11). They had a story to tell of peril that called for prayer and courage. So "with one accord," as in the days of waiting (Acts 1:14) they lifted up their voice to God. The Sanhedrin had decided against the new faith (Furneaux) and trouble was ahead. The ecclesiastical authority is here arrayed against the disciples as it was against Jesus, only here the Sadducees take the lead while the Pharisees began the attacks on the Master. This prayer Knowling terms "the earliest known Psalm of Thanksgiving in the Christian Church." God is called "Master" (*Despota*, as in Luke 2:29 by Simeon, and in II Peter 2:1 the same word is applied

to Christ). God is the maker of heaven and earth, but no "despot" in our sense of this word. Psalm 2:1 f. (ascribed to David) is quoted. The rulers, including Herod Antipas and Pontius Pilate, gathered together in this very city against Jesus "whom thou didst anoint," but they were only puppets in the hands of God. "And now, Lord, look upon their threatenings: and grant unto thy servants to speak thy word with all boldness." This is what Peter had told the Sanhedrin they would do, but he asks God to help them to be bold. Was Peter afraid of becoming afraid? At any rate they ask God for a sign of his favor: "while thou stretchest forth thy hand to heal; and that signs and wonders may be done through the name of thy holy servant Jesus" (4:30). God answered this prayer (of Peter?) for "the place was shaken wherein they were gathered together; and they were all filled with the Holy Spirit, and they spake the word of God with boldness" (4:31). They were recharged with God's power and were now ready to meet the Sanhedrin or Satan. They did not have self-confidence, but full reliance on God.

7. *Peter's Interference in the Pious Pretense of Ananias and Sapphira.*—The story moves on rapidly in the Acts with Peter constantly to the fore. The praise given by the brotherhood to Joseph, a Levite of Cyprus, and a man of property, for his generosity in selling and laying the proceeds at the feet of the apostles won for him the title of Barnabas (son of consolation) by which he is there-

after called (Acts 4:36 f.). There were others who
thus made it possible to supply the pressing needs
of the poor disciples in Jerusalem (4:32–35). But
the jealousy of Ananias and Sapphira was aroused
because no such praise came to them and yet they
did not wish to part with all their money. So Ananias
and his wife agreed together (the first "Ananias
club") to sell their property and give part as if it
were all, and yet to keep back part for themselves.
So they laid a portion at the feet of the apostles
(Acts 5:1–11), but a terrible blow befell Ananias
who came first. Peter exposed his duplicity and accused him of lying to the Holy Spirit under the influence of Satan, reminding him that he did not have
to sell his property or to give it all, only he did
have to be honest and tell the truth about it. He had
lied to God and not merely to men. On hearing this
public exposure of his hypocrisy, Ananias fell dead
at Peter's feet, whether a case of apoplexy from the
sudden shock, or a stroke of condemnation directly
from God. Clearly Peter did not kill Ananias, but
a great fear came upon all present as the younger
men bore his body outside the city walls, and buried
it. The Jews buried often on the day of death.
Ananias and Sapphira had "sought by false pre-
tenses to gain a reputation like the Pharisees for
special sanctity and charity" (Knowling). After an
interval of three hours Sapphira turned up, unaware
of her husband's death and burial. Why she had not
come with him we do not know. Furneaux finds it
inconceivable that Luke's narrative about Sapphira

should be correct, or that the body of Ananias should be hurried off to burial without notice to his family. "Such action would be, not only a violation of oriental custom, but cruel and heartless in the highest degree." But we know entirely too little about the details to pass snap judgment like that. An effort may have been made to find Sapphira. When she did appear Peter gave her an opportunity to separate herself from the lying hypocrisy of her husband. But her reply to Peter's inquiry revealed that she was as guilty as Ananias. It was easy to foresee that a like fate awaited her, and Peter predicts it and the same young men, now returned, bore her body away after she fell dead at the feet of the apostles. This was sudden and stern punishment from God upon hypocrites in the early church in Jerusalem. Does hypocrisy ever go unpunished? Sooner or later the veil is torn off and condemnation comes. The effect of this double judgment was instantaneous. It was a dangerous thing to join a group like this if a lie even to God met such a fatal reward. Miracles continued while the disciples were again with one accord in Solomon's Porch, "but of the rest no one dared to cleave to them" (5:13), remembering the fate of Ananias and Sapphira. One wonders today if there is not an element of hypocrisy and pious pretence in some of the giving in our churches. People plead undue poverty and want credit for more liberality than is due and may even pose as tithers when they are not.

8. *Under Peter's Shadow.*—The sudden exposure

and death of Ananias and Sapphira exercised a re-
straining influence upon the flippant and the insin-
cere, but it also challenged those who cared for
reality so that multitudes both of men and women
believed on the Lord and were added to the already
large church membership in Jerusalem (5:14). The
press and the excitement of the crowds remind one
of the days of Jesus in Galilee, days that Peter recalled afresh. People were bringing the sick out into
the streets and placing them upon beds and pallets
that, as Peter passed along, even his shadow might
overshadow one of them (5:15). There is an element of superstition in weak faith like this, and yet
Jesus honored the poor woman's faith who dared
only to touch the hem of his garment (Matt. 9:21;
Luke 8:44), weak faith practised by many others
(Mark 6:56). So also some later took Paul's hand-
kerchiefs to secure healing when they could not
manage otherwise (Acts 19:12). There is, of course,
no virtue or healing power in a garment of Christ
or of Paul or in the shadow of Peter or of any one.
But it is the element of faith that God honors as
he did here (Acts 5:16). There is no evidence that
Peter knew or approved the practice alluded to. It
was easy to degrade such superstitious faith into
mere magic. "Still, it was faith in the truth of a
Divine power working in their midst; and, as such,
was higher than the materialism which denies the
reality of a spiritual world intersecting the physical
world at every point" (Furneaux). Renan, for instance, denies a place in history for any narrative

with a miraculous element in it. But in all these days of power in Jerusalem Peter moves as the hero of faith.

9. *Gamaliel to the Rescue.*—The success of Peter's work in Jerusalem was too decided to go longer unchallenged. Once again the high priest and the sect of the Sadducees were filled with jealousy and laid their hands on all the apostles and placed them in public prison against the next day (5:17 f.). There was no such haste as in the case of Jesus. The jealousy here grew out of the power of the apostles with the people by their miracles and growing number of followers. Something had to be done to stop the swinging tide toward Christianity. They had tried imprisonment once before on Peter and John with poor success, but now they arrest the entire Twelve and hope for better success. But that night an angel of the Lord led the apostles out of prison and at daybreak they entered into the temple and began to teach the people (5:21). When the Sanhedrin met for the trial, the apostles could not be found in prison so that the captains of the temple and the chief priests "were much perplexed concerning them whereunto this would grow" (5:24). If they had only known how this grain of mustard seed would grow into a tree that would cover the whole earth with its leaves for the healing of the nations! Finally the apostles are found openly teaching in the temple and are brought as gently as possible before the Sanhedrin. The high priest Caiaphas sharply reminded the apostles of his command to Peter

and John (4:18) which they had disregarded: "Ye have filled Jerusalem with your teaching (a tribute to the effect of their preaching), and intend to bring this man's blood upon us" (5:28). Before Pilate they had proudly taken Christ's blood upon themselves and their children (Matt. 27:25). But now Christianity is no longer unpopular in Jerusalem. The officers of the Sanhedrin actually "feared the people, lest they should be stoned" (5:26). It is Peter who speaks for the apostles, his fifth address in Acts. Peter repeats pointedly his previous stand (4:19 f.): "We must obey God rather than man." Then he briefly repeated the charge that the Sanhedrin slew Jesus whom God exalted to be a Prince and a Saviour to give repentance and remission of sins to Israel. "And we are witnesses of these things." Peter implies that the apostles are all ready to die for the faith that is in them. The Sanhedrin (Sadducees certainly) "were cut to the heart (were being sawn in two) and were minded to slay them" (5:33). They seemed anxious to meet Peter's challenge. They did afterwards illegally stone Stephen to death (7:54–60) by mob action (lynching) and were ready to treat the apostolic group so now. But Gamaliel, a Pharisee, the first of the seven teachers to be called Rabban, teacher of Saul of Tarsus, President of the Seminary founded by Hillel (his grandfather, and afterward President of the Sanhedrin), was the leader of the Pharisees in the Sanhedrin, though Caiaphas the Sadducee presided. This illustrious man was not willing for the Sadducees to carry their hatred of

the apostles and of the doctrine of the resurrection
to such a length of madness. It is not true that
Gamaliel was half Christian, but he saw a chance to
make a plea for fairness, if not justice, and in so
doing to score heavily against the leadership of the
Sadducees who had carried on this persecution so
far. He spoke blandly and persuasively, reminding
the Sanhedrin of the fate of a rash upstart named
Theudas and of Judas the Galilean who came to
naught. Both were Messianic pretenders of whom
Josephus gives many examples, four with the name
of Simon and three with that of Judas in ten years,
among them another Theudas of a later date in the
reign of Claudius (*Ant.* xx 5:1). The advice of Gamaliel is to await results and to release these men.
If the thing is of men, it will be overthrown; but, if
it is of God, you cannot overthrow it for you will
be fighting against God. There is no question as to
the correctness of the position here taken by Gamaliel, but one must not forget that this candor is
colored by his dislike of the Sadducees and their
leadership. Gamaliel won his point, though the apostles were flogged with forty stripes save one and
released, this in addition to the futile threat which
was all the punishment that Peter and John had received before (4:21).

10. *Persecution by the State.*—Let us pass over
some years to the time when a Herod is again king
in Palestine. Herod Agrippa I is king from A.D. 42
to 44. Probably the events in Chapter 12 precede
those at the close of Chapter 11 (the visit of Bar-

nabas and Saul from Antioch). Herod Agrippa I is
in Jerusalem, possibly in A.D. 44, and gets the reaction of Sadducees and Pharisees towards Christianity. He had James, the brother of John, put to
death by the sword (12:2), the first of the Twelve to
go after Judas Iscariot, and fulfilling the baptism
of blood that James had said he was able to drink
(Mark 10:39). The deed pleased the Jews (ecclesiastical leaders) so much that Herod put Peter in
prison to be kept till after the feast of the passover
was over (12:3 f.), for he wished to observe Jewish
religious observances with due piety. He seemed a bit
uneasy about this leader of the Christians and had
him guarded by four quaternions of soldiers (sixteen
in all), one division at a time (six hours each group).
That seemed absolutely safe. Two of the soldiers
each time were chained to Peter and two kept watch
outside the cell. But God is not limited by the plans
of men. Once again an angel (5:19) appeared to
Peter, woke him up, and led him out past the guards
and through the gate which opened automatically
and noiselessly (12:10). Peter, wondering whether
he saw a vision (12:9), finally came to himself after
the angel left him (12:11) and betook himself to
the house of Mary, the mother of John Mark, clearly
a home open to him as to many other disciples who
were even then engaged in prayer for his release
from prison. The maid at the door, Rhoda (Rose),
in her joy left Peter standing outside and ran in to
tell the disciples that their prayers were answered,
for Peter was standing at the gate. It is a touch of

life when Luke adds that the disciples said: "Thou art mad," and then: "It is his angel" (12:15). The answer to their prayers had come too suddenly for their faith. Once inside Peter told his story, and bade them: "Tell these things unto James, and to the brethren" (12:17). This is James, the brother of Jesus, now one of the leaders in the Jerusalem church, and to be the leading elder when the apostles go on their preaching tours. Peter himself feels unsafe in Jerusalem "and he departed, and went to another place." Tradition mentions Antioch, where Barnabas and Saul were already at work. The truth is that we do not know. Peter will reappear in Jerusalem at the great conference on the work among the Gentiles (Acts 15 and Gal. 2). He disappears from the record as the leader in Jerusalem who has been a prisoner for Christ so often. There are other phases of Peter's activity in and around Jerusalem that must still be discussed (Acts 8 to 11), though belonging to an earlier date than the events in Acts 12.

CHAPTER XIII

EXPOSING SIMON MAGUS
(Acts 8:1–24)

1. *The Successful Mountebank of Samaria.*—The true and vivid picture drawn by Luke (Acts 8:9–11) of this first century charlatan is free from the second century legends and traditions. This fact "is evidence of the early date of the Acts" (Furneaux). The name Simon is a common one in Josephus for Messianic pretenders. The Samaritans were superstitious people and easily imposed on by such a quack. Spitta (*Apostelgeschichte*, p. 149) treats as "a perfect absurdity" the theory of Baur that the Simon Magus of the Clementine Literature is the Simon Magus of the Acts. The only two facts stated about him by Luke are that he was a magician and that he considered Philip and Peter mountebanks like himself till Peter exposed him. "In his person Christianity was for the first time confronted with superstition and religious imposture, of which the ancient world was at this period full" (Furneaux). He "used sorcery" as the word (here only in the New Testament) came to mean in the ancient Greek, though *magi* (wise men) occurs in Matthew 2:1 in a good sense. "The Magi were the priestly class under the Median and Persian Empires. The founding of their order is ascribed to Zoroaster. Their influence and learning were very great," "but, as

their scientific knowledge was most frequently used to impose on the vulgar, the word has generally a bad sense in Greek as here and 13:6 and in our 'magic' " (Page). Hence Elymas Bar-Jesus in Paphos in Cyprus (Acts 13:6, 8) and Simon here in Samaria form a lovely pair of "magi" of the typical evil kind. Jesus had preached to the Samaritans at Sychar only seven miles from the old town of Samaria which Herod the Great had rebuilt on a grand scale and named Sebaste after Augustus (*Sebastos* in Greek). Philip, the deacon of Acts 6:5 and the evangelist of 21:8, was like Stephen a preacher of great power who was undeterred by the fate of Stephen from pressing on the cause of Christ. Philip stirred great interest also by his miracles of healing (Acts 8:6–8) and it was this that attracted Simon, who had, before Philip came, "amazed the people of Samaria." This verb is repeated three times (vss. 9, 11, 13) and suggests (meaning to stand out of oneself) the wide-eyed surprise of people who almost "jump out of their skin," so to speak. There is a naïve simplicity here in accepting Simon at his face value on his own statement, "giving out that himself was some great one." P. T. Barnum once said that the American people loved to be humbugged and that he was the man to do it for them. He has plenty of imitators including men and women like Mrs. Eddy, Dowie, the House of David, etc. As Simon Magus performed his tricks, like those of modern mediums, the people lined up in near adoration: "This man is that power of God which is called

Great," a sort of emanation of God in him making him more than man, an idea that later developed into Gnosticism. Sorcery was studied and practised in Egypt and the Samaritans were open to such influences. Jerome says that the later followers of Simon Magus made him say: *Ego sum sermo Dei, ego sum speciosus, ego paraclitus, ego omnipotens, ego omnia Dei.* Simon had bewitched the Samaritans by his claims and his deeds. About A.D. 35 a false prophet announced that he would find on Mt. Gerizim the sacred vessels hidden there by Moses. Pilate sent soldiers to disperse the mob which gathered and these soldiers slew so many of them that the Samaritans complained to the Roman proconsul Vitellius with the result that Pilate was recalled to Rome for trial in A.D. 36 and was banished. Samaria was an inflammable region.

2. *Simon Thinking Philip a Greater Trickster Than Himself.*—He knew that he himself was a fraud and saw that Philip was a master while he was a tyro with all his pretensions. Simon himself "believed" probably in the reality of the deeds of Philip, though that is not certain, certainly that he wanted the "power" that Philip had, whatever it was. One may recall with profit the use of this verb in John 2:23 about the many who "believed on the name" of Jesus, but in whom Jesus "did not believe," and also in John 8:31 of Pharisees "who believed on him" apparently, but who soon took up stones to stone Jesus (John 8:59). He himself was as much "amazed" at the wonders done by Philip as the people were at

him (8:13). "He was probably half victim of self-delusion, half conscious impostor" (Furneaux). So Jesus really was the Incarnation of God, a thing that Simon claimed for himself insincerely. So he was baptized, hoping to get Peter's power by this ordinance, thinking probably that it had some magical effect. There is food for thought here for those who regard baptism as the means of securing the remission of sins. Certainly no such result followed in the case of Simon Magus. But he stuck close to Philip, hoping by close association and observation (beholding, watching) to learn the secret of Philip's power. Simon found himself completely overshadowed as a popular idol by Philip. Rackham thinks that "he himself was deeply impressed by the real spiritual power of Philip and by his signs which altogether eclipsed his own." The eclipse was undoubted, but the recognition of any spiritual power was vague and uncertain. Clearly only a superficial and outward change had taken place in Simon Magus. He was now a nominal disciple of Jesus, but as great a quack as ever.

3. *More Impressed by Peter Than by Philip.*— Philip went on his way and news reached Jerusalem that Samaria had received the word of God (Acts 8:14). The gospel was at last going outside of Jerusalem and Judea and reaching Samaria on its way to the uttermost parts of the earth (Acts 1:8), but the apostles were not taking it. It was deacon Philip as evangelist who was doing it. Philip apparently had left Jerusalem among those scattered after

Stephen's death by the persecution of Saul (8:4).
For some unknown reason the apostles were spared
in that persecution. Was it the attitude of Gamaliel
in 5:34–42? But now the church in Jerusalem sent
Peter and John to investigate what had happened
in Samaria. They had worked together before (3:1;
4:13), possibly had been sent out together by Jesus
on the tour of Galilee (Mark 6:7), when they were
forbidden to go to a city of Samaria (Matt. 10:5).
They could be trusted to deal wisely with the situation in Samaria. Peter and John at once on their
arrival approved the work of Philip and were convinced that these (not including Simon) were genuine converts. The Samaritans were technically Jews,
having been circumcised, though only half Jews in
fact. "To John it must have been a strange experience. He was sent to the very people on whom, a
few short years before, he had wished to call down
fire from heaven" (Furneaux). Peter and John prayed
that these new believers might receive the baptism
of the Holy Spirit (Acts 8:15). The reason for this
prayer is apparently the desire to be reassured that
this advance step into Samaria really did have the
approval of God. There was no doubt about the
genuineness of the baptism by Philip in the name of
Jesus, deacon though he was and not apostle. So
they laid their hands on them successively and they
received the Holy Spirit successively. In Jerusalem
at the great Pentecost as at Cæsarea (Acts 10:45
f.) the coming of the Holy Spirit and the speaking
with tongues were without laying on of hands, but

we do have this act at Ephesus by Paul (Acts 19:6), the only four instances in the Acts. Apparently the reception of this special gift of the Holy Spirit was accompanied by the speaking of tongues as at Pentecost, for Simon Magus "saw" that through the laying on of hands the gift of the Holy Spirit was bestowed and received (8:18). Many questions are raised by this Samaritan outpouring as by those in Cæsarea, Ephesus, and Corinth. There was here "the direct result of a supernatural Presence and of a special grace . . . outward visible signs of an inward spiritual grace" (Knowling). These ecstatic gifts belonged to the introduction of Christianity, but the power of the Holy Spirit abides forever. He is here with us today, if we will only let him use us for the glory of Christ.

4. *Offering Peter Money for the Power to Bestow the Holy Spirit.*—It was plain to Simon Magus that Simon Peter did something that Philip had not done as shown by the speaking with tongues. He had done his best to gain the secret of Philip's power and had failed. He was even more anxious to get what Peter had. The offer to buy the power, the gift of bestowing the Holy Spirit, reveals the utterly unspiritual character of Simon. He may have bought some of the secret books on divination and sorcery of which there were so many at Ephesus (Acts 19: 19). "It is a striking scene—the two Simons face to face, Simon Magus and Simon Peter" (Rackham). Simon Magus looked on the apostles Peter and John as on the same plane with himself, "only more ac-

complished sorcerers, who might be bribed to share
their secret with him" (Furneaux). He thought Peter
had his price and asked him to name it. "This act
has originated our word *simony*, which Webster de-
fines as 'that crime of buying or selling ecclesiastical
preferment, or the corrupt presentation of any one
to an ecclesiastical benefice for money or reward' "
(Hackett). It is a crime more common in state
churches than where separation between church and
state exists. This "treatment of spiritual functions
as a marketable commodity" (Furneaux) is not con-
fined to ministers, but in its essence is a very common sin. "Money can buy diamonds, but not wisdom, or sympathy, or faith, or holiness." It is this
offer to trade in spiritual things that has branded
the name "simony" with infamy. It is closely akin
to the offer of Judas Iscariot to betray his Lord
for thirty pieces of silver and to the sin of Ananias
and Sapphira in lying to the Holy Spirit. Simon
Magus saw the opportunity of gaining unbounded
power and untold wealth if he could only get this
power that Peter undoubtedly possessed and exercised. He only asked Peter to name his price.

5. *Fierce Denunciation by Peter.*—Peter recognized at once the enormity of the sin of Simon Magus
and spurned the temptation with vehement indignation: "Thy silver perish with thee, because thou hast
thought to obtain the gift of God with money" (Acts
8:20). "The words are no curse or imprecation, as
is evident from verse 22, but rather a vehement expression of horror on the part of St. Peter, an

expression which would warn Simon that he was on
the way to destruction" (Knowling). This language
of strong emotion expresses the intense abhorrence
excited in Peter's mind by the diabolical proposal
of Simon Magus (Hackett). Yet we must not overlook the fact that the language of Peter is in the form
of a wish for the future and includes Simon himself
as well as his money. It is interesting to call attention to Peter's words about those who followed the
way of "Balaam the son of Beor who loved the hire
of wrong-doing" (II Peter 2:15). Dante has fiercely
denounced the sin of Simon Magus and of his followers (*Inferno*, Canto xix). John concurred (vs.
24, "ye have spoken") in this language of Peter to
Simon Magus. Peter is convinced that Simon has
no part or lot in Christianity for his heart was not
right before God in spite of his profession of faith
and his baptism. He was still "in the gall of bitterness and in the bond of iniquity" (vs. 23). The only
hope for Simon lay in immediate turning from his
wickedness and prayer to the Lord "if perhaps the
thought (purpose, only here in the New Testament)
of thy heart shall be forgiven thee" (vs. 22). Peter
does not close the door of hope completely. Apparently Peter felt that this sin had come "perilously
near" (Furneaux) to the sin against the Holy Spirit
which has never forgiveness (Matt. 12:31). Peter
probably "doubted, not so much the possibility of
forgiveness, as the reality of Simon's repentance"
(Furneaux). There is no doubt whatever that Peter
was fully justified in his exposure of the sin of

Simon Magus. To allow the trail of this slimy serpent to run through early Christianity would be indeed a gall of bitterness and a bond of iniquity.

6. *Simon's Pitiful Plea for Prayer.*—He did not pray himself and did not turn from his wickedness. The rebuke by Peter "alarmed only his fears," but "produced no reformation in character or in the course of his life" (Hackett). Like Pharaoh of old "Simon was frightened, but not reformed" (Furneaux). He dreaded the fate which Peter had pointed as almost certainly his, and begged Peter and John to pray for him "that none of these things which ye have spoken come upon me" (vs. 24). "Not recognizing that penitence is a personal matter between the soul and God, he thought that he could pray by deputy" (Furneaux). He may have felt that the prayers of Peter and John would be more efficacious than his own (Knowling), but he did not himself turn to God for pardon, but only to Peter and John in his terror. The text of the Codex Bezæ adds to verse 24 the statement that Simon "did not cease weeping much." But even so, such sorrow was like that of Judas who went and hanged himself (Matt. 27:3, 5), only Simon did not feel so deeply as to do that. There is no more about him in the Acts. All that is told of him in early tradition confirms what is told here. His sorrow was not the godly sort that leads to change of life (II Cor. 7:10). He had failed to buy "power" from Peter and he relapsed into his former life of pretence and of hypocrisy, his name becoming a byword for all time.

7. *Legends About Simon's Career.*—The early Christian writers of the second and third centuries have much to say about the history of this evil man who came to be called the father of all heresy. Justin Martyr, who was himself a native of Samaria, wrote about a hundred years after this time and he says that Simon was almost worshipped by the Samaritans, that he went to Rome in the reign of Claudius (A.D. 41 to 54), and that the senate erected a statue to him as a god. But in 1574 a statue was dug up in Rome with the dedication SEMONI SANCO DEO FIDIO. It seems clear, therefore, that Justin Martyr misunderstood this inscription as referring to Simon Magus. Irenæus followed the mistake of Justin Martyr. There were some heretics in Justin's time called Simonians and these naturally claimed as their founder this wonder worker of Samaria. All this made it easy for the foolish blunder of the Clementine Homilies in the third century, which glorify Peter at the expense of Paul who is pictured as Simon Magus. Baur actually conceived the absurd notion that Luke in Acts 8 is referring to Paul by Simon Magus, though no one ever denounced sorcery more severely than Paul does in the Acts (13: 6–12; 19:11–19). That theory is now dead beyond recovery. It is not at all likely that Simon Magus held the later Gnostic theories of the second century, but he probably did have the germ of the later Gnosticism in his views about himself. He is a good example of the dog that returned to his vomit and of the sow that returned to her wallowing, a proverb

that Peter pertinently quoted of the later Gnostics
(II Peter 2:21 f.). W. M. Taylor cites Simon Magus
as a warning for all hypocrites who mock at the
mercy of God in seasons of privilege and sink into
deeper sin.

CHAPTER XIV

PETER THE LIBERATOR OF GENTILES
(Acts 9:32–11:18)

1. *Peter on a Preaching Tour.*—Foakes-Jackson in his *Peter, Prince of Apostles* (p. 74) notes that "Peter, the simple disciple, is very different from the eloquent exponent of the new faith, as he is depicted in the Acts." That difficulty exists only when we ignore the effect of the Holy Spirit on Peter. That experience gave him understanding and courage which go far to explain the powerful rôle played by Peter in Acts 2 to 5. Peter still had the same impulsiveness and timidity, a combination that continued to get him into trouble as in Joppa, Cæsarea, Jerusalem, and Antioch. The activity of Stephen stirred the Pharisees afresh after the caution of Gamaliel had set the apostles free from prison (Acts 5:40–42). It is one of the unexplained problems why the persecution by the Pharisees and Sadducees combined (the Sanhedrin), which resulted in the stoning of Stephen and the persecution of the Jerusalem church by the Sanhedrin under the leadership of Saul of Tarsus (the brilliant pupil of Gamaliel and the bright hope and rising star of Pharisaism), left the apostles alone. Luke does not make it clear why the apostles, Peter in particular, were spared in this persecution, led by young Saul,

that scattered the disciples to Judea, Samaria, Damascus, Phœnicia, Cyprus, and Antioch (Acts 8:1, 4; 9:2; 11:19). Did the position of Gamaliel play any part in it? The scattering simply spread the gospel (Acts 8:4, 11:19), and Peter and John went to Samaria to investigate the work of Philip (Acts 8:14 f.). But the sudden and unexpected conversion of Saul changed the whole situation and the church throughout Judea, Galilee, and Samaria enjoyed peace and was multiplied (Acts 9:31). Another cause of peace was the order of Caligula in A.D. 39 for his statue to be set up for worship in the temple of Jerusalem. This action diverted the anger of the Jews from the Christians. Once more therefore, after the interim of the activity of Stephen and Philip, the preaching deacons (Acts 6 to 8), and the conversion of Saul (Acts 9:1–30), Peter becomes active again in Luke's narrative. It is not fair to Peter to think that he had remained inactive during the activity of Stephen and Philip, if we may take Acts 8:25 as a specimen. Here we are told that Peter and John evangelized many villages of the Samaritans on their way back to Jerusalem. In Acts 12:17 we are expressly told that, when Peter escaped from prison and the wrath of Herod Agrippa I, he went on to another place. This was later than the present situation. When Claudius became Emperor in A.D. 41 and Herod Agrippa I King of Judea (A.D. 42–44), the persecution of the Christians started again (Acts 12:1 ff.). But here Peter in this time of peace between A.D. 39 and 42 was making a tour "throughout all parts" (Acts 9:32), evangelizing and strengthening the churches and so came down to the saints (common name in Acts and the Epistles for believers in Christ) in Lydda, the Old Testament Lod (I Chron. 8:12), near Joppa in the plain of Sharon on the way from Jerusalem to Cæsarea. It was on the way from Azotus to Cæsarea and may have been evangelized by Philip (Acts 8:40) on his way to Cæsarea where he made his home (Acts 21:8). Philip was probably Luke's source for this portion of Acts. This ministry of preaching and healing is very much like that of Jesus who went about doing good as Peter said (Acts 10:38). Æneas is a common old Greek name, probably here of a Hellenistic Jew and apparently one of the "saints" already mentioned. Peter heals him of his paralysis in the name of Jesus as he had done with the lame man at the Gate Beautiful in Jerusalem (Acts 3:2). The news of the miracle spread in every direction through the valley of Sharon and many "turned unto the Lord" (Acts 9:35).

2. *The Raising of Tabitha from the Dead.*—The news of Peter's work in Lydda reached Joppa, the port of Jerusalem (II Chron. 2:16) where a disciple (feminine form for disciple, here alone in the New Testament) lived named Tabitha, an Aramaic word meaning "gazelle" and rendered in Greek by *Dorkas* "the creature with the beautiful look" (or eyes). She may have borne both names (the Aramaic and the Greek). Her death brought great grief in Christian circles in Joppa both because of her

personal charm and because of her active beneficence. Furneaux is wrong in saying that "she is not only the first woman mentioned by name in the Christian church, but in her first came the recognition of woman's work." The names of many women followers of Christ occur in the Gospels and in the Acts. There is, for instance, Mary the Mother of Jesus (Acts 1:14), Sapphira (5:1–11). And in Luke 8:1–3 we read of the band of women who contributed towards the expenses of the work of Jesus. But it is true that Tabitha (Dorcas) was a representative of the busy type of woman worker, more like Martha than like Mary. Many women's societies have been named after Dorcas, but she did her work herself and this gave an individual and personal touch to the good deeds that won all hearts (Acts 9:39). It was natural to send for Simon Peter, though this is the first instance of raising one from the dead since Jesus ascended on high. The two brethren who came to Peter did not in so many words ask him to restore her to life, but simply said: "Delay not to come to us." It was a severe test of Peter's faith in the power of Christ, but he came and after kneeling in prayer to Christ, said to the dead: "Tabitha, arise." "Only splendid faith, or insanity, could say to a lifeless corpse, 'Rise' " (Furneaux). Peter had the splendid faith. The account here is quite parallel to the restoration of the daughter of Jairus by Jesus which Peter had witnessed. Like Jesus Peter put the people out of the room before he spoke to the corpse. He used words very much like those of

Jesus. *Tabeitha, kumi,* instead of *Taleitha, kumi.*
Like Jesus also, Peter took her by the hand and
raised her up and then called the saints and the
widows whom Tabitha had helped. "There was nothing here of the self-confident wonder-worker, but
only a humble man, putting himself in the hands of
his Divine Master" (Furneaux). Peter here appears
in a rôle like that of Paul at Troas when he restored Eutychus to life (Acts 20:10). In both instances it is Jesus Christ who brings back life to
the dead. But this miracle gave Peter new prestige
in Joppa and "many believed on the Lord." Peter's
tour was going well.

3. *Simon Peter the Guest of Simon the Tanner.*—
Peter would now be a welcome guest in any Christian
home in Joppa. The inns or hotels were such dis-
reputable places that no one lodged in them save as
a last resort. Hospitality was a necessity for the
travelling preachers (III John 6, 8, 10). It is not
surprising to find Simon Peter staying "many days"
with another Simon, for the name was very common.
What is surprising is to find the man a tanner, for
the Jews regarded this trade as utterly unclean. One
of the rabbis said: "It is impossible for the world
to do without tanners; but woe to him who is a
tanner." The handling of the skins of dead and unclean animals was to a scrupulous Jew hopelessly
unclean. And yet Peter is making his home with a
Jewish Christian engaged in this business. "It was
a ground for divorce, if a Jewess discovered after
marriage that her husband was a tanner" (Fur-

neaux). Clearly Peter was on the road to a more
liberal view than when he asked Jesus to explain the
parable about the blind leading the blind and both
falling into the ditch (Matt. 15:15) after the Pharisees had become angry over Christ's protest against
their insistence on washing the hands before eating
to escape damnation.

4. *The Vision on the Housetop.*—It was on the
housetop of the tanner's home that Peter had the
perplexing vision (Acts 10:17) or trance (10:10)
that he did not at first comprehend. Clearly Peter
was not prepared to make a complete break with his
Jewish prejudices and notions of ceremonial purification. Astounded, Peter politely, but firmly, declined the Lord's invitation to slay and eat these
unclean animals: "Not so, Lord; for I have never
eaten anything that is common and unclean" (Acts
10:14). Strangely enough to us, Peter repeated
twice more his refusal, though recognizing the invitation as from the Lord and though the Lord said:
"What God hath cleansed, make thou not common."
When it was passed, "Peter was much perplexed in
himself what the vision which he had seen might
mean" (10:17). Later, when Mark writes his Gospel, he will inject a remark (an anacoluthon) that
reflected Peter's later insight about the teaching of
Jesus concerning inward and outward defilement,
"making all meats clean" (Mark 7:19). But for the
moment Peter was hopelessly puzzled.

5. *The Call from Cornelius.*—Light came to Peter
when some men (two or three) stood at the gate and

called to know if Simon who is called Peter is lodging there. Then it was that, while Peter was pondering the strange vision, the Holy Spirit spoke directly to him and bade him expressly to go with them "nothing doubting," no longer divided in mind. The explanation by the men throws direct light on the vision, for Cornelius was a Roman centurion and, though a worshipper of God and a contributor to the Jewish worship (alms), still a heathen in actual affiliation, only a proselyte of the gate. Cornelius had not been circumcised and did not undertake to obey the whole Jewish law. There were many of these "God-fearers" among the Gentiles who attended the synagogues and believed in the one God and followed Jewish ethics and prayed to God and gave alms. But the Jews still regarded them as Gentiles because they had not come the whole way. They were not full proselytes. Apparently Cornelius had gathered a group of kinspeople around his own family. Here was surely prepared soil for Peter's sowing. God by vision and angel had prepared Cornelius for the coming of Peter to his house in Cæsarea. It was a crisis in the life of Peter. Jesus had commanded the disciples to carry the gospel to all the nations (Matt. 28:19; Acts 1:8) and Peter himself had said at the great Pentecost that the promise was "to all those afar off as many as the Lord our God calls" (Acts 2:39). But apparently it had not yet occurred to Peter that these Gentiles could or would become Christians without also becoming Jews. But the path of duty was clear to Peter, for the

Holy Spirit left him no choice. He did not know what was ahead of him and he felt it to be prudent to take along with him six Jewish Christians from Joppa (10:23, 45; 11:12). Peter had gone with John to investigate the work of Philip in Samaria and had approved it (8:14 ff.), but the Samaritans had been circumcised and so were technically Jews, though very much disliked as being half Gentiles. If Peter was crossing the Rubicon or taking a step into the dark, he wanted witnesses and fellowship. "And so we see that, impulsive and impetuous as Peter was by nature, he was not by any means destitute of prudence; for in this instance his conduct was worthy both of praise and of imitation" (W. M. Taylor). "Peter's prudence, so unlike his usual impulsiveness, in wishing to have the presence of Jewish witnesses, who might give a faithful report of anything which might occur, shows that he felt that the vision and the Divine summons to Cæsarea might be the precursors of some momentous event in the history of the church" (Furneaux). So on the following day (10:23) Peter with the six brethren made the journey from Joppa to Cæsarea where Philip dwelt later (Acts 21:8), though he does not appear in the group around Cornelius, who was expecting Peter eagerly and confidently with a considerable number of relatives and intimate friends. It was a momentous occasion. For the first time a Christian was facing a Gentile audience with the message of Christ. What did Peter have to say to such a group as this? We have seen him at Pentecost as he spoke wonderful words to Jews from all over the world, the first interpreter of Christ after the Holy Spirit came. That was the inauguration of the dispensation of the Holy Spirit under whose leadership we are still, when the "other Paraclete" entered upon his work. Now once again Simon Peter is the spokesman in the first interpretation of Jesus to a purely Gentile audience in a Gentile home. Will it be another Pentecost, a Gentile Pentecost?

6. *The Sermon in the Roman's House.*—Cornelius fell at the feet of Peter as if to worship him, but Peter would have none of this, for he was himself just a man. The visions of Cornelius and the message of the angel made him regard Peter as more than a mere man. So while talking with him Peter went on into the house of Cornelius. At once Peter explains his conduct as "an unlawful thing" (here only in the New Testament except in I Peter 4:3). There was no Mosaic law against entering a Gentile house, but Jewish oral tradition had added it to the written law. In the trial of Jesus by Pilate the Jews declined to enter the palace of Pilate, "that they might not be defiled, but might eat the passover" (John 18:28). "Any contact with a heathen might involve such defilement, that on coming from the market an orthodox Jew would have to immerse" (Edersheim). See the surprise of the Pharisee about Jesus at breakfast (Luke 11:38). But Peter reminds the group of Gentiles in the house of Cornelius that he has taken this serious, to an ordinary Jew fatal, step only under direct revelation and

command from God: "And yet unto me hath God shewed that I should not call any man common or unclean" (Acts 10:28). At length Peter is seeing the point of the vision on the housetop of Simon the tanner and the express command of the Holy Spirit. Otherwise he would naturally have objected seriously to responding to the request of Cornelius, but under the circumstances he came "without gainsaying," with no answer back to the now plain meaning of God's revelation that seemed to him on the housetop directly opposed to God's own word and will. He had then not hesitated to remind the Lord of this contradiction of the new with the old and his determination to abide by the old as the known will of God in spite of the thrice repeated vision (10:14 f.). Peter occupies a peculiar position and his apology does not wholly relieve his and our embarrassment about it. The best that one can say is that he was slowly adjusting himself to the new developments in God's revelation. Peter now desires fuller light on the reason why Cornelius sent for him (10:29), before he speaks further. Cornelius therefore proceeds to tell his experience of four days before as he was praying at the ninth hour in his own house. The angel told him to send for Peter in Joppa who would tell him what he needed to know. Cornelius commends Peter for coming (10:30-33) and expresses a readiness to hear: "Now therefore we are all here present in the sight of God, to hear all things that have been commanded thee of the Lord." If ever a preacher had an audience prepared beforehand for his message, that was true as Simon Peter began to speak.

There was little time for Peter to think of the nature of his message. He knew the gospel of Jesus which he had been preaching to Jews, but he had never before given it to Gentiles. So he opened his mouth and began with the story of Jesus Christ in outline (10:34–43) very much as a missionary today in China has to tell the essential facts in the life of Jesus on which to base his appeal for service to the Lord Jesus Christ. Peter could assume little or no knowledge of Jesus on the part of his hearers. Luke gives, of course, a mere outline of Peter's discourse which was soon interrupted as we shall see (10:44–48), but a sketch that is remarkably like that in the Gospel of Mark. Undoubtedly Mark frequently heard Peter as he presented to Jewish and Gentile audiences the salient features in the life and work of Jesus Christ. Before he begins with that, however, Peter expresses the new light that has come to him in his new environment. Inside of the Gentile's house he now of a truth perceives that God is not a respecter of persons (a word only here in the New Testament, but for kindred words see James 2:1 and 9 and Luke 20:21). Clearly this was a new discovery for Peter, not that Gentiles are saved without God in Christ, but that Gentiles can come to God in Christ without becoming Jews. This is a revolutionary idea to Peter. It is involved in the teaching of Jesus about the other sheep (John 10: 16), but he had not seen it until this moment in the

Roman's house. Jesus had brought God's message to the children of Israel, from Galilee after John's baptism, as he went about doing good, anointed by the Holy Spirit, healing the sick, for God was with him, both in the land of the Jews and in Jerusalem. "We are witnesses of all these things," says Peter. Jesus had charged them to be "witnesses." But the Jews slew Jesus on the tree (cross) and God raised him from the dead on the third day and made him manifest to witnesses prepared by God of whom Peter himself is one. It was no mere spirit whom they saw for Peter and others ate and drank with the Risen Jesus (Luke 24:42). The Risen Christ, who is Lord of all, commanded them as witnesses to proclaim him as the Judge of the living and the dead. The prophets likewise bear witness to Jesus as the Messiah and Lord, that every one who believes on him may receive forgiveness of sins through his name. This in brief was "Peter's gospel for the Gentiles" (Rackham). Peter doubtless had more to say, but this powerful and brief presentation of the message of life bore instant fruit.

7. *The Unexpected Revival.*—Peter had made no unusual adaptation of his message to these Gentiles as distinct from Jews. He had told succinctly and clearly the facts about Christ's coming, crucifixion, resurrection, mission and message about the forgiveness of sins for every believer in him. There was no doubt more detail and local color than Luke has here reproduced. But Peter treated these Romans as sinful men like the Jews and offered them Jesus as

the only hope of forgiveness for sin. The age was full of redemptive religions which proposed a series of initiatory rites and ceremonies (the so-called mystery-religions of Cybele, Isis, Mithra, etc.), but Peter offered faith in Jesus as the one means of securing forgiveness of sin. He doubtless pressed it home with passion and power to these hearts already prepared to hear the message of hope, waiting and eager to know the one definite step for them to take in the matter. Peter fortunately spoke the right word. Should not every sermon have somewhere in it such a word for one inquiring the way of eternal life? Peter apparently had much more to say when his sermon was suddenly and unexpectedly interrupted by the coming of the Holy Spirit on all those who had been listening with rapt attention to his words (10:44–48). No doubt Peter was amazed by the descent (see also Acts 8:16; 11:15) of the Holy Spirit upon these Gentiles, but we are expressly told that "they of the circumcision who believed" (10:45), the group of six Jewish Christians whom Peter had prudently brought along with him from Joppa, were astonished beyond measure. They were clearly not as fully prepared as Peter for the new day of freedom for Gentiles who believed in Jesus as Saviour and Lord. These Romans were not even Jews, let alone Christians by profession. They had not been circumcised nor baptized. And yet "the gift of the Holy Spirit," of which Peter had spoken at the great Pentecost in Jerusalem (Acts 2:38), had been poured out (the very verb used by Peter in Acts

2:33) upon Gentiles just as if they were Jews, and upon unbaptized Gentiles at that. What were they to think of this unprecedented occurrence? Had God violated all his own regulations and ordinances? There was no doubt of the descent of the Holy Spirit upon these new Roman believers for they were speaking with tongues and magnifying God in what tongues they could themselves understand (Aramaic and Greek) just as happened at the outpouring of the Holy Spirit in Jerusalem (Acts 2:4) and apparently in Samaria (8:16 f.). The amazement of the Jewish believers apparently left them speechless, though clearly it was a Gentile Pentecost like the Jewish and the Samaritan ones. "Probably nothing short of this visible manifestation would have convinced them that God was indeed claiming these Gentiles as his own" (Furneaux). It was clear also that they were already converted before the gift of the Holy Spirit came upon them, though regeneration itself is the work of the Holy Spirit also. And this new birth had come without and before baptism, a fact that seems to escape the notice of those who hold that baptism is the means of securing the forgiveness of sins. That theological conception is inconsistent with the facts recorded here at Cæsarea. Clearly then the interpretation of Peter's language in Acts 2:38 is wrong if it makes baptism for the purpose of securing remission of sin, because here we have Peter proposing baptism because these Gentiles have already received the Holy Spirit and hence are already converted and saved. The case of Saul of Tarsus is pertinent also who was converted on the road to Damascus when he surrendered to Christ (Acts 22:10), and who was filled with the Holy Spirit before he was baptized (Acts 9:17 f.). It is equally clear that Peter, if he recalled the word of Jesus to Nicodemus in John 3:5, did not interpret it as baptismal remission. Peter at once raises the question, not of finishing his sermon, but of baptism by reason of what has happened: "Can any man forbid the water that these should not be baptized, who have received the Holy Spirit as well as we?" (10: 47). Peter's question was apparently addressed to the six Jewish brethren and expects the negative answer as in Mark 14:19 and Luke 6:39. The idea is not that water was to be brought to them, but they to the water. The greater called for the less. They had received the baptism of the Holy Spirit. Why not baptism in water (Acts 1:5; 11:16)? The logic of Peter was irrevocable and conclusive. Peter and the six Jewish brethren had been baptized before the great Pentecost. No objection was made by the six brethren and so Peter directed that the new Gentile converts (Romans, the family and friends of Cornelius) be baptized, clearly by the six brethren. There was no church here to authorize the performance of the ordinances and these brethren were probably not ministers or elders of whom we do not read till Acts 11:30. But Peter gave the command and they were baptized as Philip baptized the Eunuch (Acts 8:38) in a pool or stream on the way to Azotus. Here was the making of the first Gentile

Christian church, a group of Roman believers with possibly some Greeks. There were apparently several Samaritan churches already (8:12, 25). It is worth noting that Peter, like Jesus always (John 4:2) and like Paul usually (I Cor. 1:14–17), did not do the baptizing himself. On this occasion it was wise to enlist these six Jewish brethren in this revolutionary experience of which a report must be made in Jerusalem on Peter's return there. At the request of Cornelius and the new converts Peter remained some days in Cæsarea, apparently as a guest in the home of Cornelius (10:48). Peter had surely crossed the Rubicon now and had left his Jewish prejudices and scruples behind him. It was a time of delightful fellowship while it lasted. One may think that during these days Peter possibly enjoyed the fellowship of Philip and his gifted daughters. But to Jerusalem Peter and the six brethren went in due time.

8. *Called to Account in Jerusalem.*—So sensational an event was bound to be heard of in Jerusalem and in all Judea. What the apostles and the brethren throughout Judea heard was that "the Gentiles also had received the word of God" (Acts 11:1). There was undoubted joy over this news as over the work of Philip in Samaria. But the report came from Cæsarea and not from Joppa. The brethren in Jerusalem were not acquainted with Peter's private experiences on the housetop in Joppa that helped break up the Procrustean bed of his Judaism. They knew also of Peter's impulsive character and hasty

temperament (Furneaux). Peter himself probably
felt the need of an explanation of his conduct that
"came as a surprise or scandal to many" (Rackham). Luke has had to record already in the Acts
murmuring, covetousness, and even "simony" among
the professed disciples, but now there is open strife
and contention in the church assembly itself. It
sprang from a faction as such things usually do. We
have seen already in the Acts murmuring of the Hellenistic Christians against the Aramaic (Hebrew)
Christians (both classes Jewish Christians, but one
from the Dispersion and now under Greek influences,
the other in Palestine and less so) over the help
given the Hellenistic widows and how this trouble
over money and widows led to the selection of seven
men (deacons), all Hellenistic Christians, to take
care of the problem (Acts 6:1-6). Stephen and
Philip are the outstanding men in the group. This
time the trouble starts from "those of the circumcision." Furneaux regards this phrase here as an
anachronism, for later it was used for those Jewish
Christians who insisted that all Gentiles had to become Jews as well as Christians in order to be saved
(Gal. 2:12). In fact we see here the beginning of
this time of cleavage, probably men from the sect
of the Pharisees (Acts 15:5) who were more Pharisaic than Christian, and even here distinguished from
"the apostles and the brethren" (11:1). This group
belonged to the Aramaic, not Hellenistic, wing of
6:1 f. with very pronounced views about Jewish ex-
clusiveness and they really expected all Gentiles who

became Christians also to become Jews. "To such disciples S. Peter's violation of the law of uncleanness must have been a grievous scandal" (Rackham). We do not know the names of any of the leaders, but they began a dispute with Peter as soon as he appeared in Jerusalem.

The precise point of the attack was the indisputable fact that Peter had gone into the house of the uncircumcised Cornelius and had eaten with him and his family (11:3). The charge was a violation of Jewish ceremonial customs, not of Christian principles. There was a complete ignoring of the work of the Holy Spirit in the hearts and lives of the Cornelian family. One may as well confess to a sense of shame that, so soon after the great Pentecost which came after the Great Commission from the Risen Christ for world conquest for him, the chief apostle of Christ should be arraigned before the home church in Jerusalem for preaching the gospel to the Gentiles, under the guise of taking care of Jewish social customs. The item was eating with Gentiles, but the thing aimed at was carrying the gospel to the Gentiles. Here was "hardshellism" or opposition to missions in the heart of the mother church in Jerusalem. And it has never been rooted out of Christianity. One may wonder why John or some other apostle did not at once take up the cudgels for Peter's conduct in Cæsarea. But reflection will show that only Peter could tell the actual story of his new experience both in Joppa and Cæsarea and how plainly the whole thing was the doing of God in breaking down Peter's own Jewish prejudices and in bestowing the Holy Spirit on these Romans before they were baptized. So Peter tells the story briefly and in detail to the church (some of it three times in Acts: the events in Joppa, told by Peter in Cæsarea, and again in Jerusalem), and makes it plain how it was that he finally went so far as to eat bread with Cornelius in his home.

The facts told eloquently enough the hand and leading of God in it all, but Peter definitely appealed (11:12) to the six brethren from Joppa, who had come on to Jerusalem, for confirmation of the accuracy of the narrative of the marvellous events in Cæsarea, how in particular the Holy Spirit came upon Cornelius and his household while Peter was preaching "just as on us at the beginning" (11:15). Peter wisely quoted the words of Jesus (already in Acts 1:5) about the baptism of the Holy Spirit and triumphantly demanded: "Who was I that I could withstand God?" (11:17). The effect was electric and conclusive. The hearers first became silent and then glorified God saying: "Then to the Gentiles also hath God granted repentance unto life." Nothing more was said about Peter's eating bread with Cornelius. That was a minor detail in the great spiritual revolution that had come under Peter's leadership. Peter never showed more masterful skill than on this occasion when he proved that God had opened the door of salvation to Gentiles without their becoming Jews. It is more than doubtful if the circumcision party in the Jerusalem church fully realized the significance of Peter's speech and their acquiescence in it. At any rate they were silenced for the moment by the undoubted hand of God in the case of Cornelius. For the present they are compelled to let Peter alone, but they sincerely hope that God will not go back on their Jewish convictions by any fresh developments like this.

CHAPTER XV

PETER THE CO–WORKER WITH PAUL
(Acts 15 and Galatians 2)

1. *Paul the Chosen Vessel for the Gentiles.*—Almost unwittingly Peter had been the instrument in opening the door to Gentiles in Cæsarea who were sympathetic toward the worship of God as taught and practised by the Jews, for Cornelius was considered devout by the Jews because of his prayers and his alms and his attendance on the synagogue worship. He was a "God-fearer" as such Gentiles were called. And yet after all he was not strictly a Jew and Peter had been called to account in Jerusalem by the Pharisaic element in the church, which element did not include the apostles. But Christ had already called to his service the leader of the opposition to Christianity, a Hellenistic Jew of brilliant gifts and scholarly training, probably a student at the University of Tarsus (his home town) and certainly a star graduate (Gal. 1:14; Acts 22:3) of the Pharisaic seminary of Gamaliel (grandson of Hillel), the most brilliant man of his time and destined to be the greatest preacher of the gospel for all time. This man had been at the head of the persecution of the disciples in Jerusalem and had scattered them far and wide. We do not know what Peter knew of this persecutor who held the garments of the Sanhedrin as they stoned Stephen. But now Saul has been seized upon by Jesus (Phil. 3:12) and given a direct call to be a witness of Christ to the Gentiles as Paul said in his speech before Herod Agrippa II (Acts 26:16 f.) and "a vessel of choice to bear my name before the Gentiles and kings and the children of Israel" as Jesus said to Ananias in Damascus (Acts 9:15). This man had a Jewish heritage of strict Pharisaism in a Greek environment in Tarsus, the seat of a great university, and was himself a citizen of Rome with some wealth and social prestige, a man of a wholly different type from Peter and the other apostles, who were in no sense rabbis or men of learning (Acts 4:13). But Peter did not know what the Lord Jesus was doing to carry out his own program of world evangelism which the apostles had been so slow in executing. Peter, as we look back now, already had his share in the early stages of the world expansion. "At any rate the foundations of a world-embracing Christianity were being silently laid by Peter, and presumably by the rest of the original apostles. The scene, however, was soon to be transferred from Jerusalem to Antioch and another better known champion of the faith was about to appear in the person of the great Apostle of the Gentiles, St. Paul" (Foakes-Jackson). The time will come when these two names, Peter and Paul, will be inseparably linked together. Clement of Rome and Ignatius will couple them together soon after Peter and Paul have died. Their personal contacts are not numerous, but are exceedingly important and interesting.

2. *Paul the Guest of Peter in Jerusalem.*—It is
Paul who tells us this interesting fact when these
two foremost servants of Christ met for the first
time, so far as we know. It is in Galatians 1:18:
"Then after three years I went up to Jerusalem to
make the personal acquaintance of Cephas, and I
remained with him fifteen days." At this time (some
three years after Saul's conversion), to be sure, Peter was the unquestioned leader of the Christians
and young Saul was regarded with real suspicion in
Jerusalem. Paul does not, of course, allude to that,
but Luke makes it plain in Acts how slow the brethren were there to regard him as one of the sheep
instead of a wolf in sheep's clothing. When he tried
to join the disciples, "they all continued to fear
him, not believing that he was a disciple" (Acts 9:
26). He had been away from Jerusalem some three
years, it is true, but no one seemed to know what
he had been doing in Damascus and Arabia. They
knew only too well what he had done in Jerusalem
before he had left for Damascus with papers from
the Sanhedrin to seize the disciples there. Apparently the brethren in Jerusalem regarded this approach by Saul as a new ruse to catch them again,
for the persecution had died down during his absence. It was Joseph Barnabas (son of consolation,
Acts 4:36, already called so for his generosity) who
took young Saul to himself and made him tell the
whole story of his conversion to Christ. Barnabas
was completely convinced of Saul's sincerity and so
"brought him to the apostles" (Acts 9:27), includ-

ing Peter, and vouched for the truthfulness of Saul's account of his conversion and change of front. From the human point of view it was Barnabas who stood for Saul and opened the door of opportunity for him here in Jerusalem as he did later in Antioch (Acts 11:25 f.). In a sense we owe Paul to Barnabas. It is undoubtedly true that this discovery and endorsement of Saul was the greatest thing that Barnabas ever did for Christ and for the world just as Andrew did his greatest deed in bringing his brother Simon (Peter) to Jesus. This experience has been repeated many a time by even humble ministers without great gifts, who have discovered and developed gifted and brilliant young servants of Christ who have gone far in the work of the kingdom. But Barnabas was himself a man of parts and the chief figure at this time outside of the apostolic circle, for Stephen was dead, and James the brother of Jesus came to the fore a bit later.* Clearly all this took place before Paul "visited" Cephas. It was after Barnabas had cleared up the situation about Saul that Peter extended a cordial invitation to stay with him for fifteen days. During these days Paul preached vigorously in Jerusalem in such a way as to arouse the same antagonism that Stephen had done and Paul even was willing to meet Stephen's fate (Acts 22:19–21), in part atonement for his own share in the blood of Stephen. But Jesus bade him depart and so he went reluctantly to

* See the chapter on "Barnabas the Friend of Young Preachers" in my *Types of Preachers in the New Testament.*

Tarsus for some years (Acts 9:30). But Saul's main
purpose in going to Jerusalem, when he was driven
out of Damascus, had been to have an interview with
Peter, not to be ordained by him or to receive any
sort of apostolic authority from him at all. This
Paul passionately maintains in Galatians 1:1 to 20.
Paul there answers the charge of the Judaizers that
he was not one of the twelve apostles by admitting
it and proving that he obtained his apostleship directly from God through Christ and that his apostleship was on a par with that of Peter or any of
the twelve. As a matter of fact Paul affirms that
Peter was the only one of the twelve that he saw on
this visit to Jerusalem. He did see James the brother
of Jesus (not one of the twelve) and Luke tells of
his relations with Barnabas. The other apostles (the
twelve) were apparently on preaching tours or, if
present, did not meet Paul personally (Acts 9:27),
for Luke may here use the term in a general sense
as Paul does in Galatians 1:19. Page thinks that
Luke "possesses only inexact knowledge of this period." Rackham more correctly says that Peter and
James "represented" the apostles, the rest being absent (Hackett). Rackham suggests that Luke and
Paul are referring to different occasions, an unnecessary hypothesis. Paul's "fifteen days" probably
mean only the length of his stay as the guest of
Simon Peter, not the entire time in Jerusalem. If
Paul did not obtain ecclesiastical authority from
Peter, what did he gain by the visit to him on this
occasion? There was much that any one can see at

a glance. Saul had not been a follower of Jesus during his ministry and may have known little about his teachings, about the crucifixion, resurrection, and ascension, and about the great events when the Holy Spirit came at Pentecost. He was largely in the position of Apollos of Alexandria when he came to Ephesus before he was instructed more fully by Priscilla and Aquila. Paul had clearly grasped the truth that Jesus was the Messiah and began preaching it at once in Damascus (Acts 9:22). This truth lay at the foundation of all Paul's theology and he never departed from it. He built upon it and constantly grew in his knowledge of Jesus as Lord and Saviour (Phil. 3:8–16). Paul in Galatians is answering the Judaizers who contended that he was not a competent interpreter of Christ since he was not one of the twelve apostles. In reply Paul asserts that he did not derive his gospel from any man or set of men, but by direct revelation from God through Christ (Gal. 1:1, 6–9, 11 f.). The purpose of this visit to Peter was not to receive ecclesiastical authority, but simply to learn more of the facts of the earthly life of the Master "from Peter (or Cephas, as he calls him), as from the man best qualified to inform him" (Foakes-Jackson). Paul's reception by Peter proved that Peter regarded him as a genuine apostle and not an interloper or heretic. Their paths diverge in the future for the most part, but they preach the same gospel in all essentials. The endorsement of Paul by Barnabas was followed by the warm approval of Peter. I once heard D. L. Moody give

an imaginative description of the experiences of Paul
with Peter during these two weeks. In his own graphic
way Moody pictured Peter taking Paul with him
over Jerusalem and pointing out to him the location
of various incidents, not failing to show the upper
room where Peter boasted of his loyalty, the place in
the Garden of Gethsemane where he fell asleep while
Jesus was in an agony over the sin of the world, the
places where he three times denied his Lord and Saviour, where Jesus stood when he turned and looked
at him with unutterable pity, and where he was when
Jesus himself appeared to him after his resurrection.
Hallowed days these were that knit together the
souls of these great apostles of Jesus Christ who
were to do so much for the spread of the kingdom of
God among men.

3. *Paul's Champion at the Jerusalem Conference.*
—The years move rapidly forward. There is an out-
burst of enthusiasm for Christ in Antioch as a result
of preaching to Greeks (not Hellenistic Jews, as
some manuscripts have it in Acts 11:20) on a par
with Peter's work with the Romans in Cæsarea. The
news of this revival among the Greeks reached the
ears of the church in Jerusalem (Acts 11:22) just
as the news of Philip's work in Samaria had done
(8:14) and that of Peter in Cæsarea (11:1). So
they sent Barnabas to investigate conditions in Antioch, not Peter and John as in the case of Samaria.
Peter's conduct in Cæsarea ruled him out as a partisan for Gentile freedom. But Barnabas was regarded
as a man of wisdom and tact and had the confidence

of all in Jerusalem. No one of the twelve apostles was sent nor one of the seven deacons, but this outstanding man, "a good man and full of the Holy Spirit and of faith." Possibly Peter felt it a bit that he was passed by, but it was easy to see why it was done.

Barnabas showed his wisdom by acquiescing in the manifest work of the Holy Spirit among the Greeks in Antioch as Peter had done in Cæsarea with the Romans. He did more than delay his report to Jerusalem. He sent to Tarsus for Saul who was already at work there among the Gentiles (Gal. 1:23) and brought him to Antioch with blessed results (Acts 11:25 f.). These Greek disciples here were first called Christians to distinguish them from Jews and heathen. When Barnabas did make his report to Jerusalem he took along Saul and a good collection for the poor saints in Jerusalem which fact threw a deal of light on the reality and orthodoxy of the conversion of the Greeks in Antioch. Soon Barnabas and Saul are sent out by the Holy Spirit from Antioch for a campaign among the Gentiles as recorded by Luke in Acts 13 and 14. The twelve apostles had tarried too long in Jerusalem, but we are not to think that they were doing nothing towards carrying out the commission of Jesus for world evangelism, though this new evangelist and apostle Saul (Paul) was to surpass them all in winning the Roman Empire to Christ. Luke carries on the story of the work of Paul and leaves to one side the work of Peter after the statement in Acts 12:17

that "he went to another place" after leaving Jerusalem. Tradition tells of his preaching in Antioch,
Asia Minor, Babylonia, Egypt, Rome. He had along
with the other apostles already left Jerusalem before
Barnabas and Saul returned from Antioch to Jerusalem for they reported to elders of the church there
(Acts 11:30), the first mention of this type of officers in the churches. But Peter came back to Jerusalem from time to time.

When Paul and Barnabas, for this is the order in
the Acts after Paphos in Cyprus where Paul (no
longer termed Saul) took the lead in rebuking Elymas Bar-jesus and winning Sergius Paulus, the proconsul, to Christ, returned from this great tour
through Syria, Cyprus, Pamphylia, Galatia (Pisi-
dia, Lycaonia, Phrygia), there were probably more
Gentile than Jewish churches, none of which had
become Jewish. The Pharisaic wing in the church in
Jerusalem, that had brought Peter before the church
for his conduct in Cæsarea (Acts 11:1 f.) and had
kept still about Barnabas and Saul in Antioch because of the money (11:29 f.), determined to submit
no longer to such deliberate and extended propaganda to turn the cause of Christ over to uncircumcised Gentiles. Their submission about God's doing in Cæsarea (Acts 11:18) was concerning an individual case and they had not meant it to be used as a
basis for what Paul and Barnabas had done. So, in
the midst of the great rejoicing at Antioch over
God's blessing on the campaign of Barnabas and
Saul which the Antioch church approved (Acts 13:

1–3) but to which they had made no financial contribution, some of the sect of the Pharisees in the church in Jerusalem (15:5), probably the same brethren of the circumcision (11:2 f.) who had raised the issue with Peter, came down from Jerusalem and "began to teach" the brethren (Greek Christians in Antioch): "Unless ye become circumcised according to the custom of Moses, ye cannot be saved" (Acts 15:1). The implication of this teaching clearly was that the Gentile Christians in Antioch and in all the other churches established by Paul and Barnabas (Acts 13 and 14) were still unsaved. There is no evidence at all that these regulators of the Gentile Christians were sent from the church in Jerusalem, least of all that Peter, John or James had anything to do with their coming or their attitude. They were self-appointed regulators of the kingdom who have had a long line of successors. These Pharisaic Christians knew little as yet of the mettle of Paul who knew Pharisaism in all its implications. Paul saw at once that to make the Gentile Christians Jews was to make Christianity merely a sect of Judaism with all the bondage of Pharisaic rules and rites fastened upon Gentile Christians. He had not so learned Christ and had shaken off the legalistic bondage of Pharisaism. The sharp dispute resulted in victory for Paul and Barnabas in Antioch, but with the wise decision to carry the whole question to the great Jewish church in Jerusalem that there might not be two types of Christianity (Jewish and Gentile). The church in Antioch did not recognize any authority

by the Jerusalem church over them, but the apostles
were there and the Judaizers came from there. So
it was eminently wise to have a conference. Delegates
(Barnabas, Paul, Judas, Silas, Titus and probably
others) were sent along to Jerusalem.

It was a great moment in the history of apostolic
Christianity. Scholars are not agreed about all the
facts involved. One of the chief problems is whether
the accounts in Acts 15:3–35 and Galatians 2:1–10
refer to the same event or to two separate visits by
Paul to Jerusalem. The arguments for identity are
to me conclusive as I have set them forth in my
Epochs in the Life of Paul and the objections seem
to me more or less whimsical and some of them
trivial. Paul in Galatians only mentions the visits to
Jerusalem when he met apostles and so passes by
that in Acts 11:29 f. Besides in Galatians he is
chiefly concerned with the recognition of his equality
as an apostle by Peter, James and John and that
was won in the private conference as told in Galatians 2:1–10. In the Acts Luke presents the public
aspects in two separate meetings, one in 15:4 f.
when the Judaizers renewed their dogmatic position
as at Antioch (15:1) and probably alluded to by
Paul in Galatians 2:2 ("I set before them the gospel
which I preach among the Gentiles"), the other in
15:6–29 when Luke expressly says that the apostles
and the elders were gathered together as in a separate meeting after the explosion in verse 5. In between these two public meetings is the natural place
for Paul's conference with the leaders as told in

Galatians 2:1–10. It was exceedingly important that the Big Three in Jerusalem (Peter, James the brother of Jesus, and John the Beloved Disciple) should see eye to eye with Paul and Barnabas. They all knew and trusted Barnabas, but so far as we know, this was the first and only meeting between Paul and John. Evidently Paul called this private conference after the first public meeting that there might be no misunderstanding. Peter was the obvious leader among the apostles, but James and John were "pillars" (Gal. 2:9) also, all reputed to be "somewhat" (Gal. 2:6). It was a sensitive situation with apparent differences of opinion. Bigg thinks that in Galatians 2:6 "there is an embarrassment, there is even a touch of anger in St. Paul's language." There is embarrassment clearly, but not anger. Bigg thinks also that "even the Twelve at the time of the council regarded him with a certain uneasiness and coolness." This again seems to me an exaggeration of the facts. There were others invited to the conference who represented a compromising attitude. Some of the Judaizers, "false brethren" (Gal. 2:4), had apparently slipped in unawares and these exerted some influence on the timid element. Paul was outspoken and courageous in his presentation of freedom in Christ (Gal. 2:4) and refused to agree to the plan of the timid brethren to circumcise Titus, a Greek Christian whom Paul had brought down to the conference, and then to pass some pious resolutions for Gentile liberty. Paul was adamant and would not yield an inch for an hour. He wanted to win Peter, James, and John. The compromisers did not matter. In the end Paul won. The Big Three gave Paul and Barnabas the right hand of fellowship and acknowledged their apostleship to the uncircumcision as on a par with that to the circumcision by Peter, James, and John (Gal. 2:7–9). In other words they all preached the same gospel of grace for both Jew and Gentile. They agreed to a division in a general way in the sphere of activity, not in doctrine, something like our home and foreign missions. It was a great and glorious victory for the gospel of grace. It meant evangelical Christianity for the Gentiles, not a sacramental Judaized Christianity. It was agreed that Paul and Barnabas should go on helping the poor saints in Jerusalem.

The second public meeting that followed was more or less routine and ratified completely the position already taken by the leaders. Wisely James presided. Plenty of opportunity was granted for "much questioning" before Peter arose to speak (Acts 15:7–11). He pertinently rehearsed his own experience at Cæsarea and before the Jerusalem church when the Roman Christians were not required to become Jews. It was a telling argument. Besides, Peter reminded the conference how the Holy Spirit came on the household of Cornelius as at Pentecost and how even we Jews had to believe on Jesus as Saviour in order to be saved. It was therefore wrong and useless to put the yoke of Judaism on the Gentiles when it had failed to save the Jews. Peter thus took a bold and unequivocal stand by the side of Paul and Bar-

nabas who then rehearsed again the story of God's
dealings with the Gentiles. After due deliberation
James himself spoke and showed how all this was
in accord with the prophets for the Gentiles to be
taken into the kingdom of God. So James offered a
resolution of freedom for the Gentiles from the bondage of the Jewish ceremonial law, only they were to
avoid the Gentile sins of idolatry and fornication
and to respect Jewish scruples about things stran-
gled and blood (or murder according to some manuscripts). This decision was unanimous (Acts 15:25),
completely silencing the Judaizers for the moment.
The approval of the Holy Spirit was also claimed
for the result (15:28).

A letter was sent to Antioch, apparently written
by James and with marks of the style of the Epistle
of James and the leaders sent along with it (15:22,
27), Judas and Silas. There was denial of any part
in the embassy of the Judaizers to Antioch (15:24),
and full endorsement of Barnabas and Paul. It was
a great day for evangelical Christianity and there
was much rejoicing in Antioch over the result. By
and by Peter went up to Antioch to rejoice with them
and accepted invitations to the homes of Greek Christians in Antioch (Gal. 2:12) as he had done in
Cæsarea.

4. *Peter Rebuked by Paul in Antioch.*—All went
well at Antioch with Paul and Peter till "some from
James" came up from Jerusalem. This language
could mean that they were sent by James to investigate the conduct of Peter in his social relationships

with the Greek Christians in Antioch, rumors of which may have reached Jerusalem. As a matter of fact the conference in Jerusalem did not pass on this phase of the problem, but Peter was evidently following the lead of Paul and Barnabas and was mingling freely at meals in the homes of the brotherhood in Antioch. It is possible that these Judaizers from Jerusalem had no real right to use the name of James at all, but saw a loop-hole after their ignominious defeat in Jerusalem for reopening the problem on the social issue, the very one first raised against Simon Peter (Acts 11:1 f.). Lightfoot considers it "not improbable, however, that they came invested with some powers from James which they abused." It is inconceivable that James, who presided over the conference in Jerusalem and whose resolution settled the controversy, should have sent spies up to Antioch to get Peter, Paul, and Barnabas into trouble. Peter's vision in Joppa had prepared him for his conduct in Cæsarea and in Antioch. These Judaizers undoubtedly threatened Peter with a report to James that he had gone beyond the Jerusalem agreement and reminded him of his previous trial before the church on this very charge which had been excused as an exceptional experience under God's special direction. Once again, as in the open court of Caiaphas, Peter turned coward and "drew back and separated himself, fearing them of the circumcision." The tenses are probably inchoative imperfect, "he began to draw back (slyly and shamefacedly) and to separate himself" (the very word used of the Pharisees who drew themselves away from defilement). Peter had not changed his principles, but he did change his conduct. "When in this instance he separated himself from the Gentiles, he dissembled his convictions" (Lightfoot). Paul felt it keenly and all the more so when the other Jewish brethren in Antioch drew the same line "and dissembled likewise with him; insomuch that even Barnabas was carried away with their dissimulation" (Gal. 2:13). This is a euphemistic translation, for the Greek verb for "dissembled" means "they acted the hypocrite with him," and the word for "dissimulation" is plain "hypocrisy." And that is what Peter had done and "even Barnabas" had been led astray. For the moment it was *Paulus contra mundum*. He had the insight into the real issues involved and the courage to stand alone for them even against his best beloved brethren. It is plain from the outcome that Paul won back to his position and to his fellowship both Barnabas (Acts 15:36–41) and Peter (I Cor. 9:5). This incident reveals a fundamental weakness in Peter's nature as compared with Paul's, the occasional cowardice and surrender to untoward environment. It is at this point that Paul's granite character towers above Peter's as well as does his stronger intellectual grasp of doctrine and wider mental training. It is certainly clear that Paul did not regard Peter as in any sense a pope or autocrat nor did Peter pose in that capacity. Paul's language was plain and severe, but necessary to save the situation for the truth and freedom in Christ. He fought and won the fight for all of us and Peter came back to Paul's side as his helper. You could always count on Peter's coming back when he blundered. It was not a hopeless debacle.

5. *Paul Commending Peter's Work.*—Many years after the sad occurrence in Antioch Paul was writing a letter to the church in Corinth and was making an argument about liberty in the matter of eating meats offered to idols provided it was not in an idol temple or feast (I Cor. 10:14–22) and provided a brother with scruples did not make a point about it (10:25–30). The meat itself might be good and uncontaminated, but it was not worth making a brother stumble about (8:13). This is a point that those who clamor for personal liberty to drink overlook, the peril to the weaker man even granting no harm to the moderate drinker which is by no means so certain. But Paul himself does not wish to be a stumbling-block to the weaker brother. He illustrates his rule of love by marriage. He has as much right as Peter and the brothers of the Lord to "carry around" (to lead around) a wife on his preaching tours, though he has no wife. He saves money by not having a wife, though he may once have had one, certainly so if he was ever a member of the Sanhedrin (Acts 26:10 f.). This incidental reference to Simon Peter shows clearly that Paul is familiar with the preaching work of Peter and rejoices in it. After Acts 12 Paul is Luke's hero and he has no more about Peter save his championship of Paul's position at the conference in Jerusalem (Acts 15:7–11). But this one word by Paul shows that the so-called breach between Peter and

Paul of which Baur made so much in the nineteenth century is purely imaginary. The rift at Antioch was closed completely.

6. *Peter Praising Paul.*—Assuming the genuineness of II Peter which many modern scholars deny (see Chapter XVIII for discussion of the problem), we have Peter's cordial praise of "our beloved brother Paul" (II Peter 3:15). These gracious words have been used by Baur and others as conclusive proof that Peter did not write this Epistle because of Paul's plain talk and bold stand against Peter's cowardice in Antioch. It is assumed that Peter would never forgive so grave and sharp a rebuke as Paul then administered to him. But that argument overlooks one of the best elements in Peter's character— his rebound and his generosity. He did turn after his denials of Jesus and did come back to strengthen his brethren in Christ. This very weakness gave him added sympathy and power for such service. He had once asked Jesus if he should forgive a brother seven times (Matt. 18:21 f.), only to be told that he must do it seventy times seven. There are difficulties beyond a doubt in accepting the Petrine authorship of this Epistle, but this is not one of them that counts for anything. Peter finds some hard things in Paul's Epistles, as forsooth we do today, things that the unlearned "twist" as they still do Paul's Epistles and other Scriptures. It is a more serious criticism that Peter seems to regard Paul's Epistles as a definite body of writings and on a par with the Old Testament Scriptures. It is entirely possible that Paul's

Epistles formed the first group of the New Testament writings to be treated as a unit, as they occur in all the early Greek manuscripts. Paul clearly regarded his own writings as having the help and guidance of the Holy Spirit. Men will differ about the value of Peter's witness for Paul in these verses. As for myself, I consider it proof of the nobility of Peter and of his power to recognize the greatness of Paul who had now towered above him as the apostle to the Gentile world, the Roman world. This passage removes any suspicion of jealousy or resentfulness on Peter's part toward Paul.

7. *Pitting Peter Against Paul.*—So far as we know, Peter and Paul never met again after the interview in Antioch, though legend is busy with stories about their contacts and even antagonisms including the death of both together in Rome with the *Quo Vadis* addition. "If the New Testament is to be our guide, Paul and Peter, after meeting at Antioch, worked quite independently, and never met again" (Foakes-Jackson). There is no evidence that Paul ever spoke slightingly of the twelve apostles, for his allusions to the "false apostles, deceitful workers, transforming themselves into apostles of Christ" (II Cor. 11:13) are to the Judaizers, not to the twelve apostles. In II Corinthians 12:11 he terms these Judaizers "super-extra apostles" in ridicule. Foakes-Jackson thinks that there is possibly a touch of sarcasm in Galatians 2:6 towards Peter, James, and John, "those who are reputed to be something," and in 2:9, "those who are reputed to be pillars," as if

they were the only "pillars," but that is not Paul's necessary meaning. The Judaizers tried hard to drive a wedge in between Peter and Paul, but without success. They were independent in ecclesiastical standing, but one in essential doctrine and message, Peter mainly to Jews though not wholly so, Paul mainly to Gentiles though always beginning his work in the synagogues with the Jews and the "God-fearers." Some antipathy did arise in the second century between followers of Peter and Paul. "That there was antagonism between a school of Peter and that of Paul cannot be denied. Marcion with his exaggerated Paulinism, and the Ebionites with their Judaizing tendencies prove this" (Foakes-Jackson). But there is no historical foundation for the picture of the bitter conflict between Paul (as Simon Magus) and Peter in the Clementine Homilies and Recognitions. This antagonism is purely arbitrary since Clement of Rome in his letter to Corinth in A.D. 96 and Ignatius in his letter to Rome in A.D. 112 both couple Peter and Paul together as the leading apostles with no hint of opposition. There is no real proof that they ever met again after the incident in Antioch. And yet Baur in the nineteenth century won to his side a great flock of scholars to the view that this supposed opposition between Peter and Paul was the real key to the historical interpretation of the New Testament. "Briefly stated, it is that there were in the New Testament days two rival forms of Christianity, that of Peter the companion of Jesus, and that of Paul who had not known Jesus, but had

evolved a Christ out of his inner consciousness"
(Foakes-Jackson). One may put it to the credit of
Baur that this wild theory, as we see it now, did a
vast deal for the historical study of the sources of
our knowledge of the New Testament times. The
scales have now tipped heavily against Baur's thesis
as against that of Strauss about Jesus. There is no
doubt that Paul felt keenly (see Galatians) the attempts made by the Judaizers to discredit his authority as not equal to that of the twelve apostles, and
that Peter was cut to the heart by Paul's rebuke at
Antioch. But the twelve apostles took their stand
with Paul against the Judaizers and Peter saw that
Paul was right in his rebuke at Antioch. Paul is con-
ciliatory and Peter is responsive and these two great
spirits do not deserve to be pitted against each other
as in some of the early legends and in the over-specu-
lative theory of Baur. In the end, as at the beginning, Peter stands by the side of Paul, the greatest
apostle of Jesus Christ, and with John, the Eagle
flying by their side and above them in some of his
interpretations of Christ.

CHAPTER XVI

PETER'S CONNECTION WITH JOHN MARK
(I Peter 5:13)

1. *Mark Peter's Spiritual Son.*—In I Peter 5:13 Peter says, "Mark my son." The meaning is obvious here that Peter had won Mark to Christ as Paul did Timothy and Titus. Origen indeed thinks that Peter terms Mark his son because he wrote his gospel as an interpretation of Peter's message. The circumstances are unknown to us, though we do know that he was the son of Mary of Jerusalem whose home was a meeting place for prayer for many of the saints when Peter was released from prison by the angel (Acts 12:12) to which home Peter went at once on his escape. It is easy to see that Peter was at home here and so knew John Mark well. Some modern scholars imagine that John Mark was the young man who fled in the Garden of Gethsemane when Jesus was arrested (Mark 14:51 f.). This theory supposes that the last passover meal had been observed by Jesus in Mary's home, her husband being "the goodman of the house" (Mark 14:14), and that Mark followed Jesus and the apostles from the house at some distance out of curiosity, though Papias seems to say as does Jerome that Mark had neither

heard nor followed Jesus in person. But there seems
no doubt at all that Mark was one of Peter's trophies
for Christ. We know also that Mark was a cousin of
Barnabas (Col. 4:10), a disciple of wealth from
Cyprus before he gave it all away. The hospitality
of Mary implies that she also had some means and
may also have come from Cyprus where Mark may
have been born.

2. *The Training of John Mark.*—Much of this
was by contact with the Christian leaders in his
mother's home. Here Peter had his share of influence
on the young disciple along with Barnabas and many
others. It was Barnabas who saw possibilities of service in John Mark and took him along with him
when he and Saul returned to Antioch from Jerusalem (Acts 12:25). Wise preachers are always on
the lookout for young people who can do useful work
for Christ. So, when the Holy Spirit sent forth Barnabas and Saul on their first mission tour, they had
John Mark as "attendant," literally "under-rower"
(a metaphor from the triremes with several tiers of
rowers). Mark was at the call of Barnabas and Saul.
All went well till at Paphos Saul (now Paul) as-
serted definite leadership against Elymas Bar-jesus
and it became "Paul's party" ("those around Paul,"
Acts 13:13). Hence at Perga in Pamphylia where
they faced the mountains and robbers and mosquitoes
and things, Mark in disgust deserted the campaign
and went back home to Jerusalem (Acts 13:13). Paul
held this timidity against Mark and refused to accept him as a colleague in the second mission when

Barnabas urged him strongly (Acts 15:37-39). Paul was not willing to risk again one who was a quitter in a crisis. So Paul and Barnabas parted over Mark. Paul took Silas and Barnabas took Mark who made good with him on this second trial.* We know that Mark made good this time because Paul later praises him in Rome (Col. 4:10) and in Paul's last letter during his second imprisonment in Rome he urges Timothy in Ephesus to pick up Mark and bring him along to Rome "for he is useful to me for ministry" (II Tim. 4:11). The once useless Mark has become useful to Paul. There is comfort here for every preacher. It is even possible that Paul may have read Mark's Gospel and had it among the books left at Troas (II Tim. 4:13). There are many stories about Mark's work with Barnabas in Cyprus and, after the death of Barnabas, of his preaching in Alexandria, but we really know very little. We can be certain that Barnabas gave John Mark the opportunity and the discipline that he needed.

3. *Mark's Relation with Peter.*—The New Testament tells us nothing beyond the bare statement in I Peter 5:13. It is not absolutely certain where Peter and Mark were at this time, probably in mystical Babylon or Rome, though the actual Babylon (chiefly in ruins) remains possible. It is a matter of opinion and mine inclines to Rome as in John's Apocalypse because the Neronian persecution against Christians began in A.D. 64. Peter, if in

---

* See my *Making Good in the Ministry,* for a sketch of this phase of Mark's career.

Rome, may have desired to conceal that fact from Nero and his agents (informers). Several of the early writers, Irenæus, Clement of Alexandria, Jerome, speak of Mark's being in Rome. But, whatever is true about their statements we have Paul's for the fact that Mark was at Rome during his first Roman imprisonment (Col. 4:10), though Peter may not have been there at this time. There are numerous statements in the early writers to the effect that Mark was the "interpreter" of Peter. This term is used of Mark by Papias, Irenæus, Jerome. Irenæus uses the word of Mark's connection with Peter before he wrote the Gospel. Epiphanius merely calls Mark "a follower" of Peter while Eusebius says that Mark was the "familiar acquaintance and attendant" of Peter. We know that Peter and John were not technical schoolmen (Acts 4:13). Both used the current *Koiné* Greek, but were more at home in the Aramaic. It is entirely probable that often Peter preached in Aramaic whereupon Mark would act as his dragoman and put it into vernacular *Koiné*. It is also likely that Mark was Peter's amanuensis often. In the case of the First Epistle Peter seems to say that Silvanus (Silas) was his amanuensis (I Peter 5:12), though the language may simply mean that Silvanus was the bearer of the Epistle while Mark was the actual amanuensis. There seems to be no doubt whatever of the actual and apparently prolonged connection between Peter and John Mark. One may conjecture that it began near or after the death of Barnabas. Certainly Mark was a far finer minister for service when Peter took him over than when he deserted Paul at Perga. John Mark had great opportunities for learning how to work for Christ from Paul and Barnabas and finally Peter, three of the finest spirits ever in the Christian ministry. He is a good model for many other noble ministers who have spent their lives largely in assisting men of greater gifts and higher station. And yet no one can say that Mark's life was a failure or his work slight because he was always overshadowed by greater lights. He left a monument to his own industry and fidelity that probably has carried Peter's influence further than anything that Peter himself ever did.

4. *Writing His Gospel under Peter's Influence.*— There seems no doubt at all that Mark has reproduced in his Gospel the substance and often the very language of Peter in his discourses. He heard Peter preach many times and knew Peter's story of the life and work of Jesus. In fact the rough outline of Mark's Gospel corresponds with the sketch of Peter's discourse in the house of Cornelius as reported by Luke (Acts 10:34–43). The statements of the early writers do not agree in the precise relation of Peter to Mark's Gospel, though all affirm that he was the actual instigator of the work either directly or indirectly. Eusebius says that Mark "made memoirs" of the discourses of Peter concerning the doings of Jesus." This is the view of Jerome also, that Mark "narrated those of his deeds which he had heard his teacher preaching," but Jerome also speaks of

"Peter narrating and Mark writing," as if he thought that Peter practically dictated the Gospel to Mark. Eusebius pictures Peter as the real author of the substance of the book: "Mark indeed writes this, but it is Peter who so testifies about himself, for all we have in Mark are memoirs of the discourses of Peter." Tertullian affirms that "it may be ascribed to Peter, whose interpreter Mark was." Clement of Alexandria says that, after Peter had preached the gospel in Rome, many besought Mark to write down what Peter had spoken which he did: "When Peter became aware of it he neither eagerly hindered nor promoted it." Irenæus says that Mark wrote it apparently in Rome, after Peter had left Rome: "Even he has delivered to us in writing the things which were preached by Peter." Clement of Alexandria is quoted by Eusebius as saying that Peter was so pleased with Mark's Gospel that he "authorized the writing to be read in the churches."

Without trying to decide upon the actual facts in these various statements we can easily see that Mark wrote his Gospel under the inspiration of Peter, whether under the actual "guidance of Peter" as Origen affirms or not. The contents and character of Mark's Gospel confirm in a remarkable way the idea that Mark made shorthand rapid and vivid reports of Peter's sermons. Papias says that Mark's Gospel is accurate, but not strictly chronological. And yet both Matthew and Luke follow the broad outline of Christ's life in Mark's Gospel. There are numerous evidences of details that clearly come from

Peter and often Mark sees things through Peter's
eyes as I have tried to show in my *Studies in Mark's
Gospel*. The pictures drawn by Peter in his preaching are preserved by Mark with freshness and vivid-
ness. This reportorial aspect of the book in vernacular *Koiné* explains also the frequent use of the dramatic historical present tense in narrative and the
common imperfect in the midst of aorist tenses. Mark
sees the thing going on as Peter saw it when he told
it in his graphic sermons. It is clear that Peter's
preaching is faithfully reproduced in Mark's Gospel.
It does not follow that Mark had no other sources,
especially for the closing chapters. We must leave
undecided the question whether Peter himself ever
read Mark's Gospel or not. There is no known reason
why that could not have happened. What is true, as
has already been stated, is that Mark's Gospel has
done more to carry on and to spread over the world
the preaching of Peter about Jesus than anything
that Peter did himself. The claims of the Roman
Catholics that Peter founded the church in Rome,
became the first pope, and has transmitted his power
through the Roman Catholic hierarchy may be dismissed as legend and mere tradition. A Roman Catholic scholar, Doctor James A. Kleist, has called his
edition of Mark's Gospel *The Memoirs of St. Peter*
(1932). Something can be said for this title if we
understand that it is Mark's "memoirs" of what
Peter preached. Streeter (*The Four Gospels*, p. 63)
says: "Mark reads like the shorthand account of an
impromptu speaker, with all the repetitions, redun-

dancies and digressions which are characteristic of living speech. And it seems to me most probable that his Gospel, like Paul's Epistles, was taken down from rapid dictation by word of mouth."

CHAPTER XVII

THE INTERPRETER OF CHRIST IN TIME OF PERSECUTION
(First Epistle of Peter)

1. *Peter the Author of the Epistle.*—That is a dogmatic statement of what I regard as true. The Epistle claims to be from Peter so that it is either genuine or pseudonymous, not anonymous (I Peter 1:1). In brief the external evidence can be cited. Bigg gives II Peter 3:1 as the first direct evidence for the Petrine authorship of I Peter, which carries no weight with those who deny the genuineness of II Peter. But the so-called Epistle of Barnabas has many points of contact with I Peter in language and imagery like that of Clement of Rome. "Papias bishop of Hierapolis (*c.* 140) uses testimonies from I Peter" (Foakes-Jackson) and Polycarp (died 155) makes "actual quotations" (Bigg) from I Peter. Clement of Alexandria "quotes very freely from every chapter of the Epistle" (Bigg). Irenæus uses I Peter and "I Peter has a place in the canon of Origen, and perhaps II Peter" (Foakes-Jackson). Bigg accepts the genuineness of I Peter while Foakes-Jackson says (*Peter, Prince of Apostles,* p. 110): "Enough has been said here to show that there is no question as to the reception of I Peter at a **very** early date." And yet he adds (p. 119): "That

Peter could have written the letter is hard to believe. The author is not the Peter of the Gospels and hardly the Peter of the Acts." Foakes-Jackson finds his difficulty (p. 118) chiefly "because of the character of the persecution described as taking place in Asia at so early a date," but he adds: "Still, it must be remembered that our ignorance of what happened in the early days of Christianity is so profound, that it is impossible to declare dogmatically that nothing of the kind occurred in the apostolic period." That is more to the point. The versatility of Peter is the outstanding thing about him and the conciliating and loyal spirit of the Epistle is wholly in harmony with Peter's speeches and conduct in the Acts. It is quite gratuitous in the face of the overwhelming external evidence for the early recognition and use of I Peter to reject it in the face of our "profound" ignorance of the apostolic period. The known fact of the persecution of the Christians in Rome by Nero in A.D. 64 is supported by the numerous attacks on Paul in Asia, Macedonia, and Achaia and by the general persecutions revealed in the Apocalypse and in the correspondence between Pliny and Trajan in the second century. The most natural thing in the world was for the five Roman provinces named in I Peter 1:1 to imitate the example of Rome and persecute Christians to curry favor with Nero and Rome. The Roman provincial rulers quickly caught on to the fashion of Rome. The Epistle itself has abundant earmarks of Peter's language in the speeches in the Acts and of his hortatory style without the great argumentative and doctrinal power of Paul.

2. *The Date of the Epistle.*—If the Epistle was written by Peter, as is here assumed for the reasons already given, then it was, of course, written before his death. There is not real agreement as to the date of Peter's death. Some argue for A.D. 64 during the persecution in Rome by Nero. Others more plausibly argue for A.D. 67 or 68 before Nero's death on June 8, 68. Eusebius (*H. E.*, II:25:5) is the chief authority for the martyrdom of Peter and Paul in Rome. He wrote his *Ecclesiastical History* about A.D. 330 and quotes Tertullian of North Africa for the statement that Peter was crucified, and he adds "head downwards, while Paul was beheaded." Origen is quoted by Eusebius as saying that Peter "in the end was crucified at Rome head downward, for so he desired to die" and that "Peter appears to have preached in Pontus, Galatia, Bithynia, Cappadocia, and Asia" as is implied in I Peter 1:1. Clement of Alexandria is quoted by Eusebius as speaking of Peter's encouraging his wife as she was led to execution. The so-called Acts of Peter gives the story of Peter meeting his Lord at the gates of Rome (*Quo Vadis*). The precise year of Peter's death cannot be settled with our present knowledge, but the probability is that it was in Rome by or before A.D. 68. The Epistle was certainly written after Nero began his persecution of the Romans in A.D. 64 and also after Peter's preaching in the five Roman provinces mentioned in I Peter 1:1 which probably took

place before A.D. 64. So then I Peter was written between A.D. 64 and 68, probably 65 or 66.

3. *The Readers of the Epistle.*—The Epistle is addressed to "the elect sojourners in the dispersion in Pontus, Galatia, Cappadocia, Asia, and Bithynia." The natural inference is that Peter himself had preached in these regions. Paul had preached in the provinces of Galatia and Asia, but Peter had apparently followed him there, probably while Paul was a prisoner in Cæsarea and Rome, and had preached in the outlying regions of Pontus, Cappadocia, and Bithynia where Paul did not go, so far as we know. In a general way Peter felt that his work was to the Jews as Paul's was to the Gentiles according to the Jerusalem agreement (Gal. 2:9), but each ministered to both classes, as a matter of fact. It is clear that some of the readers of Peter's Epistles were Gentiles from 4:3 f. Apparently Peter has in mind all real followers of Christ who are "elect and sojourners" and who are scattered in the Diaspora (the Jews outside of Palestine). They are "pilgrims" on earth on the way to heaven. There are Christian communities dotted all over Asia Minor and Peter is addressing these. In James 1:1 the Diaspora probably includes only Jewish Christians, but Peter seems to use the word for all believers, whether Jews or Gentiles. Sometimes Jewish synagogues may have become Christian in a body (Bigg). In other cases the church would be half Jewish, half Gentile. Peter treats them all alike as elect and pilgrims.

4. *The Immediate Purpose of the Epistle.*—That

is plainly to strengthen and sustain the Christians
in the five regions named in verse one of chapter one
(Pontus, Galatia, Cappadocia, Asia, and Bithynia)
who were undergoing fiery trials (I Peter 1:7) and
persecutions so that it was now a crime to be known
as a Christian (I Peter 3:16). Suffering is now the lot
of the Christian who must learn how to be happy in
suffering and not to fear death for Jesus' sake (I
Peter 3:13 f.). Death matters little for those doing
good as the example of Jesus shows for us all (I Peter
3:17–22). Peter himself knew what persecution was
at the hands of the Sadducees in Jerusalem who used
the Sanhedrin to arrest, imprison, and flog the apostles. Then Herod Agrippa I did his turn. Finally the
Pharisees joined with the Sadducees in the stoning of
Stephen and a short reign of terror came under "the
fiery energy of Saul" (Bigg). Paul after his conversion met persecution from Jew and Gentile in
Galatia, Asia, Macedonia, and Greece. It was nothing new for persecution to arise in these regions, only
it was now on a large scale as a definite and general
propaganda to exterminate Christianity. Nero had
set the fashion in Rome and the provinces quickly
followed suit. The Acts and Paul's Epistles agree in
numerous allusions to the persecutions against him.
Luke does not tell us of Peter's travels in these
regions and so we are not able to check up the refer-
ences in I Peter by any statements in the Acts.
In the Epistle to the Hebrews (about A.D. 69) the
Jewish Christians are warned against apostasy and
are reminded how they took joyfully the confiscation

of their property (Heb. 10:32–34), and they were
in peril of death. "Ye have not yet resisted unto
blood" (Heb. 12:4). "The time has arrived when
Christians saw their property confiscated by law,
and when not apostles only, but everybody must
make up his mind whether he was or was not ready
to shed his blood for the Name's sake. The State has
drawn the sword" (Bigg). That was done by Nero,
and his followers. Only it is probable that matters
in the provinces had not gone to the extreme of Nero
in Rome or of Pliny in the time of Trajan. The
Christian is under suspicion and is in peril, especially
if some other charge can be produced against him.
Christians are called evil-doers (I Peter 2:12) and
suffered reproach in the name of Christ as the apostles did in Jerusalem (Acts 5:41). They were to
suffer for righteousness' sake (I Peter 3:14) as Jesus
taught (Matt. 5:10–12). Christians were to be ready
for answer to every one who challenged their hope in
Christ (I Peter 3:15) and to arm themselves with the
same mind that Jesus had who met death for us (I
Peter 4:1). The Rescript of Trajan in answer to the
appeal of Pliny for instructions gives a graver picture than is drawn in I Peter and more like that
in the Apocalypse of John. "But the reader who will
consider the Rescript of Trajan, the way in which
Tacitus speaks of the Neronian persecution (*Annals*,
XV, 44), the language of the Apocalypse and even
of the Epistle to the Hebrews, will feel that the First
Epistle of St. Peter must come in point of date before them all. At the time when it was written Baby-

lon had not yet unmasked all its terrors, and the
ordinary Christian was not in immediate danger of
the *tunica ardens,* or the red-hot iron chair, or the
wild beasts or the stake" (Bigg). But it was bad
enough when Peter wrote, for, when the Roman official authorized or winked at persecution, anything
was possible. What Peter is most concerned about is
that, if suffering has to come, the Christians shall be
guilty of no real crime like murder, robbery, or any
such evil deed (I Peter 4:15) or even of meddling in
other people's affairs (literally a bishop or preacher
spying into the affairs of others). If suffering or
persecution has to come at the hands of the state, let
it be "as a Christian" with no other charges possible.
Then one should not be ashamed, but rather glorify
God that one is counted worthy to suffer for the
Name of Christ (Acts 5:41). Some, when tested thus,
renounced the name of Christ and said *"Anathema
Iēsous"* (I Cor. 12:3), traitors to the cause of
Christ. Polycarp, when thus urged to say *Kurios
Kaisar,* each time replied *Kurios Iēsous* (I Cor.
12:3) and lost his life for his loyalty. No doubt Peter
had a pang in his own heart when he recalled his own
triple denial of knowing Jesus as Lord. But that
pang would only add fresh urgency and power to his
exhortation for loyalty to Jesus in time of persecution and trial. Such a time is on today in Russia,
and a somewhat similar situation has existed for a
long time in India, Japan, and China. It requires
courage to bear the name of Christ in these lands
that include two thirds of the population of the

earth. And it calls for courage in many circles in our own land to wear nobly the name of a disciple of Christ Jesus in spite of taunts and social ostracism. So then I Peter has a message for us all today.

5. *The Leading Ideas in I Peter.*—It may be said at once that this Epistle, like Peter's speeches in the Acts, does not exhibit the masterly argumentative grasp of the Pauline Epistles. Peter deals mainly with exhortation and yet he weaves in much doctrine and really bases his various exhortations on important doctrines. Even in the salutation (1:1 and 2), besides the Trinity, he refers to holiness or sanctification and the atonement.

The second paragraph (1:3–12) is really one long sentence connected by relative pronouns in praise of God's grace (many-colored grace, 4:10) and goodness. In this sentence he speaks of regeneration (3), the resurrection of Jesus (3), our living hope (3) which is a favorite idea (1:13, 21; 3:15), the blessed inheritance kept for us through faith in salvation ready to be revealed at the last time (4 f.). The second coming of Christ is presented as revelation (1:5, 7, 13). Peter urges joy in trials (1:6) as James had done (1:2) and speaks of many-colored trials (1:6) like James (1:2) and uses the very phrase for the proof of faith (1:7) employed by James (1:3), evidence that Peter knew the Epistle of James. Peter gives the testing of gold by fire as an illustration. In verse 8 Peter has language that reminds one of what Jesus said to Thomas about the happiness of those who believe without seeing (John

20:29), a probable reminiscence by Peter of Christ's own words. Peter makes a striking comment about the prophets who did not always perceive to what time their prophecies concerning the Messiah pointed (1:10–12), a gentle hint to those modern scholars who deny any Messianic reference in a prophecy beyond what the prophet himself understood.

The rest of the Epistle from 1:13 is exhortation, either of a general nature to an exalted life (1:13–2:10), to special classes (2:11–3:12), or to courage in the trials and persecutions which confronted believers (3:13–5:11) and a brief closing greeting in 5:12 to 14. "Wherefore" because of God's proven goodness, he urges hope in that grace for the future. The metaphor of girding up the loins of the mind (1:13) is pointed and pertinent in order to have such sustaining hope. As children of obedience they are not to fashion themselves by the lusts of their life of ignorance, but to be holy according to the command and likeness of God, who as Father is impartial (without respect of persons) in his judgments (1:14–17), and to pass the time of their pilgrimage (our word "parish") on earth in fear. In truth they were redeemed or bought by the precious blood of Christ, not by money as a slave was set free (1:18), and this by no accident, but by the eternal counsel of God who raised Jesus from the dead so that we have a sure basis for our faith and hope in God in this time of persecution. Peter, like Paul, takes the same view of Christ's death as Jesus announced himself (Mark 10:45; Matt. 20:28). Here again Peter's exhortation to hope and faith rests on God's love as shown in the atoning death of Jesus Christ.

Peter now takes up the idea of the new birth (mentioned in 1:3) and urges that, having "been begotten again" through the word of God they are to purify their souls by obedience to the truth and to love one another from the heart fervently (1:22–25). The lack of such cleansing of soul explains the absence of love from the heart. Peter carries on the idea of the purifying process under the metaphor of laying aside like old clothes (like Paul in Col. 3:8 f.) all sins, and as newborn (just born, see 1:23) babes longing for the spiritual milk without guile (un-adulterated) that they may grow thereby, a whole-some lesson for all spiritual dietitians who have tasted that the Lord is gracious and who wish more of such food (2:1–3).

The mention of the Lord Jesus gives Peter the occasion for one of his noblest passages (2:4–10) in which he pictures the kingdom of God as a spiritual house in process of building (the very verb used by Jesus to Peter of Christ's spiritual house or kingdom (Matt. 16:18 f.). The saints in the five regions are addressed (I Peter 1:1) as "living stones" (2:5) in this spiritual house, with Christ as the "living stone" (2:4), the corner-stone in Christ's own image (Mark 12:10 f.; Matt. 21:42; Luke 20:17), which the builders (the experts, the Jewish rulers) rejected, though elect and precious with God (I Peter 2:4, 6 f.; Psalms 118:22 f.). This spiritual house Peter also calls an elect race, a royal priesthood, a holy nation, a people for God's own possession, that they might proclaim the excellencies of God who brought the "no people" to be "God's people" out of darkness into his marvellous light (I Peter 2:9 f.).

Peter repeats the picture of his readers being sojourners (as in 1:17) and pilgrims (as in 1:1), a favorite metaphor and one used here to argue abstinence from the lusts of the flesh in the warfare of the soul which reminds one of Paul's bold figure in Galatians 5:16–24, of the battle line drawn between the spirit and the flesh. The enemies of the followers of Christ will be only too ready, as they inspect (old word to put the eye on, in New Testament only here and 3:2; and see II Peter 1:16) their lives, to charge them with being evil-doers (old word in John 18:30 of Christ and again in I Peter 2:14 and 4:15), if guilty; if innocent they may glorify God in the day of visitation, "an unmistakable echo of Matthew 5:16" (Bigg).

Like Paul (Rom. 13:1–7) Peter (2:13–17) is on the side of law and order and not of anarchy. He urges this "for the Lord's sake" for law is meant for the punishment of evil-doers. Peter himself refused to obey the Sanhedrin when that body stepped in between the rights of the soul and God (Acts 4:19–21), but with that exception the way to put to silence (to muzzle, like an ox, I Cor. 9:9) the ignorance of foolish men is to go on doing good, not using freedom as a cloak (or veil) for wickedness, but rejoicing to be "God's slaves" finding personal liberty in doing God's will. Verse 17 is a noble motto for every Christian: "Give honor to all men, keep on loving the brotherhood (note this word for all Christians), keep on fearing God, keep on honoring the king (or whatever ruler we may have)."

After these general exhortations Peter now addresses various special classes. The first one is the domestic servants (like Latin *domesticus* from *domus*, used by Jesus in Luke 16:13), whose Christian duties are portrayed in 2:18–25. Peter does not hesitate to use the word *despotais* ("despots") of the masters of the domestic servants. But the word has no essentially bad meaning, for it is applied to God (Luke 2:29) and to Christ (II Peter 2:1). Here Peter distinguishes between the good and gentle and the froward (the crooked). There are still both classes of masters in home and in industry as also two classes of servants and hence the present-day labor problem in home and in business. Peter employs the hard word "subjection," though he might allow for exceptions in matters of duty to God and family. He finds "grace" (vss. 19 and 20) with God if for conscience toward God one suffer wrongfully. Unlike Paul (Col. 4:1; Eph. 6:9; I Tim. 6:17–19) Peter has no direct word to the masters themselves, but he dignifies the position and privilege of employees as servants of Christ by presenting the example (copy-plate in writing) of Jesus himself for servants to follow in his steps, for he was buffeted, but he did not strike back, nor did he answer back when reviled, nor did he commit sin or deceit, but himself bore on the tree (cross) our sins, in order that renouncing sin we might live to righteousness for Christ, "by whose wound ye were healed." Many of these domestic servants had received lashes (*bruises*) from their masters and mistresses. These wandering sheep, to carry on Isaiah's image, have turned now to the shepherd and bishop of their souls (2:25) who as the good shepherd did lay down his life even for these servants (John 10:17 f.).

The wives come next (3:1–6). Curiously enough some women who resent the headship of their own husbands in the family voluntarily submit themselves to the influence of other men. Peter gives a noble motive for gentle decorous obedience on the part of wives. It is that some husbands who are disobedient to the word and will of God may be won without controversy (or talk) by beholding the pure conduct of their wives. Many a wife has pursued this plan and has finally won her husband to Christ. Peter presents as the ideal for wives, not the ornament (old use of the word, our kosmos, world) of fine clothes, but the hidden man (like Paul's use in Eph. 3:16, the inward man) of the heart. Peter surely is right in putting the emphasis on such inward graces in contrast with gaudy display of finery. He presents Sarah's obedience to Abraham as a model for young wives who may wish to adorn themselves as the holy women of old who hoped in God used to do. No such organization as the Daughters of Sarah has ever been started. Peter's message is still pertinent if one allows for various points not clearly stated.

Peter's word for husbands (3:7) is quite short, but sharp and pertinent. He urges that husbands live with their wives "according to knowledge," which certainly means with sense and wisdom. He exhorts honor for the wife as "unto the weaker vessel," not in mental gifts or in moral and spiritual quality, but in the very function of motherhood that belongs to her, "as to the female." Men, not merely husbands, should remember this when they keep their seats while women are standing in the street cars. Husband and wife are "joint-heirs of the grace of life." Peter adds a motive for such reverent respect on the part of husbands, "to the end that your prayers be not hindered." "Cut-in" is the literal meaning of the word. Some husbands may here find the explanation of some unanswered prayers. Their treatment of their wives has cut in on the line of communication with God.

Peter then has a word for all classes (3:8–12), carrying on his commands without the imperative, only adjectives and participles, that express sympathy, affection, humility, reciprocity of blessing, "not rendering evil for evil, or reviling for reviling" (like 2:23 about Christ and like Paul in I Thess. 5:15 and Romans 12:17). To support this idea about thus inheriting a blessing he quotes Psalms 33 (34): 12–16.

Peter pictures "zealots for the good" as immune to real harm, quoting Isaiah 50:9. If ye should suffer for righteousness' sake, happy are ye, even if death comes. "Sanctify Christ as Lord in your hearts." Then you will be ready always for an answer concerning the hope that is in you. This is the Christian *apologia*, to be able to put to shame revilers by a noble manner of life. Peter repeats his point of 2:15 that it is better to suffer, if that is God's will, when doing good than when doing evil. He introduces again (cf. 2:21–25) the example of Christ (3:18–22) who once for all died concerning our sins, righteous for unrighteous, put to death in the flesh, but made alive in the spirit. At this point comes the most disputed passage in the Epistle and almost in the New Testament, the preaching of Jesus to the spirits in prison. Some modern scholars cut the Gordian knot by inserting "Enoch" after *en hōi kai* (left out by similarities of letters and sound). This theory, makes Enoch, not Jesus, the preacher to the spirits in prison. Both Goodspeed and Moffatt put it so in their translations. Others take it as it is and interpret it to mean that Jesus did go after his death and preach to those now in prison (or hell) to whom Noah preached before the flood came. That is a possible meaning of the passage, though one wonders why Jesus preached only to this group. Some argue from this interpretation for a second chance in the other world for all lost souls, what is called the larger hope. But there is only precarious scriptural exegesis for this hope. Others take it to mean that in spirit during the time of Noah Jesus preached to the people of Noah's time who are now spirits in prison. One element of uncertainty about any certain exegesis of the passage is Peter's reminiscential and incidental way of going off at a word.

Here at the word "spirit" he turns to what Jesus did in spirit, in verse 21 the relative "which" refers back to "water" in which Noah's family were saved. Then at once Peter turns to *baptism* in his time, an antitype not actual cleansing, but an appeal of a good conscience to God. Clearly Peter is not a sacramentalist, whatever may be his meaning about the preaching of Christ in spirit to the spirits now in prison.

Peter is not done about bodily suffering. It "is grace with God" (2:20) and better if we are doing good by making ourselves cease from sin (4:1). It all depends on how one looks at his sufferings. So Peter once more introduces the example of Jesus (4:1–6) and urges his readers: "Arm ye yourselves with the same mind." The best spiritual weapon in times of persecution is this clear confidence in God such as Jesus showed always. He uses a military metaphor of spiritual weapons that reminds us of Paul's great passage in Ephesians 6:10–20 about "the panoply of God" which we are to put on in order to stand against the wiles of the devil. So here Peter reminds his readers that they should live the remainder of their lives doing the will of God. Surely the time past is enough to have wrought the will of the Gentiles in all manner of nameless sins. Now they have to endure the mockery and sneers of their former companions in vice who will have to render an account to God who judges the quick and the dead. The words of Peter here have pith and point for all young Christians who break away, as they should, from evil habits of worldly friends.

Peter suddenly says (4:7) that "the end of all things is at hand." He has alluded to the last time (1:5), to the revelation of Christ (1:7, 13), and to God as Judge (1:17; 4:5 f.). He does not say how near the end is nor does he pretend to know (cf. II Peter 3:8). The main thing is to be ready for Christ's coming and to hasten it by pious living (II Peter 3:11 f.). So Peter here (4:7–11) urges watchfulness and love for one another, for love covers a multitude of sins like a veil thrown over the sins of others (cf. James 5:20). He urges hospitality, a sorely needed grace in those days without decent hotels, and that each shall exercise his special gift as a steward of God's many-colored grace, a beautiful phrase that reminds one of Paul's discussion of the varied gifts of the spirit in 1 Corinthians 12. The phrase "the oracles of God" is interesting. "The Christian's talk is to be modelled on the Bible" (Bigg). In Romans 3:2 and Hebrews 5:12 "the oracles" means the Hebrew Bible while in Acts 7:38 Stephen uses the phrase in reference to the Ten Commandments. But God supplies each gift and the strength for it through Jesus Christ to whom be the glory and the power for ages of ages (a beautiful doxology to Jesus just as to God).

Peter now (4:12–19) warns his readers not to count it strange (the same word used in 4:4 about their former evil companions who think it strange, when they no longer run with them) because of the burning (picture of the refiner's fire in testing metals, as in Prov. 27:21, and already in I Peter 1:7) which is coming upon them for testing (as in 1:7), "as though a strange thing was happening to you." Peter pleads that they regard persecution and sufferings as a perfectly normal thing in the life of a follower of Christ. By this means we become partners or partakers in the sufferings of Christ, a thing to cause joy now and still more at the revelation of his glory (4:13). Like James (1:2) Peter felicitates any one for any reproach in the name of Christ as a Christian, only not as a murderer, a thief, an evil-doer, or as a busy-body or meddler in other people's affairs (4:14–16). It is useless to pose as a persecuted saint if one has been guilty of such sins and crimes. We have no right to complain of keen criticism by the worldly, for it is time for judgment from God to begin from the house of God. But it will not end there, for the wicked cannot escape God's judgment in the end. Meanwhile those that suffer according to the will of God should present their souls to our faithful Creator in well-doing.

Peter has a fine word for elders (5:1–4) and calls himself a fellow-elder instead of apostle (1:1) as John calls himself elder in II and III John. There is no feeling here of superiority on Peter's part, but rather of genuine fellowship with other ministers who like him are to be witnesses (Acts 1:8) for Christ, in Peter's case of the actual sufferings of Christ with the hope of being also a sharer in the coming glory of Christ. Peter's exhortation to the preachers is: "Shepherd the flock of God among you," using the very word that Jesus had used to him by

the Sea of Galilee (John 21:16). He undoubtedly has
that incident in mind and adds some items growing
out of his own rich experience. They are to do the
shepherding not from compulsion, but gladly; not
for shameful gain, but readily; not as lording it over
the heritage (clearly Peter was no pope), but becoming models (types) for the flock, for the sheep
usually follow the shepherd (good or bad). From
the Chief Shepherd ye will receive the unfading crown
of glory when he comes. Surely Peter has learned
how to strengthen his brethren now that he has really
turned back to the Master (Luke 22:32).

Peter inserts a timely word (5:5) to younger men
in correspondence to the original meaning of *pres-
buteroi* (5:1) as older men, not as mere officials (cf.
our aldermen). The word is submission to elder men
as normally possessing wisdom and leadership like
that once supposed to belong to the Elder Statesmen
of Japan. It is not always true, but it is a reflection
on age when it does not bring wisdom and it robs
youth of what it is entitled to from age. When youth
has to provide wisdom as well as energy and enthusiasm against the follies of old men, as sometimes happens, it is sad indeed.

But Peter has a word for all classes, and it is
humility (5:5–10), a grace that Peter did not once
possess, one that he had to learn by bitter experience, but that he has learned at last. His first command is: "Gird yourselves with humility" (a rare
word, gird, here only in the New Testament, to tie
a knot as of a girdle or apron). Beyond a doubt

Peter is thinking of the night when Jesus arose from the passover meal at which the apostles had been wrangling over the post of honor, took a basin and a towel, and came to Peter to wash his feet over Peter's protest, giving him and the rest an example in humility that has borne fruit in Peter's life (John 13:1–20). He quotes Proverbs 3:34 and repeats the exhortation to humility under God's mighty hand, a timely and comforting word in the time of persecution. Peter calls the devil a roaring lion (5:8) as John terms Jesus the Lion of the tribe of Judah (Rev. 5:5), the Lion that is also a Lamb slain and victorious. But the only thing to do with the devil as a lion is to resist him and to take our share of sufferings that come for a little while, for triumph comes in the end, victory with Christ.

It is possible that Silvanus (Silas, Paul's friend) is both the amanuensis and bearer of this Epistle (5:12). Peter states that the purpose of the Epistle is to show that this (truth expounded by him) is the true grace of God. Mark is with Peter in Babylon (either literal or Rome as is likely). Who "the co-elect lady in Babylon" is we do not know. The natural meaning is that she is Peter's wife (I Cor. 9:5) as Bigg holds, although it remains possible that the church in Rome is thus referred to. It is also possible that the Elect Lady in II John 1, 13 means church, though here again the reference may be to an actual woman. Certainly Peter's wife was a woman of prominence enough to justify this veiled allusion to her as is shown by her martyrdom.

At any rate, whatever is true about this matter, there is no doubt to persecuted saints then and now about the clearness and courage of Peter. The whole Epistle is an exposition and an application of the words of Jesus in the Beatitudes (Matt. 5:10–12) as illuminated by Peter's own experience and that of multitudes of the followers of Christ.

CHAPTER XVIII

THE TRUE CHRISTIAN SCIENCE
(Second Epistle of Peter)

1. *The Claim to Authorship.*—The writer claims
to be "Simon (some manuscripts Symeon, the Aramaic form as by James in Acts 15:14) Peter" (as
in I Peter 1:1) and so more precise than in I Peter.
This fact has, forsooth, been used against the genuineness on the ground that the writer is too anxious
to prove that he is Simon Peter. But, if he had not
claimed to be Peter, that would have been used
against the Petrine authorship. As in I Peter 1:1
Peter asserts that he is an "apostle of Jesus Christ"
and he adds "slave" (*doulos*) also as Paul does
(Romans 1:1) and James also (1:1). The Epistle
therefore is either genuine or pseudonymous, not
anonymous like Luke's Gospel, the Acts, I John.
There are those who take it to be a "pious fraud"
and yet worthy to be in the New Testament. For
myself I could not so treat it if I were convinced
that it was not written by Simon Peter. The ele-
vated spiritual tone of the Epistle is one thing to
be considered in connection with the writer's claim.
The book is far and away above the pseudonymous
books that bear the name of Peter like the Gospel
of Peter, the Acts of Peter, the Apocalypse of
Peter. "Yet the fact that they (Jude and II Peter)
were received by the church makes them of impor-

tance, especially in view of the rejection of writings under the name of Peter—writings which the church rejected despite their popularity" (Foakes-Jackson). In addition the writer narrates personal experiences of Peter as his own, in particular the Transfiguration of Christ (1:16–18; Mark 9:2–8), and the plain words of Jesus about Peter's death (1:14; John 21:18 f.).

2. *The Direct Reference to the First Epistle.*— In II Peter 3:1 the writer says: "This now, beloved, a second epistle I am writing unto you." The natural and obvious allusion is to the First Epistle which we possess. This reference is again turned against its genuineness as being a thing that Peter would not do, though Paul did that very thing (I Cor. 5:9) to an epistle not preserved to us. To be sure, I Peter can be genuine and II Peter spurious, but II Peter is not spurious because of this allusion to I Peter.

3. *The Readers.*—They are, of course, the same as those of I Peter—"the elect sojourners of the dispersion in Pontus, Galatia, Cappadocia, Asia, and Bithynia." It is therefore a general Epistle, like I Peter and like Galatians (to the churches in Galatia), and not just to one particular church. Spitta and Zahn object that the readers are not the same because the two Epistles do not treat the same topics, surely a feeble objection. In both of these Epistles (*en hais,* plural relative in II Peter 3:1) Peter says "I stir up your pure mind by putting you in remembrance, to recall the words spoken beforehand by the holy prophets and the command of

the Lord and Saviour through your apostles" (II Peter 3:2). Peter seems to allude to his own preaching in these regions and he puts the preaching of the apostles on a par with the words of the holy prophets and calls the messages "by your apostles" as really "the command of the Lord and Saviour." This is what Peter claimed and what Jesus promised would be true. And yet here again it is gravely argued that Peter as an apostle would not so include himself in the group of "your apostles." But Paul, who certainly claimed to be an apostle on a par with the twelve apostles, speaks of strangers and pilgrims, fellow-citizens with the saints and members of the family of God, as "built upon the foundation of the apostles and prophets, Christ Jesus himself being the chief corner-stone" (Eph. 2:19 f.), the very same reference as that here by Peter, only Peter names "prophets" before "apostles" and is not using the metaphor of a building as Paul does. Jude (17) has almost Peter's very words save that he speaks only of "apostles" and not of "prophets."

4. *The Relation of the Epistle to That by Jude.* —There is an undoubted connection of some kind. Scholars are very much divided whether Peter makes use of Jude or Jude is familiar with II Peter 2. Some, like Kühl, argue that the second chapter of II Peter is an interpolation, "always a last and desperate expedient" (Bigg). There is a general parallelism in contents between Jude and II Peter 2, though in Jude there is no mention of Cain, Lot, Balaam, Korah, and Jude quotes Enoch by name.

Peter and Jude may have had some other common source or one may have used the other. There is no way of reaching a clear decision. My own feeling is that Jude, as the briefer and fresher Epistle, comes just before II Peter, but that is a matter of feeling, not of proof. This use of Jude by Peter cannot be used against the genuineness of II Peter.

5. *The Reference to Paul's Epistles.*—This reference is in II Peter 3:15 and 16. The objections are mainly two. One is that Peter, after Paul's treatment of him at Antioch when Paul virtually called him a hypocrite to his face (Gal. 2:11–14), would never have spoken of Paul as "our beloved brother Paul" as the writer does here (3:15). That objection overlooks one of the finest traits in Peter's character, his elasticity and willingness to forgive. Some men might and would cherish resentment in such a case, but not Peter. The other objection lies in the implication that Paul's Epistles are on the same plane "as the other scriptures" (3:16). It is urged that such language is an anachronism in the first century A.D. and is only possible in the second. But here again two things are overlooked. One is that Paul's Epistles in the earliest manuscripts and translations form a separate collection and this custom began very early, how early we do not know. There is absolutely nothing to show that it was impossible or improbable by A.D. 67. We do know that at the very start Paul calls attention to his signature as proof of genuineness in each Epistle (II Thess. 3:17; Col. 4:18) and that attempts were

made to palm off Epistles as Paul's that were not
genuine (II Thess. 2:2). We know also that Paul's
Epistles were sometimes copied and passed from
church to church as Paul urges in the case of Colos-
sæ and Laodicea (Col. 4:16). The other thing is the
importance that Paul attached to his Epistles (I
Thess. 4:15; II Thess. 3:11 f.; I Cor. 7:25, 40).
Peter simply accepts Paul's Epistles as having the
Spirit of God in them like the Old Testament in
spite of the difficulties in them which some men twist
as is done today. There is no evidence here that
Peter has in mind a New Testament canon which
came much later, but he does recognize thus early
that the wisdom given to Paul was of God. There is
no known reason why Peter could not have written
thus about Paul's Epistles.

6. *The Difference in Language Compared with
That in I Peter.*—Here is a more serious obstacle
for there is a real basis of fact both in the vocabulary and in the style. As to the vocabulary I Peter
has some 361 words not in II Peter, while II Peter
has 231 words not in I Peter. I Peter is also longer
than II Peter. In the New Testament there are 686
hapax legomena and 54 of them are in II Peter
alone with only 3 chapters. I Peter has more quotations from the Old Testament while II Peter has
frequent allusions to the Old Testament words and
phrases. And yet there are similarities of various
kinds. Both have a dignity of style and a tendency
to iambic rhythm. Both have frequent repetition of
words and both show apparent acquaintance with

the Old Testament Apocrypha. The idiomatic use and non-use of the Greek article is common to both as is the sparing use of Greek particles while both show a fondness for the plural of abstract substantives. It is argued from these facts by some that the only explanation is difference of authorship, though some scholars deny the Petrine authorship of both Epistles. Different men do show differences of style, but the same man reveals variety of style in treating different subjects and at different stages of his life. But there is another quite plausible explanation of the difference here, one that applies to Paul's Epistles and to the Johannine writings also, and that is the use of different amanuenses. Apparently Silvanus (Silas) is the amanuensis as well as the bearer of I Peter according to 5:12. We have no intimation as to the amanuensis used by Peter in II Peter if he used any. There is a certain oratorical rotundity in II Peter with some unusual idioms that may be marks of Peter's own style without an amanuensis. The explanation may be like the difference between John's Gospel (21:24 "we know") and the Apocalypse (alone on Patmos). We know that both men had been fishermen and without the culture of the schools (Acts 4:13). The fact that Peter used John Mark so much as "interpreter" shows that he felt more at home in the Aramaic than in the *Koiné*. We know also that even his Galilean Aramaic pronunciation had a provincial accent. II Peter may, in fact, give us more of Peter's actual style than I Peter.

7. *The Date.*—This question is linked with the authorship. If Peter wrote it, he wrote it before he died and so before A.D. 68 at the latest. If the Epistle is not genuine, there is no way to decide the date, though there are indications of its use by Clement of Rome, Ignatius, Aristides, Justin Martyr, Irenæus. Clement of Alexandria accepted it and apparently wrote a commentary on it. Origen was disposed to accept it, though Eusebius put it among the disputed books. It was accepted in the canon by the council at Laodicea (372) and at Carthage (397). Jerome put it in the Latin Vulgate, though the Peshito Syriac did not have it. Bigg in the *International Critical Commentary* accepts it as the work of Peter, though it is rejected by F. H. Chase and J. B. Mayor. It is the most disputed book in the New Testament, though to my mind the balance of probability is in its favor and for a date not later than A.D. 67.

8. *The Purpose Is Loyalty to Christ in the Midst of Heresy.*—Peter desires to remind the readers in the five regions in Asia Minor (I Peter 1:1) of the words of the apostles of Christ, since they already know that scoffers are coming who will ridicule the promises of Christ's coming back again (II Peter 3:3 f.). Paul had warned the elders of Ephesus at Miletus of wolves that would ravish the sheep (Acts 20:29 f.) as he did also vigorously in Colossians, Ephesians, and the Pastoral Epistles, as John did in his Epistles, and as Jude did in his short Epistle. These Gnostics boasted of a superior knowledge

(*gnōsis*) of Christ and Christianity with mystic initiatory rites, kin to those in the worship of Cybele,
Isis, Mithra, etc. By the second century these mys-
tery-cults or religions challenged Christianity on a
wide scale.* Already in the middle of the first century inroads have been made in Asia Minor by these
cults and the exponents are seeking to absorb Christianity in their various systems. As Paul in Colossians and John in his First Epistle, so here Peter
pleads, not for ignorance or obscurantism, but for
more knowledge, for real (additional) knowledge as
the answer to these conceited champions of secret
and occult practices. Peter urges "full knowledge"
of Christ (in 1:2, 3, 8; 2:20). He puts "knowledge"
in his temple or pillar of graces (1:5 f.) and makes
knowledge of Jesus Christ the goal of our growth
in grace (3:18). So here (3:3) he appeals to their
knowledge of the teachings of Christ by the apostles
as the bulwark against these perverters of truth who
are in reality "ignorant" (2:12) as Paul also affirms
of them (I Tim. 1:7 "not knowing either what they
say or whereof they confidently affirm"), though they
call themselves Gnostics (the knowing ones). So I
call the Second Epistle of Peter the True Christian
Science (knowledge) in contrast with the false so-
called Christian Science of the Gnostics and of Mrs.
Eddy whose "Christian Science" is neither "science"
(knowledge) nor Christian. It is true neither in sci-

* See H. A. A. Kennedy, *St. Paul and the Mystery-Religions*,
1913; S. Angus, *The Mystery-Religions and Christianity*, 1925;
S. Angus, *The Religious Quests of the Græco-Roman World*,
1929.

ence nor religion. People were deceived by the Gnostics as some are deceived now by the plausible platitudes and inanities of Mrs. Eddy. This description of II Peter will be made good by the brief exposition that is to follow.

9. *Leading Ideas in II Peter.*—There is no separate greeting apart from the rest of the Epistle, for the prayer about grace and peace being multiplied (as in I Peter 1:2) is not a separate sentence here, but part of a long sentence in verses 1 to 4. But Peter is addressing Christians whom he terms "those who have obtained a like precious faith with us." The adjective here can mean either equal in value or equal in honor because of the twofold use of honor or price. Either idea makes good sense here and one may recall I Peter 2:7 and II Peter 1:4. The point is that the faith of the readers has precisely the same worth and honor as that of Peter. The "righteousness" here is not that of Peter or of the readers of the letter, but that "of our God and Saviour Jesus Christ," for so it has to be translated with the one article, precisely as in II Peter 1:11 we have "of our Lord and Saviour Jesus Christ" where the same idiom occurs. The insertion of "the" in the American Standard Version before "Saviour Jesus Christ" in 1:1 is wrong from the standpoint of grammar and is pure ungrammatical Unitarianism.* Peter

---

* See A. T. Robertson, *Grammar of the Greek N. T. in the Light of Historical Research,* 5th ed., p. 786. Even Schmiedel (Winer-Schmiedel, *Grammatik,* p. 158) says "Grammar demands that one person be meant." See precisely the same idiom in 2:20; 3:18; and Titus 2:13.

prays for the multiplication of grace and peace "in the full knowledge of God and of Jesus our Lord." The manuscripts here vary greatly, possibly the short reading, "of our Lord," being the original, and the longer ones variations. There are two articles here in the text, but even so it is possible for only one person (Jesus) to be meant. At any rate "the full knowledge" of God and Christ (or of Jesus our Lord and God) is insisted on at the very start as the answer to the pretensions of the Gnostic heretics. The antidote is more knowledge of Christ, not less. The whole of Chapter 1 is an exhortation to greater knowledge of Christ. In Chapter 2 Peter gives a vivid picture of these Gnostic heretics very much like that in Jude's Epistle. In Chapter 3 he has a practical and timely discussion of the promise of Christ's second coming which is applicable to our cwn time.

Peter goes on in verses 3 and 4 of Chapter 1 with the exhortation to full knowledge of Christ by using the genitive absolute construction the perfect middle participle, "seeing that his divine power hath granted." Hence he is able to bestow on us "all things for life and godliness." Once again Peter uses full knowledge which comes through Christ who called us as he had done Peter. He does it through the glory and virtue which belong to his divine nature, through which (his glory and virtue) he has granted us "the precious and very great promises" for which word see 3:13. Christ's purpose, Peter adds, is "that ye may become partakers of the divine

nature." Note Peter's use of "become." It is not the
Stoic doctrine that all men are so, but that by the
new birth men may become so. We are all children
of God in one sense, but in the spiritual sense here
meant only those who are partners in the divine nature by the work of the Holy Spirit (II Cor. 13:14;
Phil 2:1). "Having escaped," Peter explains, not "by
escaping," the corruption in the world.

In verses 5 to 11 Peter gives a list of graces or
virtues like those in James 1:3; I Thessalonians
1:3; II Thessalonians 1:3 f.; Galatians 5:22 f.;
Romans 5:3 f.; 8:29 f. Peter links these together
with the preposition "in" like a string of pearls or
"on" like a pillar or tower. Somewhat analogous to
the Stoic "progress" (Bigg). The point of this paragraph is to urge that the readers do their part or
share in this growth in divine likeness "for this very
reason," referring to the gift from Jesus Christ just
mentioned (vss. 3 and 4). He urges that they bring
in alongside, because of what Christ has done, use
"all diligence" or eager haste and so supply the list
of virtues which he names as their part in the divine
program for growth in Christ likeness. Faith comes
first in Peter's list of graces to be supplied by his
readers as with Paul (Eph. 2:8) and on faith rests
virtue or moral energy, "right conduct under discipline" (Bigg). On virtue rests knowledge or understanding skill (John 15:15; I Cor. 16:18). On
knowledge rests self-control or holding oneself in
(Gal. 5:23), a self-mastery the very opposite of the
modern self-expression (psychoanalysis or opposi-

tion to inhibitions) or the covetousness of the heretics. On self-control rests patience or endurance
without murmuring (James 1:3). On patience rests
godliness or godlikeness connected with life in verse
3. On godliness rests brotherly love or love of one's
brothers (the brotherhood in Christ) as in I Peter
1:22. On brotherly love as the capstone or climax
rests love unmeasured as in I Peter 1:8, love for
Christ and for all men, the greatest of all as Paul
has it (I Cor. 13:13). It is a beautiful picture, as
Peter draws it, but he adds another touch, for that
grace must not simply exist, but must abound or
overflow in order to render us fruitful for the full
knowledge of our Lord Jesus Christ. Peter now adds
a vivid warning that without them one is near-sighted
and blinks one's eyes and turns away from the Light
of the World and forgets the cleansing of one's sins
of the long ago. Hence Peter renews (verse 10) his
exhortation to diligence (1:5) "to make your calling and election sure." Peter believes in election as
God's part, but he insists on diligence as our part.
Thus we shall not fail and shall have a rich entrance
into the eternal kingdom of our Lord and Saviour
Jesus Christ (1:11).

In verses 12 to 18 we have some of Peter's personal experiences told in vivid fashion. He is always
ready to do his part to remind his readers about
these things, though they are well-established in the
truth (doctrinal and moral). So he considers it right,
his duty in fact, to keep on stirring them up by
way of remembrance so long as he is in this taber-

nacle, earliest metaphorical use of the word though
Paul has a like word in this sense (II Cor. 5:1, 4),
kin to the common word used by Peter on the Mount
of Transfiguration (Mark 9:5). Peter makes an
allusion to his death under the metaphor of laying
aside the tabernacle with direct allusion to Christ's
words to him by the Sea of Galilee (John 21:18 f.),
which he knew by personal experience before John
wrote them down. Once Peter had boasted to Jesus
of his willingness to die for him (Mark 14:31; John
13:37), but now he makes humble reference to
Christ's words and he knows that it will be soon. So
he faces it calmly and plans to make preparation
for them to have a reminder of all these things after
his departure or "exodus" (the very word used by
Luke in 9:31 as the subject of the talk between
Jesus and Moses and Elijah). It is even possible that
Peter is thinking of the Gospel of Mark, already
written, as one of the means by which this purpose
would be realized. At any rate Peter wishes his readers to know that he did not follow in his teaching
and preaching "cunningly devised fables," myths al-
legorized with all sorts of far-fetched interpretations like the Gnostics and other heretics. But Peter
spoke as "eye-witnesses (literary plural, old word
like I Peter 2:12; 3:2, used of the initiates into
Eleusinian mysteries) of his majesty" (*megaleiotē-
tos*, late and rare word), in Luke 9:43, of the greatness and grandeur of Jesus on the Mount of Transfiguration. Peter is a witness from personal knowledge (cf. Luke 1:2). So he dares to speak of the

voice borne to Christ on the Mount "by the Majestic Glory." The words quoted by Peter are the same as those in Matthew 17:5 except in different order and the use of different prepositions. Mark (9:7) and Luke (9:35) add "Hear." Peter could very well have seen these Gospels, though he did not need any written report, for he was there himself, as he insists "when we were with him in the holy mount" (1:18).

In verses 19 to 21 Peter speaks of the word of prophecy about Christ (I Peter 1:10) made "more sure" by the voice of God on the Mount of Transfiguration. So Peter urges that his readers give heed to this prophetic word thus made more sure "as unto a lamp shining in a dark place" (dark murky place, here only in N. T.) "until the day dawn and the day-star arise in your hearts." This is a beautiful picture of prophecy like stars pointing the way through the night till the Sun of Righteousness rises in their hearts and it is daylight forevermore. Peter says that they know the origin and source of prophecy of scripture in a passage (vss. 20 and 21) that is usually misunderstood and misapplied by the words "of private interpretation." Alford rightly insisted that *ginetai* here does not mean "is" (*estin*), as it never does in fact in spite of what Bigg says, and despite frequent mistranslations of *ginomai* as being the same as *eimi*. The difference is clearly shown in the use of *ēn* (was) in John 1:1 and *egeneto* (became) in John 1:14, both of the Logos. As Alford insists, *ginetai* here followed by the ablative

case *epiluseōs* means "comes from, springs out of."
This is made certain by verse 21 which explains
(*gar*, for) the meaning of verse 20: "For no prophecy was ever brought by the will of man, but men,
moved by the Holy Spirit, spoke from God." That
is to say, prophecy has divine, not human origin. So
then verse 20 means: "Knowing that no prophecy
of scripture ever comes from one's own disclosure."
One does not pump up a prophecy of himself. *Epi-
lusis* occurs only here in the New Testament, but
the verb *epiluō* to unloose, to untie, occurs in Mark
4:34, where it can mean that Jesus disclosed parables to the disciples, and in Acts 19:39 where it
means to decide. It is the misinterpretation of verse
19 (private interpretation) that the Roman Catholics use to prove the peril of an ordinary man reading the scriptures without a priest to tell him what
it means. But the passage is not about interpretation of prophecy, but about the source of prophecy.

Chapter 2 is the portion of II Peter that is so
much like the Epistle of Jude in its vivid portrayal
and denunciation of the Gnostic heretics. He begins
with the statement that there arose false prophets
among the Jewish people in bold contrast to the true
prophets of God just described in 1:19–21. He will
resume discussion of the old days in verse 4, but he
first portrays the false teachers (a late compound,
here alone in the N. T.). Here (vss. 1–3) Peter uses
future tenses of them, but in 15 the aorist (wandered astray), and in 17 the present tense (are).
Clearly some of them were already on hand playing

havoc in the churches in these five regions. The picture at first is like that drawn by Paul of the Judaizers in the Jerusalem conference, "the privily brought in false brethren" in Galatians 2:4. These false teachers "will privily bring in heresies of destruction," language that shows how gravely Peter regarded their dangerous teaching, "denying even the Master that bought them." Paul took this same view of the Gnostics who depreciated Christ to the rank of one of their *œons* as we see in Colossians where he exalts Christ as equal with God (Col. 1:15–19; 2:9). Perhaps Peter recalls by his use of this language his own denial of Christ. The worst of it is that many will follow these false teachers in their teachings and in their lascivious doings so that the way of truth will be blasphemed. With forged words in their covetousness they will make merchandise of their dupes. That was true in Peter's day and it is true in ours in the east and in the west. Gullible people easily fall victims to these charlatans in religion and in medicine. The only hope is that God's judgment does not linger and destruction does not slumber for such quacks.

Peter has a long conditional sentence of the first class (assumed as true) in verses 4 to 8 with the aorist tenses, and the conclusion in verses 9 to 11. The argument is that, if God did not spare angels when they sinned (but handed them over to punishment), and did not spare the ancient world of Noah's time (though he did spare Noah), and did condemn Sodom and Gomorrah (though he rescued

Lot), the Lord knows how (9 to 11) to rescue the godly and to punish the unrighteous. God himself is Peter's ground of confidence in the midst of conditions in his day. He is our hope today. The God of all the earth will do right. There is a like argument in Romans 11:21 in briefer form which should be compared with this. Peter uses a rare word for casting into hell, here alone save a scholion on Homer, though *tartaros* is in Homer, Pindar, Job, Philo, inscriptions as the abode of the wicked dead. In Enoch 20:2 it is the abode of the fallen angels. Noah is called a preacher of righteousness and Lot righteous. The word for turning into ashes occurs in Dio Cassius of an eruption of Vesuvius. Lot vexed his soul by the sins of Sodom, but he lived on there till God drove him out. Peter really begins his description of these false teachers in verse 10 and resumes it in verse 12. Here they are called unrighteous men who walk after the flesh and despise the lordship of Christ. Hence they are daring, self-willed, tremble not to rail at dignities, a thing that angels do not do. This tone of superiority (the superiority complex) is characteristic of such conceited charlatans.

From verses 12 to 22 Peter piles up epithets upon epithets in his description of "these men," these false teachers (vs. 1). We need only touch upon the main ones. They are as "creatures without reason," senseless animals, "railing in matters whereof they are ignorant," a common failing of such pretentious wiseacres. They are "spots and blemishes revelling."

These "religious" teachers "have eyes full of adultery and cannot cease from sin, enticing unsteadfast souls." How modern all this portrait seems. They wandered after the way of Balaam who loved the hire of unrighteousness, who was even rebuked by a dumb ass. These men are springs without water, mists driven by a storm. With great swelling words they entice to lasciviousness those trying to escape from sin. They promise liberty while themselves the slaves of corruption. For, Peter explains, by what a man is overcome by the same is he enslaved (2:19), a saying illustrated today by the victims of drink, lust, gambling, dope. Alas, says Peter, for those who, having once known (*en epignōsei*) our Lord and Saviour Jesus Christ, are entangled (as in a web or noose, II Tim. 2:4) again in such sins and overcome (2:20). With solemn impressiveness Peter adds: "For it were better not to have known the way of righteousness, than, after knowing it, to turn back from the holy commandment delivered unto them" (2:21). He illustrates this truth by two proverbs (wayside sayings) about the dog returning to his vomit and the sow to wallowing in the mire. Peter knows human life and that warning by him is pertinent. He himself sinned, but came back to his Lord. But Peter does not wish his readers to run that risk with the heinous teaching and lives of the Gnostics before them.

In Chapter 3 he discusses chiefly the problem of the second coming of Christ. The reference to a First Epistle by Peter in 3:1 is naturally taken to be our

I Peter, though some scholars imagine it to be a lost epistle, a wholly gratuitous idea. The stirring up by way of remembrance is the same language used in II Peter 1:13 and here applied to both Epistles as his purpose, the same idea of exhorting and testifying occurring also in I Peter 5:12. The word here for "sincere" or "pure" is used by Plato for ethical purity and in the New Testament only here and in Philippians 1:10. The purpose in this stirring up in the two Epistles is to bring to their remembrance the words spoken before by the holy prophets and also the command of the Lord and Saviour by (*hupo* not repeated, but probably understood from the use with *prophētōn*) your apostles. This last reference includes Peter also as Paul probably included himself in the foundation of the apostles and prophets in Ephesians 2:20. The phrase "knowing this first" occurs in II Peter 1:20. Peter makes a prophecy of his own about these mockers, a good example of Peter's play on words (used of the play of children in Isaiah 3:4, then of ridicule as in Luke 14:29). When these last days will be Peter does not indicate (cf. Jude 18; James 5:3; I Peter 1:20). In Hebrews 1:2 the phrase is used for the New Testament dispensation in contrast with the old. Peter affirms that these mockers were already asking in ridicule of Christ's promise to return: "Where is the promise of his coming?" (3:4). This is precisely the objection made today against the personal return of Jesus that he has not yet done so, though nineteen hundred years have gone by since his ascension to heaven.

Jesus had made this promise of his Parousia (Matt. 24:3). Already scoffers were scoffing though only one short generation (less than forty years) had passed by. Peter accuses these scoffers of willing ignorance ("for this escapes them being willing"), as often happens, of the fact that, as God once destroyed the world by flood, so he can destroy it again by fire (3:5–7). God holds the universe in the hollow of his hand. He created it by his word and he can destroy it in the same way. Clearly Peter does not believe in the eternity of matter as Plato taught it and as some nineteenth-century materialists held. But the main point in Peter's reply is in verses 8 and 9 in his exhortation: "But forget not this one thing." (But let not this one thing escape you.) What is "this one thing"? It is found in a quotation from Psalms 89 (90):4, "That one day is with the Lord as a thousand years, and a thousand years as one day." God's clock is not like men's and he runs the universe by his own clock. This item is one that men easily forget. Hence men are wide of the mark who accuse God of being slack in fulfilling his promise about Christ's second coming. By God's clock it may still be not yet two days (a thousand years as one day). Peter's point here applies also to a literal interpretation of the thousand years in Revelation 20:4–6. It may be only a day or each day may be a thousand years. Dogmatism is ruled out by this view of the symbolism. The essential truth is that Christ is coming again in God's own time who is patient with men that all may come to a change of life. But the day of the

Lord will come as a thief comes (vs. 10), the very
metaphor used by Jesus in Peter's hearing (Luke
12:39; Matt. 24:43), also by Paul (I Thess. 5:2),
and later by John (Rev. 3:3 of Jesus; 16:15). This
day of judgment will be the time when the heavens
shall pass away with a great noise, the elements melt
with burning heat, and the earth be burned up. Some
scientists forecast such an end to the earth by col-
lision with a star. But Peter's appeal is intensely
practical. In view of the sudden and final dissolution
of earthly things we ought to lead holy and godly
lives (3:11), "looking for and hastening the coming
of the day of God." This we can do by pious living,
not by charts for God to run the world with. Peter
holds out the promise of "new heavens and a new
earth wherein dwelleth righteousness" (3:13). The
promise rests on Isaiah 65:17 f. and 66:22. It is
repeated in Revelation 21:1. This blessed hope will
be realized in heaven at last and some even hope that
this earth will become the future heaven of the righteous. But at present righteousness is not generally
"at home" in this present earth in individuals, families, or nations.

Peter renews his exhortation to holy living that
they may be found in peace when Christ comes and
to account the Lord's long-suffering as salvation with
an affectionate allusion to Paul's Epistles in which
he also deals with disorders growing out of miscon-
ceptions concerning the second coming of Christ as
in I Thessalonians 4:13–18; II Thessalonians 2:1–
12; I Corinthians 15. Peter's praise of Paul in spite

of Galatians 2:11–14 has been sufficiently discussed in this chapter. Peter admits difficulties in Paul's Epistles which are hard to understand. The Thessalonians misunderstood Paul's preaching about the second coming and Hymenæus and Philetus did so about the resurrection (2 Tim. 2:17) as men had done with the Old Testament and do yet, as they "twist" God's Word to their own destruction. God's Word is a live thing and dangerous to tamper with for it searches one's inward soul (Heb. 4:12 f.). He ranks Paul's Epistles with the Old Testament Scripture.

Peter's final word is that, with all this knowledge beforehand, they may not be carried away by the error of these Gnostics and so fall from their own steadfastness. The rather they should keep on growing in grace and in the knowledge of our Lord and Saviour Jesus Christ. There is no limit to one's growth, for Christ is too wonderful and too high for us to exhaust in a lifetime or in eternity. With Peter, as with Paul (Phil. 3:8–14), his major passion is precisely this pursuit of the knowledge of Jesus Christ, still "the most excellent of the sciences." "To him be the glory both now and forever. Amen."

CHAPTER XIX

PETER'S CONNECTION WITH ROME
(I Peter 5:13)

1. *Prejudiced Problem.*—The question of Peter's presence or death in Rome is linked in most minds with the assumptions of the Roman Catholics that Peter was the founder of the church in Rome and was the first pope of Rome followed by an unbroken line of popes who have thus carried on through the ages the exclusive power of the keys committed by Jesus to Peter to be transmitted by him to his successors. There are so many inferences in this involved claim that it is not always easy to keep them separate. "That Peter was bishop of Rome as well as the representative of the Lord in the Apostolic College and of the Church for all time is an article of faith in the Roman Communion" (Foakes-Jackson). On the other hand Protestants deny that Jesus gave such exclusive ecclesiastical power to Peter alone in Matthew 16:18 f. and least of all the power to transmit it and that Peter was the first pope in Rome. Some Protestants even deny that Peter ever was in Rome at all in their zeal to disprove the claims of the Roman Catholics about Peter as the first pope. "Of course, we can see that the questions of Peter's residence at Rome and the primacy of the

pope are two separate and entirely unconnected
things" (W. M. Taylor). At any rate, we can try to
keep distinct these two problems. For myself it is
sufficient to deny as destitute of proof the claim that
Peter was the first pope at Rome charged with supreme authority by Christ to transmit his exclusive
authority to his successors in Rome. That claim
rests on a complete misunderstanding of Christ's
words in Matthew 16:18 f. and is destitute of historical evidence. It rests on legends and ecclesiastical
prejudice. Certainly the other apostles did not recognize Peter as supreme during Christ's life or afterwards. Peter was spokesman at the great Pentecost
and was the leader with John for a while in Jerusalem. But Peter himself was arraigned by the
Judaizers before the church in Jerusalem for his conduct in Cæsarea (Acts 11:1–18) and was threatened by the Judaizers in Antioch so that he was
guilty of such cowardice there that Paul reproved
him to his face as a hypocrite (Gal. 2:11–14). In
the Jerusalem Conference (Acts 15:6–29) James,
the brother of Jesus, and not Peter presided, though
Peter was present and spoke. And James is the leader
in Jerusalem when Paul returns after his third mission tour (Acts 21:18). But it is quite open to frank
and fair investigation, quite apart from the Roman
claim about Peter as pope, to consider the evidence
concerning Peter's presence or preaching in Rome or
even founding the church there. In the New Testament Peter does not appear in any sense as pope or
autocrat by claim on his part or by recognition on

the part of others. The question remains therefore for us to see whether Peter ever went to Rome.

2. *He Was Not in Rome When Paul Wrote the Epistle to the Romans.*—This was about A.D. 57. There is already a church in Rome and Paul is sending this great Epistle by Phœbe, a deaconess of the church in Cenchreæ (Rom. 16:1), assuming Chapter 16 to be a genuine part of the Epistle, as I believe. It seems hardly possible that, if Peter was in Rome at work, Paul should ignore him when he names so many brethren and sisters with special messages to each. Besides, Paul had been anxious for a long time to come to Rome, but had been hindered so far (Rom. 1:9–13; 15:22–29), but he was definitely planning to come after his visit to Jerusalem that he might have fruit among them also as among the rest of the Gentiles (1:13), for he was ready to preach the gospel in Rome also (1:15). The church in Rome is already well established and instructed (15:14 f.), but still Paul wishes to come, though his chief ambition has been to preach the gospel where Christ was not yet named (evangelism in other words) and not to build on the foundation of another man (15:20). If Peter had founded the church in Rome, or was in Rome at this time, it is hard to conceive how Paul could have avoided making some mention of Peter's name when he came so close to a situation that called for it. We may assume, therefore, in the absence of definite testimony to the contrary, that Peter did not found the church in Rome as clearly Paul did not, for Paul had not yet been to Rome. It is hard to

prove a negative, but we seem to come fairly close
to it here, namely, that up to A.D. 57 Peter had not
been in Rome. We know that he had left Jerusalem
temporarily after the escape from prison (Acts
12:17), but he was back again at the Jerusalem
Conference (Acts 15:7–11; Gal. 2:8–10). We see
him afterwards in Antioch with Paul (Gal. 2:11–14).
We know that he was out in the field preaching Christ
(I Cor. 9:5) and he apparently spent some time in
Asia Minor (I Peter 1:1). But there is no proof as
yet that Peter had been to Rome.

3. *Peter Was Apparently Not in Rome during
Paul's First Roman Imprisonment.*—That is to say,
if we can judge by the absence of any mention of
Peter by Paul in the Epistles (Phil., Philemon, Col.,
Eph.) which he wrote during this period (A.D. 60–
63), assuming again that Paul wrote these Epistles
from Rome as I hold to be true in spite of the claims
put forth for Ephesus and Cæsarea. There are several places where Paul could hardly escape mention-
ing Peter's name, if he were in Rome (Phil. 2:19–30;
Philemon 23; and in particular Col. 4:10–14). In
Colossians Paul especially commends Mark to the
Colossians and sends Mark's greetings (Col. 4:10).
We know that Mark was with Peter for some time in
"Babylon" (I Peter 5:13), but surely this was not
the time. Otherwise it would seem a positive dis-
courtesy for Paul to overlook Peter after speaking
so kindly of Mark. There is mention of Mark also in
Philemon 24. There is not the faintest suspicion that
Paul knew of any connection of Peter with the church

in Rome during these years or even before this time.

4. *But Peter Was in Rome When He Wrote I Peter if He Means Rome by Babylon in I Peter 5:13.*—There is no way to decide beyond controversy whether Peter means the actual Babylon or is using the name in a mystical sense for Rome as is done repeatedly in the Apocalypse of John. John did it because of the persecution under Domitian. There is no reason whatever why Peter could not do so when writing his First Epistle in Rome during the persecution under Nero which began in Rome itself and spread rapidly to the provinces. Nero began his persecution of Christians in A.D. 64 after he burned the city in order to lay the blame on them and remove it from himself. If Peter was actually in Rome, say in A.D. 65 or 66, along with Mark and Silas (Silvanus), there was every reason for him to conceal that fact by using mystical Babylon for Rome. Paul, of course, was not in Rome at this time. This view, which I hold, denies the opinion of some scholars that both Paul and Peter were put to death in Rome in A.D. 64. Interpreting Babylon as Rome in I Peter 5:13 admits that Peter did go to Rome. There is little doubt that the unwillingness to admit Peter's presence in Rome at all is a main reason with some for insisting on the interpretation of Babylon as literal Babylon. To be sure, if Babylon in I Peter 5:13 is actual and literal Babylon, it still remains possible that Peter was once in Rome. The only difference is that, in that view, there is no direct New Testament statement to that effect. If we admit or

claim, as I do, that Peter here means Rome by Babylon, this is an end to the controversy on that point. But it is proof only for those who accept this interpretation and so is not objective historical evidence in the ordinary sense of the term.

5. *Many Other Testimonies to Peter's Presence in Rome.*—These possess varying value, but they all agree on the main item that Peter did visit Rome one or more times. The so-called First Epistle of Clement of Rome to the church in Corinth (about A.D. 95 or 96) seems to say that Peter suffered martyrdom in Rome: "Let us set before our eyes the good apostle Peter, who, through unrighteous envy, endured not one or two, but numerous labors, and having suffered martyrdom departed to the place of glory due him." This language seems to mean that Peter suffered martyrdom in Rome. Ignatius of Antioch, writing to the church in Rome (about A.D. 115), says: "Not as Peter and Paul do I command you," though he does not say that Peter had been in Rome. Papias (about A.D. 130) is quoted by Eusebius as interpreting Babylon in I Peter 5:13 to mean Rome, which view, of course, means that Papias believed that Peter went to Rome. Justin Martyr lived in Rome, and was martyred there (A.D. 165), but, though he speaks of Simon the magician, he does not mention Peter. Irenæus (about A.D. 190) speaks of both Peter and Paul being in Rome, "having founded and established the church," a statement that we have already seen to be impossible from Paul's Epistle to the Romans. Eusebius quotes Hegesippus (about the

same time as Irenæus) as saying that Peter visited Rome. Eusebius also quotes Clement of Alexandria (about A.D. 200) as saying that Peter followed Simon Magus to Rome and Origen (about A.D. 252) as saying that Peter was crucified at Rome head downwards. Dionysius of Carthage (about A.D. 170) alludes to the martyrdom of both Peter and Paul in Rome. Tertullian (about A.D. 200) is the first writer who speaks of Peter's death by crucifixion in Nero's reign. Jerome makes Peter arrive in Rome in the second year of Claudius (A.D. 42–43), a most unlikely date. The *Liber Pontificalis* states that Peter's Roman Episcopate lasted twenty-five years, an "unhistorical" (Chase) tradition. But out of this welter of tradition the one thing that seems to have support is the fact that Peter at one time or another went to Rome. The most likely time is after Paul's departure from Rome (A.D. 63) and after A.D. 64 when Nero began his persecution. Peter was thus in Rome when, say A.D. 65, he wrote his First Epistle (I Peter 5:13), concealing his identity as far as possible. Then in A.D. 66 or 67 he wrote the Second Epistle from Rome also.

6. *But No Proof That Peter Founded the Roman Church.*—Irenæus does say that Peter and Paul founded and established the church in Rome, but that statement is untrue concerning Paul as his Epistle to the Romans proves and there is no evidence given by Irenæus to prove his statement about Peter. If he is clearly wrong about Paul, he is likely wrong about Peter. The presence of Peter in Rome

during the Neronian persecution does not at all prove that he was the founder or the organizer or even the bishop of the church there.

7. *Some Evidence That Peter Was Put to Death in Rome.*—We have already seen several such statements by Tertullian, by Origen who says that "at last, having arrived in Rome, he was crucified head downwards, having himself requested that he might so suffer." The Chronicon of Eusebius (Armenian version) puts the martyrdom of Peter under Nero the thirteenth year of Nero's reign (A.D. 67–8), the probable year also when Paul was beheaded by Nero's orders, though apparently before Paul's death. It seems hardly likely that Peter was in Rome when Paul wrote II Timothy in view of 4:9–18. The probability is that Peter had met his death before Paul wrote this Epistle to Timothy with the plea for Mark to come along in haste with Timothy before winter. Archæologists have seemed to recover the probable places of burial of both Peter and Paul in Rome. Foakes-Jackson is prepared to agree to the evidence on this line from the catacombs, the inscriptions, the church sites: "For the archæologist the presence and the execution of SS. Peter and Paul in Rome are facts established beyond a shadow of doubt by purely monumental evidence." But he instantly admits that the known evidence on which the archæologist rests his case "is decidedly slight" and "with more rhetoric than inscriptions." Ambrose gives the legend of Peter's death preserved in the words *Quo Vadis?* The story is that some of the Christians at

Rome, say in A.D. 67, persuaded Peter to flee from Rome to escape Nero's wrath, for Nero's attention had at last been attracted to him. At the gate of the city, as he was fleeing, Peter met the Lord Jesus and said to him: "Lord, whither goest thou?" The Risen Christ replied: "I go to Rome, there once more to be crucified." It was more than enough for Peter who returned at once and was crucified head downwards as unworthy to be crucified in the same manner as his Lord. That is a beautiful legend, but Peter did know only too vividly the words of Jesus to him by the Sea of Galilee: "When thou wast young, thou girdedst thyself, and walkedst whither thou wouldest; but when thou shalt be old, thou shalt stretch forth thy hands, and another shall gird thee, and carry thee whither thou wouldest not" (John 21:18). Peter had lived to be an old man. He had borne his witness to Jesus as Christ and Lord. He had forged to the front as the preacher to the Jews as Paul had to the Gentiles. He had won his place beside Paul and John in the great trio of ministers of Jesus Christ in the first century and in all the centuries. Their gifts differed, but they still feed the souls of uncounted millions of believers in Jesus as Lord and Saviour. Paul towers highest in his intellectual prowess and energy of achievement. John soars as an eagle in the serene upper air or looks with clear and penetrating eye down into the crystal water of life. Peter has a human touch of weakness and sympathy, of hesitation and resilient hopefulness that draws us all close to him and to the presence of the Christ whom he loved and served so nobly and so long. "And so we take our leave of thee, thou generous, impulsive, wayward, impetuous, yet true-hearted man of God! We have come to know ourselves better through our acquaintance with thee, and even thy backsliding has shown us new depths of mercy in the heart of Christ" (W. M. Taylor). Simon did become the Rock that Jesus foresaw in him. He was slow in the making, but hard rocks are not made in a day. He did learn how to become a fisher of men and caught them alive for Christ. He did turn and strengthen his brethren as Jesus foresaw that he would do. He did shepherd the flock and feed the lambs. He did use the keys in his hands to unlock the door of the kingdom of God (the church of Christ) for all who would listen to his words. He has been misused by some who have sought to monopolize his name for ecclesiastical ends that he would have scorned, for he termed himself a fellow elder with the other elders or bishops or shepherds of Christ. But Peter's life is an open book written in imperishable words and deeds recorded in the New Testament to cheer us all on our way with Christ.

A BRIEF BIBLIOGRAPHY ON PETER
AND HIS EPISTLES

Not including lives of Christ and Paul, books on the Apostolic
Age, cyclopædia articles, commentaries on the
Gospels and Acts.

Abbott, E. A., *The Expositor* (January to March, 1822).

Baldwin, H. A., *The Fisherman of Galilee* (1923).

Barnes, *St. Peter in Rome and His Tomb on the Vatican Hill.*

Beck, J. T., *Erklärung der Briefe Petri* (1895).

Bennett, W. H., *New Century Bible* (1901).

Bigg, C., *The Epistles of St. Peter and St. Jude* (1901) [*International Critical Commentary*].

Birks, H. A., *Studies in the Life and Character of St. Peter* (1887).

Blenkin, G. W., *First Epistle General of Peter* (1915).

Brown, John, *Expository Discourses on First Epistle of Peter* (1852).

Brun, A., *Essai sur l'apôtre Pierre* (1905).

Buckland, A. R., *Devotional Commentary on Epistles of Peter* (1913).

Camerlinck, *Commentarius in epistolas catholicas* (1909).

Couard, *Commentaire* (1895).

Couard, *Simon Petrus der Apostel des Herrn.*

Dallmann, William, *How Peter Became Pope* (1862).

Davidson, John, *St. Peter and His Training* (1905).

De Zwann, J., *2 Peter en Judas* (1909).

Dietlein, W. O., *Der 2 Brief Petri* (1851).

Edmundson, George, *The Church of Rome in the First Century* (1913).

Elert, *Die Religiosität des Petrus* (1911).

Erbes, Karl, *Die Todestage der Apostel Paulus and Petrus* (1899).

Fillion, L., *Saint Pierre* (1906).

Foakes-Jackson, F. J., *Peter, Prince of Apostles* (1927).

Foster, Ora D., *The Literary Relations of the First Epistle of Peter* (1913).

Fouard, C., *St. Peter and the Early Years of Christianity* (1892).

Gallagher, M., *Was the Apostle Peter Ever at Rome?* (1894).

Goutard, L., *Essai critique et historique sur la première épître de S. Pierre* (1905).

Green, S. G., *The Apostle Peter: His Life and Letters* (1880).

Greene, R. A., *Saint Peter* (1909).

Griffith-Thomas, W. H., *The Apostle Peter* (1904).

Grill, *Der Primat des Petrus* (1904).

Grosch, H., *Die Echtheit des Zweiten Briefes Petri* (1889).

Guignebert, C. A. H., *La Primauté de Pierre et la Venue de Pierre à Rome* (1909).

Gunkel, H., *Die Schriften d. N. T.* 3 Auflage (1917).

Hart, J. H. A., *Expositor's Greek Testament,* edited by W. R. Nicoll (1910).

Henkel, K, *Der Zweite Brief des Apostelfürsten Petrus* (1904).

Henriott, *St. Pierre* (1891).

Hoffman, J. C., *Der Zweite Brief Petri und der Brief Judä* (1875).

Hort, F. J. A., *Commentary on I Peter 1:1–2:17* (1899).

Howson, J., *Horæ Petrinæ* (1883).

Hundhausen, *Die beiden Pontifikalschreiben des Apostelfürsten Petrus* (1878).

James, M. R., *The Second Epistle of Peter and the Epistle of Jude [Cambridge Greek Testament,* 1912].

Janvier, *Histoire de Saint Pierre prince des Apôtres et premier pape* (1902).

Jenkins, R. C., *The Apostle Peter: Claims of Catholics* (1875).

Johnstone, R., *The First pistle of Peter* (1888).

Kasteren, Van, *De Eerste Brief van d. Apostel Petrus* (1911).

Keil, C. F., *Commentar über die Briefe des Petrus und Juda* (1883).

Kleist, J. A., *The Memoirs of St. Peter* (1932). Mark's Gospel.

Knopf, R., *Der Briefe Petri und Juda* (1912)

Kögel, J., *Die Gedankenheit des Ersten Briefes Petri* (1902).

Kühl, E., *Die Briefe Petri und Judæ (Meyer Kommentar,* 6 Aufl. 1897).

Lietzmann, H., *Petrus und Paulus in Rom.*

Lightfoot, J. B. and Lumby, J. R., *St. Peter and St. Jude* (1881) *[Speaker's Commentary,* edited by F. C. Cooke].

Lumby, J. R., *Expositor's Bible* (1893).

Masterman, J. H. B., *Epistles of St Peter* (1900).

Mayor, J. B., *The Epistle of St Jude and the Second Epistle of St. Peter* (1907).

McInnis, J. M., *Simon Peter: Fisherman and Philosopher* (1928).

Meyer, F. B., *Peter: Fisherman, Disciple, Apostle* (1920).

Moffatt, James, *Epistles of Peter* in *Moffatt New Testament Commentary* (1930).

Monnier, J., *La première épître de l'apôtre Pierre* (1900).

Ninck, J., *Simon Petrus, Fischer aus Galiläa* (1903).

Perdelwitz, Richard, *Die Mysterienreligionen und das Problem des ersten Petrus briefes* (1911).

Plummer, A., *The Second Epistle of Peter and the Epistle of Jude* [Vol. 3, *New Testament, Ellicott's Commentary for English Readers*].

Plumptre, E. H., *Epistles of St. Peter and St. Jude* [*Cambridge Bible for Schools and Colleges*] (1879).

Reagan, J. N., *The Preaching of Peter the Beginning of Christian Apologetics* (1922).

Robinson, C. G., *Simon Peter, His Life and Times* (1889).

Robson, E. I., *Studies in the Second Epistle of St. Peter* (1915).

Ross, J. M. E., *The First Epistle of Peter* (1913).

Salmond, G. D. F., *Peter* [*Popular Commentary on the New Testament,* edited by Philip Schaff] (1883).

Scharfe, E., *Die petrinische Strömung der neutestamentlichen Literatur* (1893).

Schmid, *Petrus in Rom* (1879).

Schott, Theod., *Der zweite Brief Petri und der Brief Judä* (1863).

Schweenhorst, H., *Das Verhältnis des Judasbriefes zum zweite Petrusbriefe* (1904).

Seely, *The Life and Writings of St. Peter.*

Southouse, A. J., *The Making of Simon Peter* (1906).

Snyman, D. R., *The Authenticity of the Second Epistle of Peter* (Thesis in 1923 for the Th.D. degree at Southern Baptist Theological Seminary).

Soden, von H., *Hand Kommentar* (3 Aufl. 1899).

Spence, *Scenes from the Life of St. Peter.*

Spitta, F., *Der zweite Brief des Petrus und der Brief des Judas* (1885).

Strachan, R. D., *Expositor's Greek Testament,* edited by W. R. Nicoll (1910).

Taylor, W. M., *Peter the Apostle* (1875).

Thompson, *Life-Work of Peter the Apostle.*

Upham, F. B., *Simon Peter, Shepherd* (1910).

Ullmann, C., *Der 2 Brief Petri Krit. Untersuch.* (1821).

Usteri, J. M., *Wiss. und prakt. Komm. über den 1 Petrusbrief* (1887).

Völter, D., *Der 1 Petrusbrief* (1906).

Warfield, B. B., *A Defence of 2 Peter* (*Southern Presbyterian Review,* January, 1882 and 1883).

Weiss, B., *Der erste Petrusbrief und die Kritik* (1906).

Weiss, B., *Der petrinische Lehrbegriff* (1855).

Werdermann, H., *Die Irrelehrer des Judasbriefes und 2 Petrus-briefes* (1913).

Wiesinger, J. T. A., *Der zweite Brief des Apostels Petrus und der Brief des Judas* (1862).

Williams, N. M., *Peter* (*American Commentary on the New Testament*, Ed. by Alvah Hovey).

Windisch, H., *Die Katholische Briefe Handbuch zum Neuen Testament* (2 Aufl. 1930).

Wohlenberg, G., *Der erste und zweite Petrusbrief und der Judasbrief* [*Zahn Kommentar*, 2 Aufl. 1915].

INDEX OF SUBJECTS

INDEX TO NEW TESTAMENT PASSAGES

COMPILED BY REV. JOSEF NORDENHAUG, PH.D., OSLO, NORWAY

MATTHEW